Transgender Identities in the Press

Also available from Bloomsbury

Constructing the Welfare State in the British Press, Malgorzata Paprota
Corpus, Discourse and Mental Health, Daniel Hunt and Gavin Brookes
Discourse and Identity on Facebook, Mariza Georgalou
Using Corpora to Analyze Gender, Paul Baker

Transgender Identities in the Press

A Corpus-based Discourse Analysis

Angela Zottola

BLOOMSBURY ACADEMIC
LONDON • NEW YORK • OXFORD • NEW DELHI • SYDNEY

BLOOMSBURY ACADEMIC
Bloomsbury Publishing Plc
50 Bedford Square, London, WC1B 3DP, UK
1385 Broadway, New York, NY 10018, USA
29 Earlsfort Terrace, Dublin 2, Ireland

BLOOMSBURY, BLOOMSBURY ACADEMIC and the Diana logo are trademarks of
Bloomsbury Publishing Plc

First published in Great Britain 2021
This paperback edition published in 2022

Copyright © Angela Zottola, 2021

Angela Zottola has asserted her right under the Copyright, Designs and
Patents Act, 1988, to be identified as Author of this work.

For legal purposes the Acknowledgements on p. vii constitute
an extension of this copyright page.

Cover design: Rebecca Heselton

All rights reserved. No part of this publication may be reproduced or transmitted
in any form or by any means, electronic or mechanical, including photocopying,
recording, or any information storage or retrieval system, without
prior permission in writing from the publishers.

Bloomsbury Publishing Plc does not have any control over, or responsibility for,
any third-party websites referred to or in this book. All internet addresses given
in this book were correct at the time of going to press. The author and publisher
regret any inconvenience caused if addresses have changed or sites have
ceased to exist, but can accept no responsibility for any such changes.

A catalogue record for this book is available from the British Library.

A catalog record for this book is available from the Library of Congress.

ISBN: HB: 978-1-3500-9754-4
        PB: 978-1-3502-1130-8
        ePDF: 978-1-3500-9755-1
        eBook: 978-1-3500-9756-8

Typeset by Integra Software Services Pvt. Ltd.

To find out more about our authors and books visit www.bloomsbury.com
and sign up for our newsletters.

Contents

List of tables	vi
Acknowledgements	vii
1 Introduction	1
2 Transgender identities and the press	13
3 A matter of choices: Identity labels in English	45
4 Semantic prosodies in the press	77
5 Differences and similarities in the representation of trans identities	107
6 Conclusion	171
Notes	182
References	186
Index	203

List of tables

2.1	Newspaper circulation rates in the UK	35
2.2	Distribution of articles across newspapers and years in the TCUK	37
2.3	Distribution of articles and word tokens across sub-corpora and years in the TCUK	37
2.4	Newspaper circulation rates in Canada (2015)	40
2.5	Distribution of articles across newspapers and years in the TCC	42
2.6	Distribution of word tokens across newspapers and years in the TCC	42
3.1	Frequency of search words in the TransCorUK by year	68
3.2	Frequency of search words in the TransCorCan by year	69
4.1	*Personal details* in the TCUK	83
4.2	*Personal details* in the TCC	93
4.3	*Implying verbs* in the TCC	99
5.1	*LGBTIQ+ group and labels* in TCUK	108
5.2	*LGBTIQ+ group and labels* in TCC	117
5.3	*Entertainment and celebrities* in the TCUK	124
5.4	*Entertainment and celebrities* in the TCC	138
5.5	*Crime stories* in the TCUK	142
5.6	*Laws and rights* in the TCUK	149
5.7	*Laws and rights* in the TCC	154
5.8	*Awareness and support* in the TCUK	159
5.9	*Awareness and support* in the TCC	165

Acknowledgements

This book is partially based on work started during my doctoral research at the University of Napoli Federico II. I am very grateful to Vanda Polese and Paul Baker for their advice and guidance during that time of my life and for the continuous encouragement and inspiration in the following years as well.

To my colleagues and friends Giuseppe, Lucy, Antonio and Stefano for discussing with me ideas and allowing me to learn from them, your contribution to my growth is incommensurable and invaluable, for this I thank you.

Thanks are due to the two anonymous reviewers for their helpful and stimulating comments.

I would also like to thank the team at Bloomsbury, in particular Andrew Wardell and Becky Holland who have reassured and supported me in the long process that led to the publication of this book since my very first email.

Finally, I would like to thank Andressa, without your support, both moral and practical, this work could not have been completed.

1

Introduction

Laws, rights and guidelines: What is the current situation for transgender people?

Two of the key terms in this work are *identity* and *transgender*. For this reason, I believe it is appropriate to open this reading by defining both. In this book, I aim to reflect on the use of language in relation to transgender identities, and it seems only fair to begin this discussion by looking at these terms starting from their most basic description, their vocabulary entry.

> **Transgender, adj. and n.**
> **A.** adj.
> 1. Designating a person whose sense of personal identity and gender does not correspond to that person's sex at birth, or which does not otherwise conform to conventional notions of sex and gender.
> Although now typically used as an umbrella term which includes any or all non-conventional gender identities, in wider use *transgender* is sometimes used synonymously with the more specific terms *transsexual* or *transvestite*.
> 2. Of or characterized by transgenderism; of or relating to transgender people.
> **B.** n.
> 1. A transgender person; (sometimes) *spec.* a person who is transsexual or transvestite. Also occasionally (with *the* and *plural* agreement): transgender people as a class.
> Cf. note at sense A. 1.
> 2. Transgenderism; transgender identity, experience, etc. (OED Online 2018)
>
> **Identity, n.**
> **1.**
>   a. The quality or condition of being the same in substance, composition, nature, properties, or in particular qualities under consideration; absolute or essential sameness; oneness.

b. An instance of this quality or condition.
   c. Recurrence of the same; repetition. Also: an instance of this. *Obsolete.*
   d. The selfsame thing. *Obsolete. rare.*
   e. *Logic.* law or principle of identity: the principle expressed in the identical proposition *A is A.*
   f. Absence of distinction between people of different ethnic groups. *South African.*

2.
   a. The sameness of a person or thing at all times or in all circumstances; the condition of being a single individual; the fact that a person or thing is itself and not something else; individuality, personality.
   b. Who or what a person or thing is; a distinct impression of a single person or thing presented to or perceived by others; a set of characteristics or a description that distinguishes a person or thing from others.
3. Personal or individual existence. *Obsolete. rare.*
4. *Mathematics.*
   a. The equality of two expressions for all values of the variables.
   b. An equation that holds whatever values are assigned to any of the variables in it.
5. *New Zealand* and *Australian.* A person long resident or well known in a place; a local eccentric; such persons collectively. Frequently as old identity.
6. The condition of being identified in feeling, interest, etc.; identification *with.*
7. *Mathematics.*
   a. An element of a set which, if combined with any element by a (specified) binary operation, leaves the latter element unchanged;
   b. A transformation that gives rise to the same elements as those to which it is applied. (OED Online 2018)

I will come back to the definition of identity later. Let us now focus on the definition of transgender. My attention is drawn first by the fact that the definition includes two parts; the first considers the term as an adjective; the second considers it as a noun. The following chapters of this book will explain at greater length how problematic this second definition is. The definition brings us back to the long-standing dichotomy between gender and sex. An individual's sex is mainly defined by their anatomy – which reproductive organs and chromosomes the person is born with. The gender of an individual defines their identification within recognized or emerging roles that are associated to behaviours and internal and external appearance socially associated to female, male or non-binary (i.e. identifying as neither female nor male) individuals.

The association of sex and gender has been contested since the 1960s, and until today this discussion continues to evolve, including new terminology and new understandings of gender and sexual identities.

This evolution brought forward a new dichotomy which sees the juxtaposition of the terms transgender and cisgender; both terms include a prefix deriving from Latin, *cis-* and *trans-*, the former means on 'the same side of/on the side of' while the latter 'cross to or on the farther side of/ beyond/ over' (OED Online 2018). The two prefixes have been used in combination with the term gender for decades. The adjective transgender is now used as a collective/umbrella term to indicate an individual whose gender identity and biological sex do not correspond. The term cisgender is used to define people whose gender identity matches their biological sex. To use more inclusive definition, and one we endorse in this work, the term 'is used to refer to people who do not identify with a gender diverse experience, without enforcing existence of a "normative" gender expression' (Green 2006: 247). The term cisgender has a more recent history, being used in this connotation since the 1990s by trans studies scholars (Aultman 2014: 61). The term transgender, in the connotation described here, has been used since the 1980s, but its history can be traced back in literature to the 1960s (Williams 2014). The term *transgender* underwent many changes in its connotation and use. It has been associated over time to different terms such as *transsexual* or *transvestite*. Today, it is socially recognized as an adjective rather than a noun, and the distinction between this and other terms has been made clear. In the following chapters, I will also observe that a number of other terms have alternated over time in association to transgender identities (i.e. female-to-male [FTM], male-to-female [MTF], trans).

The second term widely used in this book is *identity* or rather *identities*. It is then necessary to give a definition to the concept of identity and position the perspective of this study toward this definition. The dictionary entry, in a way, already explains the choice of using the noun in its plural form. There are seven entries to the noun, and most of them are subdivided in further definitions, to signal the complexity of this term and all that it entails. The second definition given by the OED is the most appropriate to be considered in this work.

The concept of identity has been theorized in many different ways and from different perspectives. One of the definitions that this study relates to is the one proposed by Bucholtz and Hall (2005: 586), who describe identity as 'the social positioning of self and other'. This definition puts identity in a broad context, where social implications play a pivotal role. At the same time, if we want to give a more detailed description of identity, we could think about it as 'a set of traits, capacities, attitudes [...] that an individual normally retains over a considerable period of time and that normally distinguishes that individual from other individuals' (Shoemaker 2006: 41). This suggests that identity is not a fixed concept but a subjective one, always evolving, not 'static' (Llamas and Watt 2010), and 'always "in process"', as Stuart Hall (1996) posits. Thus, it seems appropriate to agree with the fact that 'different persons can have the same identity – or at any rate, there can be as much similarity between the identities of different persons as there is between the identities of the same person at different times' (Shoemaker 2006: 47).

Due to the context in which they develop, some identities are similar to others, while others are different. There is a tendency of grouping similar identities together, as the data considered for this work proves. While this practice can be useful in some cases, it can also cause the opposite effect in others. Chapter 5, for example, highlights that the collective representation of identities is not always the best choice, especially when considering that identity and language, as the means used to represent it, are being constantly negotiated and reshaped (Llamas and Watt 2010) and cannot be classified according to any specific general category. Each identity can be part of an indefinite number of groups, at the same time or at different times of its existence, based on kinship, relationships, physical appearance or sexual preference.

Bucholtz and Hall (2005: 585) maintain that identity is 'a relational and sociocultural phenomenon'. They continue by arguing that identity is constructed through and in interaction. Therefore, it is a result of discursive practices as identity is manifested, described, and represented through discourse. The essence of identity, engendered within discourse, accounts for the historical and institutional era it is generated in, the discursive strategies and choices employed in its construction, and also the style or enunciation used — according to the type of discourse, written or spoken (Hall 1996). Identity is constructed through the definition of the difference, when one identity is compared to an *Other* self, the definition of this identity builds on these differences and has a series of ideological and power relations at its basis.

The concept of identity becomes even more intricate when associated with gender. Expanding the reflection to these two terms in combination, as they are used throughout this book, transgender identities 'represents [the] identities of many individuals who transcend gender norms in different ways' (Burnes and Chen 2012: 117). It refers to those people who do not conform to their biological sex, and includes all variations that this label can include, ranging from people who choose medical interventions to those who rely on less invasive practices which allow them to fully acknowledge their identity by differentiating themselves from the binary and heteronormative concept that society has of men and women.

Transgender identity goes beyond 'gender norms on both internal (intrapsychic) and external (social, relational, and community) spectra' (Burnes and Chen 2012: 113). It subverts what society considers the norm in order to express people's feelings of incongruence between what they perceive as their identity and their biological sex. It is not only the physical appearance that makes the identity. It is first and foremost the way in which language is used to describe it, as 'bodies do not derive their meanings from pre-linguistics natural order, but are imbued with meaning through discourse' (Hall and Zimman 2010: 166).

Transgender individuals are nowadays legally recognized in many countries around the world. In Europe, almost all countries have laws that regulate gender identity recognition, with places such as Malta and Ireland at the forefront (Sherpe 2015; Polese and Zottola 2019). Other countries such as Ukraine require people to undergo a psychiatric evaluation while others such as France make a distinction between minors and individuals over the age of eighteen. In this book, I focus on two specific countries, the United Kingdom and Canada, where the situation is quite different.

In the United Kingdom, the first legal document which in a way referred to trans people was the Sex Discrimination Act issued in 1975. This document attested that it was illegal to discriminate a person on the grounds of their anatomical sex. This document was amended in 1999 to specifically include people who have undergone gender reassignment surgery. In 2004 the Gender Recognition Act (henceforth the GRA) was promulgated after the European Court of Human Rights ruled that the UK government, through this law, infringed basic human rights in the case of *Goodwin v United Kingdom*. Goodwin, a British trans woman, applied for a state pension but was denied access to it at the women's age. The GRA recognized that transgender people could change their legal gender in the United Kingdom, allowing trans people to acquire a new birth certificate and be legally recognized in their identifying gender. This process does not require the individual to have gone through gender reassignment surgery. The GRA specified that any individual who wanted to have their identifying gender legally recognized would need to have been diagnosed with gender dysphoria and have been living in the identifying gender for at least two years. In July 2018 the government began a consultation to reform the GRA 2004. Anti-discrimination laws were put in place through the Equality Act issued in 2010.

In Canada, the situation is different as the laws vary in each of the ten provinces and three territories. Significant changes in the legislative organization with regard to transgender people have occurred since 2015, but some of the provinces began these amendments even earlier. Of the ten provinces of Canada, Manitoba and Ontario in 2012, Alberta in 2014, Newfoundland and Labrador and Nova Scotia in 2015, and Prince Edward Island in 2016, have made it illegal to require gender reassignment surgery in order for gender identity to be legally recognized. Each individual born in those provinces can apply to have their identifying gender recognized on their birth certificate by submitting a statement where they affirm they identify as male or female. The individual's statement needs to be accompanied by one written by their physician. In British Columbia since 2014, Saskatchewan since 2016, and New Brunswick since 2017 individuals born in these provinces are no longer required to have gender affirmation surgery to apply for a different birth certificate. Additionally, in Saskatchewan, since 2018, gender is no longer included on birth certificates (with regard to this, each province has a different regulation, but I will not go into detail here). In the province of Quebec, since 2015, individuals who were born in or have been resident in the province for at least one year can apply to change their birth certificate. As for the three territories, Nunavut since 2015, Northwest Territories since 2016, and Yukon since 2017 have all banned the requirement for gender affirmation surgery to apply for a birth certificate update. Since 2017 all provinces and territories have defined illegal and prosecutable discrimination against gender identity and expression by explicitly addressing the issue in the Canadian Human Rights Act. Much of the analysis on the Canadian data collected revolves around these legal issues.

A turning point, in the legal recognition of transgender identities, can be identified outside of the legal environment. In fact, in June 2018, the World Health Organization (WHO) changed its definition of transgender and transsexual identities. Until then trans people were considered a medicalized category and gender dysphoria was defined as a mental disorder. Since 2018 gender dysphoria has been declassified to a sexual health disorder and no longer connected to mental health.

The last point to touch upon in this first introductory section is guidelines for the use of inclusive and non-discriminatory language and terminology. A large number of guidelines can be found online, these have been put together by transgender people, cisgender people who identify as allies and by groups that work to support the transgender community. Some of the material retrievable online is specific to the workplace. Other resources discuss the use of pronouns or were created by universities. In this book, I mainly refer to guidelines offered by four organizations: GLAAD (n.d.-a), founded in 1985, which has been working ever since toward the cultural change and acceptance of the LGBTIQ+ (lesbian, gay, bisexual, transgender, intersex or queer/questioning) community within society (GLAAD n.d.-b); the National Center for Transgender Equality (2020a), founded in 2003 by transgender activists; All About Trans (2020), which aims to positively change the way in which the media perceives and represents transgender people; and the *Beaumont Society*, founded in 1966 in the UK to support transgender people across the country. The perspectives on the use of terminology referring to transgender people are many and vary from person to person; for this reason, I choose here to refer to the suggestions found in these guidelines, always to ensure the highest standards of inclusivity. As I acknowledge the fact that transgender identities are so varied, I also appreciate that the concept of a transgender community is a social construct that cannot be representative of all transgender people because of the very – fluid – nature of these identities.

This study aims to observe the way others, namely the press, describe and represent identity, namely transgender identity. In using the term *transgender* as an umbrella term, as postulated in this introduction, and in line with other scholars who looked into the discussion of transgender identity (Baker 2014b; Borba 2019; Jones 2019), I acknowledge that transgender identity is not a fixed concept.

Alongside the issues clarified so far, the word *gender* in this book is intended to mean non-binary and not heteronormative, inclusive of all the existing shades in defining identities. As this work develops, we must bear in mind that 'identity labels are only "real" for the here and now' (Baker 2008: 194).

To conclude this section, I must also include a more personal reflection. I do not identify as transgender, but I do see myself as a transgender ally. As a cisgender person I acknowledge that my understanding of the issues related to transgender identities is only partial due to the fact that I have not experienced them first hand. Knowing this, I also believe this research can have the potential to contribute to a better understanding of the underestimated negative effects that the use of discriminatory language and non-inclusive practices has on the transgender community at large. In light of this underlying statement to my work, everything that has been written and analysed has been done with the best intention and to the best of my knowledge. Should any reader disagree with my analysis or interpretations, please bear in mind that there is no intention to make generalizations on behalf of the transgender community or any transgender individual. I aim in this work to look at language use and possibly highlight ways to engage with more inclusive and non-discriminatory linguistic practices.

Aims of the research

In 2015, when I first began this research project, I was astound by the power of media discourses to quickly change and impact society so strongly, focusing on some matters while backgrounding others and immediately channelling the attention of the masses on specific topics. Current media platforms such as Twitter, for example, can direct the attention of large numbers of people onto specific issues in a mere matter of hours. Once a piece of news is identified as newsworthy, it can quickly spread around, possibly overshadowing other information, which might be even more relevant at that specific moment.

By 2015, I noticed that the issue of transgender identities had grown exponentially in popularity. One of the contributing factors to this phenomena, I believe, was the increasing number of TV series and films featuring transgender characters – among these: *Orange is the New Black* (2013), *Transparent* (2014), *Dallas Buyers Club* (2014), *Sens8* (2015), *Boy meets Girl* (2015) and *The Danish Girl* (2015). These productions worked as a sounding board, presenting stories that people could relate to or at least understand: no complicated talk, no boring legal procedures, just people going through something in their lives. These productions showed how transgender people are among us and live *normal*[1] lives just like everybody else. These productions not only brought up the topic, gave space to transgender identities but also engendered a discussion about trans lives outside of the transgender/ LGBTIQ+ community.

At the same time, transgender people had been receiving more attention in other media outputs, such as newspapers and magazines, as well as television programmes. More specifically, I noticed that some news stories[2] were particularly drawing the media's attention such as the transition of former athlete Caitlyn Jenner, or issues concerning gender-neutral toilets in the United States, which prompted a worldwide discussion. At first glance, the terms *transgender* and *transition* appeared to be referenced in contexts associated with scandals or the violation of transgender people's rights. My curiosity, as a researcher and as a linguist, was triggered by the increased interest taken by the media on the representation of these identities. Thus, I started my investigation in order to gain a better understanding of the impact that the linguistic representation of these identities may have had on users of such platforms. The idea of building the TransCor (Transgender Corpus) developed from the desire to learn more about the issue, and to uncover the main linguistic strategies used to (re)produce such representations. Moreover, the TransCor served as a valid collection of data that allowed me to analyse the use of language in the press from a critical viewpoint. As I kept thinking about this project and reading about transgender identities, I elaborated some hypotheses on the findings that I would gain through the analysis of the data collected. My initial aim was to find, if it was the case, validation of these hypotheses about the representation of transgender identities.

As the current political situation becomes more terrifying by the minute, influencing not only the economy but also society's perspective on many issues such as gender identities, I believe this research can be beneficial to the understanding of the role of language in these events. Inspired by the major works conducted on the use of language in the representation of gender identities, this study is a contribution to creating further awareness on the implications of the use of language in the representation of identities. My purpose is to shed light on the linguistic practices to which we are exposed daily, and which consciously and unconsciously work in the background of our mind, shaping our knowledge of the world.

As I started reading about transgender identities, it became even more clear to me – and the analysis of the data collected for the study confirmed this – that there is nothing more personal and subjective than identity. It is impossible to make any generalization about identity, especially gender and sexual identities. As I hinted at in the previous section, 'Laws, rights and guidelines', labels and definitions may not have the same value or connotation for all individuals, even if two people might identify using the same term. That is to say that one person who identifies as transgender might feel about their own identity differently compared to another person who also identifies as transgender, just as it could happen for any other gender and sexual identity. Thus, the choices I made regarding terminology seek to be as representative and non-discriminatory as possible. However, in the light of what has been said previously, I acknowledge the fact that it would be impossible to use a type of language that could be wholly inclusive and represent each and every individual, due to the fluidity of gender and the variety of gender expressions. In defining myself as an ally to transgender people and always making an effort to use inclusive and non-discriminatory language to the best of my knowledge, this study acknowledges the fact that when talking about identity representation we are stepping on very sensitive ground, therefore, discussing gender identity is not an easy task.

Against this backdrop, the following section discusses the research questions that guided and shaped this study.

Research questions

This study is born out of the belief that the choices made by the press – such as picking terminology, building specific types of representation, constructing social and gender identities are given through discursive practices, and how cultural practices are brought into being through linguistic interaction and semiotic manifestations in newspapers – directly influences public opinion and the way society deals with and perceives transgender identities.

In light of this, and the other issues discussed in 'Laws, rights and guidelines' above, this study evolves around the following research questions (RQs):

1. How is language used in the British and the Canadian press to represent transgender people between 2013 and 2015?
    a. In the British press, to what extent does language change with reference to the main class distinction between popular and quality press?
2. In what ways do newspapers differ in terms of language when covering news stories about transgender people with reference to:
    a. frequency and context of use of naming strategies (nouns and pronouns); and
    b. semantic prosodies (e.g. use of descriptors, such as adjectives or descriptions of grammatical agency via verbs).
3. How do the findings relate to the social context and social practices in the UK and Canada?

As it is clear from the first RQ, which can be considered as the primary, overarching RQ, this study attempts to investigate how transgender people are represented in the British and the Canadian press from a linguistic point of view in a period of three years, from 2013 to 2015. This involves the analysis of the use of terminology related to transgender identities, the lexical choices related to the description of this identity and the political and ideological stances conveyed by each specific choice. In particular, in sections which deal with the British press, a further distinction will be taken into account, the analysis of the popular versus quality press (RQ1a).

The second RQ looks into more general patterns of language used in the representation of transgender individuals. Here, I take into consideration how language can be employed and manipulated at various levels in order to represent transgender identities according to the specific political and ideological stances fitting the newspapers under investigation. Attention is paid to the lexical choices adopted by the press by looking at the frequency and context of naming strategies such as nouns and pronouns. In particular, this investigation tries to verify whether the press is using terminology in a consistent way, and what are the implications behind these choices. Moreover, by examining semantic prosodies, I will try to uncover specific patterns of meaning associated with transgender people in the press. For example, I will focus on how the use of descriptors such as adjectives or the use of verbs to express grammatical agency influence the way the readers perceive a particular representation of transgender people. Transgender people are analysed as social actors, looking at the way the patterns of meanings associated with these individuals can be considered as positive or negative, by considering the type of evaluation that emerges from this representation retrieved from the British and Canadian press.

The third and final RQ tries to relate the findings to the context in the UK and in Canada, taking on a more critical and reflective perspective. I will try to consider whether the interest taken by the press regarding transgender people is likely to be temporary or if it signals a change toward a more conscious and inclusive discourse concerning these identities.

The study was initially conceived to analyse the British data only, however, in light of the results of the analysis, I believed it would be beneficial to compare these results to practices adopted in other countries. Given the positive sociopolitical situation in Canada, and the advances made in this country in relation to transgender identities, this country appeared to be a perfect fit to compare the different representational choices made by the press. The comparison was very fruitful, the Canadian press presented several patterns and language choices that struck me for their inclusivity and for being highly ethical, even in very slippery contexts.

Outline of the book

This book is organized into six chapters. The first being the introduction that the reader is currently exploring, and which tries to discuss the background of this study and present a general contextualization with regards to transgender identities.

Chapter 2 retraces the history of studies on language, gender and sexuality and addresses the development of the field. It also focuses with more detail on transgender studies and the contribution to the field with a linguistic perspective. The chapter introduces the data analysed, describing it and explaining the collection process and the different methodological tools from the field of Corpus Linguistics adopted in the analysis.

In Chapter 3, I begin with a definition of *discourse* and the relevance of this basic concept within the book. The chapter aims to provide a general introduction to the methodological approach used in the analysis, namely corpus-based discourse analysis. To do so, I introduce both Critical Discourse Analysis and Corpus Linguistics, provide a critical discussion on previous studies that apply this methodology. The chapter also introduces the field of News Discourse by briefly describing first the development of both the British and the Canadian press, and second addressing the peculiarities of the language of the press. The chapter ends with an overview of the use of identity labels in the TransCor and introduces the analysis that is further described in the following chapters.

In Chapter 4, the concept of semantic prosody, used throughout the analysis, is described in greater detail. The collocation analysis is also introduced, with a focus on two semantic categories of representation: *personal details* and *implying verbs*. The chapter concludes with a discussion on the theory of social actor representation and the taxonomy suggested by Van Leeuwen (1996), which is used as an analytical tool throughout the analysis.

In Chapter 5, the main semantic categories of representation, retrieved through the use of collocation analysis are presented. The chapter discusses each category of representation identified for the British data first and then for the Canadian data. Examples are provided from both data sets, and a concordance analysis is used to support some of the claims made in the analysis. The categories of representation discussed in this chapter can be roughly divided into two main groups, those that reinforce a type of collective representation: *LGBTIQ+ group and labels* and *entertainment and celebrities*; and those which discuss laws and rights for transgender people: *laws and rights* and *awareness and support*. The chapter also discusses one last category of representation which was only retrieved in the British data: *Crime Stories*.

Chapter 6 concludes this work by bringing together the main findings presented throughout the previous chapters. This section also offers a reflection on both the methodological tools employed in this work and the implications of the findings within broader society.

2

Transgender identities and the press

Transgender, transsexual, trans: (Mis)representations and (mis)understandings

Gender identities and the way they intersect with language have in the last two decades been increasingly under the microscope of linguistic analysis. Identity is evolving into 'an altogether more complex phenomenon as a result of the mobility and diversity in the social worlds' (Preece 2016: 3). While its complexity increases so does anything associated with it, for instance gender. Identities, such as gender identities, are embodied within language, primarily because categorization can be done solely through language. As Joseph puts it, 'labels that people attach to themselves and others to signal their belonging' are actualized through language (Joseph 2016: 19). This embodiment within languages is also determined by the fact that words are the vehicles to express 'indexed ways of speaking and behaving through which [people] perform' their affiliation (19). Lastly, it is because other people interpret this performance by understanding that language (19). These labels become a tool for people and are used to make sense of and fit gender identities into recognized categories. These categories are, and actually have been for a while now, at a crossroads, as the expression of gender keeps changing, adjusting and continuously evolving as years go by, remarkably as Western society has become more and more aware of the relation between gender and sexuality. There is an evolution, which feels much like a quiet revolution, going on as gender identities open to new, different and more complex definitions and we lean toward more inclusive, not strictly categorizing discourses. The meaning that the word *gender* will have in this chapter, and throughout the research, as anticipated in the introduction, is non-binary and not heteronormative and inclusive of all the existing shades in defining gender and sexual identities.

This chapter aims to describe the relationships between language, gender and sexuality and how these intersections relate to the research presented in this book by critically addressing some of the key findings that literature has pointed out so far. The study of language in reference to gender can be traced back to the beginning of the twentieth century. At that time, research in this area consisted mainly of looking at the difference between the way men and women spoke and behaved when communicating.[1]

Until the early 1990s, studies on gender were mainly studies about women. Some scholars had looked into the language of gay men, and the relationships between language and sexuality. However, these aspects were considered something distant from studies on gender and language. Research conducted on the representation of other gender identities, or people with non-heterosexual sexual preference, were mainly based on the use of lexicon; one of the most investigated examples is the language of the gay community. Cory (1965) was one of the first scholars to publish research on gay people's language, while among the most recent studies, it is possible to mention the study on Polari, a language variety used by the gay community in the UK, conducted by Paul Baker in 2002.

There were two significant shifts in research concerning language, gender and sexuality at that time. First, the introduction of the concept of *community of practice*, theorized by Eckert and McConnell-Ginet in 1992, who put forward the hypothesis that language use is directly related to the context in which it is produced and that people belonging to the same community can use language in the same way. The second shift concerned the type of analysis applied to language, with the introduction of the notion of 'indexicality':

> Indexicality concerns the semiotic process that exists within interaction, whereby speakers connect particular linguistic features with representations of the social group that are stereotyped as using them (Irvine and Gal 2000). [...] Indexicality, then, is the process by which particular ways of using language point towards, or indicate, culturally recognizable identities. (Jones 2016: 213–214)

Another major shift in the study of language and gender occurred at the beginning of the 1990s when William Leap launched the first Lavender Language and Linguistics conference in Washington, DC, in 1993, which signalled the beginning of the study in what is known as 'lavender linguistics' (Baker 2008: 68). Lavender Linguistics embraces the study of language used in the LGBTIQ+ community and has come a long way since 1993. At that time, research mainly focused on gay and lesbian communities. Despite this limitation, the beginning of this new strand of linguistics was already a step forward if compared to previous research in which the lesbian community was rarely considered. The field has today evolved into a more inclusive range of topics which comprise the study of the language used to talk about and represent all different gender and sexual identities. In other words, this can be considered as the beginning of the era in which analysis of language in reference to gender started to give greatest importance to the way in which, to use Milani's words, 'individuals *do* gender in *different* ways by creatively deploying linguistic means which will allow them to orient themselves to available images or models of masculinity and femininity in a specific socio-cultural context' (2010: 119, emphases in the original).

The last significant change, which sets the basis for the understanding of *gender* that many scholars agree with today, arrived with the new wave of post-structuralist theories. More specifically, the groundbreaking studies by Judith Butler (1988, 1993, 1997, 2004) in the 1990s were and still are amongst the most relevant. Major influences also came from philosophers such as Roland Barthes (1964) and Jacques Derrida (1967). Barthes believed that any given text has a range of possible interpretations according to the reader's point of view. At the same time, Derrida's line of thinking stems from Ferdinand De Saussure's (1916) concepts of 'signifier' and 'signified'. De Saussure believed that the meaning of each signifier, or object/word/term, has to be agreed upon by society; differently from his inspirer, Derrida believed that meaning can change over time and is dependent on the context in which it is produced.

These perspectives imply a sort of deconstruction and (re)construction of meaning according to the context and the perception of the 'shared representation' (Milani 2010: 119) of the person interpreting the text. In a similar understanding, we can position Butler's concept of gender as performative, as 'a re-enactment and re-experiencing of a set of meanings already socially established' (1988: 526). She argues that language can be used to construct gender and used to convey a specific performance. These theories are presented for the majority in her two books *Gender Trouble* (1990) and *Bodies that Matter* (1993). The performativity feature of gender makes its construction a never-ending process, as anyone can perform their gender in a different way drawing on different social meanings. Another point made by Butler is that no group is a unified group, and thus it is not possible to generalize on the representation of identities. This point, also made earlier in this chapter and which will become evident later, fully applies to the transgender community as well. Gender and sexual identities are a personal matter. One person performs their gender in a unique way and for as much as some identities might have common characteristics what is true in the representation of one's identity might not be true in the representation of another person's identity.

Many other scholars, such as Jacques Lacan (1977), Luce Irigaray (1985) and psychoanalyst Sigmund Freud (1953), have influenced Butler. However, it was from Michel Foucault (1980) that she got the inspiration for her theory about society and hegemonic power. Foucault (1980) maintained that specific gender performances are naturalized in society following a hegemonic heteronormativity. Accordingly, Butler suggests that specific gender performances are privileged compared to others, in the sense that those gender identities that are considered *natural* are in a position of power with respect to others. Butler proposes a deconstruction of gender and therefore of those gender stereotypes which are linked to the traditional limitations that lie at the basis of inequalities toward gender identities.

This perspective proposed by Butler on performativity and the social construction of gender, and the definition of identity as something that can be continually changed and modified, influenced the views adopted by scholars, setting the basis for a new era on the studies of language related to gender and sexuality.

Like an ever-growing wave, following the development of Lavender Linguistics in the 1990s, the subsequent decades have seen the rise of a new current in the linguistic field: Queer Linguistics. One of the notions that played a pivotal role in the development of Queer Linguistics is post-structuralism. Identity, from a post-structuralist point of view, is defined according to its opposite: one thing is something that it is not. A number of thinkers quoted so far, such as Irigaray (1985) and Derrida (1976), as well as others such as Helen Cixous (1975), agree that society makes sense of the world by imposing categories onto things. Queer Linguistics has the main aim, in order to make sense of society, of deconstructing those categories, dismantling the binary structure in which identity is put into and understanding the way language is used to construct diverse identities. Queer Linguistics is based on the fact that identities are fluid and multiple (Baker 2008: 192) and does not focus on the study of what mainstream society considers as queer but on any identity that distances themselves from mainstream categories. When it comes to gender identities, the term 'queer' was adopted to indicate this kind of research as an umbrella term that could encompass a range of marginalized identities together with those already stereotypically defined as queer by society. As Livia (2000) remarks, the term has been semantically widened going from referring more specifically to gay people to becoming a hypernym to indicate any sexual and gender identity, as anyone can be someone else's queer person.

One of the perks that Queer Linguistics has added to the study of language, gender and sexuality is that it reinforced the idea that the field needed to move from gay and lesbian identities to all those identities which in one way or another are considered to be outside the boundaries of the heretonormative, mainstream and binary categories in which society is enclosed, rejecting the idea of normalization and binary categorizations (Milani 2017). As Motschenbacher suggests,

> For Queer Linguistics all identity categories are problematic because they normatively regulate and exclude those who do not fully meet their normative requirements […] It concerns all linguistic mechanisms that lead to heterosexuality being perceived as the naturalised norm, which in turn is to be destabilised and confronted with non-heteronormative alternatives. (2010: 10–11)

As Baker points out, Queer Linguistics should not be merely a replacement for studies and theories developed so far but an additional point of view to consider in the analysis of the relationship between language, gender and sexuality (Baker 2008: 196). The analysis presented in this research can be positioned within the field of Queer Linguistics to the extent that it critically addresses the way language is heteronormatively used to represent identities that do not adhere to heteronormative categories.

Stephen Whittle, professor of Equalities Law at Manchester Metropolitan University and transgender activist, begins the foreword of the book he edited with Susan Stryker in 2006, *The Transgender Studies Reader*, by saying that 'trans identities were one of the most written about subjects of the late twentieth century' (Stryker and Whittle 2006: xi). Here, we go against this current, as I believe that when it comes to this matter the literature in the field of linguistics is still not as extended as other topics or, to be more precise, it is not as popular and advertised as other fields of inquiry related to identity, gender and sexuality.

Indisputably, the literature surveyed shows that studies on transgender identities from a linguistic viewpoint are mostly all recent since it is only in the past two decades that this topic started flourishing among the interests of scholars who dedicated their research to language, gender, sexuality and identity.

Based on Lakoff's (1975) and Tannen's (1990) studies on women's language, some books were published with the aim of giving advice to transgender women on how to change their communicative behaviour in order to resemble cisgender women as much as possible. One famous example is Lou Sullivan's *Information for the Female to Male Cross Dresser and Transsexual* (1990). But still, this had little to do with transgender identity and how this is linguistically constructed and represented, which is the aim of the analysis presented in this book.

Some of the first studies on the linguistic representation of transgender identity can be traced back to Kira Hall and her research on Indian hijras (Hall 1997, 2002, 2013; Hall and O'Donovan 1996) and to Don Kulick (1998) who investigated the language and identity representation of *travesti* in Brazil.

More recently, in 2014, Duke University Press launched the *Transgender Reader Quarterly* (*TSQ*), the first non-medical scientific journal on issues related to transgender people, edited by Susan Stryker and Paisley Currah, which as of writing is at its seventh volume. Before this, the only academic journal focusing specifically on this topic was the *International Journal of Transgenderism*, a medical journal launched by Routledge in 1998, which this year has changed its name to the *International Journal of Transgender Health*. The journal mainly discusses issues related to gender dysphoria, gender reassignment and the psychological effects of such medical processes on patients. From a linguistic point of view, it is possible to affirm that the opening statement of this section is still very applicable. In fact, if it is true that scholars have been researching about transgender people for the past twenty or even thirty years, it is even more recent that linguists took an interest in this topic.

Apart from the medical journal cited above, the list of other works from a medical and psychological perspective is long (see, for example, Delemarre-van de Waal and Cohen-Kettenis 2006). The same can be said for the field of cultural studies and history, with the work of scholars such as Sandy Stone (1991), Susan Stryker (1994, 1998, 2008) and Vivienne Namaste (2000); and also in the field of law with scholars such as Stephen Whittle (1995, 1996, 1998a, b; Witten and Whittle 2004). In the past decade, we have seen the rise of studies that have tried to bring all these topics together, such as *The Transgender Studies Reader*, of which Stryker and Whittle published the first volume in 2006. Whittle describes the book as:

> The Transgender Studies Reader is an effort to afford the student and teacher with a passage through the complexities of gender theory. It illustrates how trans people were problematized by science and society, and how trans people have responded by using the same intellectual tools that have oppressed them to place the 'Other' in the problematized position. This process has not been easy. Our collection also illustrates the call to arms that has been issued by activist trans academics to make the study of the self and the Objective Other a reputable field. (2006: xiv)

In 2013, a second volume came out edited by Stryker and Aren Aizura with the aim of complementing the first one and expanding the horizon to more recent works and emerging trends. Both volumes give little to no space to linguistic perspectives. In the last few years, we have witnessed the rise of interest from scholars who prefer a more interdisciplinary approach to the study of transgender identities, with works such as the investigation carried out by Ruth Pearce (2018), who takes a sociological perspective in the analysis of gender identity clinics and health-related issues, problematizing the role of clinicians as gatekeepers, or the latest collaboration on cultural, political and sociological aspects of trans identity (Pearce et al. 2019). From a non-academic perspective, autobiographies written by transgender people have become increasingly popular as well (see among others: Jacques 2015; Baker 2017; Kiss 2017; Burns 2018).

In 1997 Kira Hall and Anna Livia edited the book *Queerly Phrased*, a collection of essays on language, gender and sexuality, as the subtitle reveals. It is not the first collection on language and gender studies, but one of the first displaying research on transgender identity, with an essay by Bagemihl on the linguistic reaction of lesbian and gay people to transsexual identity and a further investigation by Hall on Indian hijras.

A couple of years later, in 1999, Don Kulick wrote 'Transgender and Language: A Review of the Literature and Suggestions for the Future', tracing a sort of literature review of the various studies related to language and transgender people's identity found in academic research up to that time.

Starting from the beginning of the twentieth century many aspects of transgender identity have been considered, especially as it becomes more and more apparent that binary heteronormativity was shaping the world in every aspect and that non-heteronormative identities were struggling to find a safe space in which they could freely express themselves. As suggested by Petra L. Doan (2010), the binary heteronormative vision of the world influences every aspect of life; even the way space is conceptualized. Doan analyses the way transgender and gender-variant people suffer from the heteronormative shaping of spaces in society. Transgender identity is also studied from a cross-cultural point of view, for example the study by Kira Hall (1997) mentioned above.

Among those scholars who have dedicated their research to the way transgender identities are represented in non-Western cultures and society is Niko Besnier (2003), who investigated the linguistic construction of transgender identities in Tonga. Besnier analyses the way the English language influenced the Tongan society, which remains essentially monolingual. He concludes that among the minorities using English in that society a big part is constituted by transgender individuals who find in this form of code-switching an escape from marginality and oppression (Besnier 2003: 296).

In 2016, the whole November issue of *TSQ* was dedicated to another aspect of transgender studies: ways in which transgender identities are translated. The issue opens with the study on the translation of the biography of the East German artist Charlotte von Mahlsdorf by Brian J. Baer (2016), who concludes that the translation of the memoir reflects a specific way of framing queer identities in Western society. The issue continues with interesting parallelism between the marginalization of transgender studies and translation studies, with a subsequent destructuralization of both fields and the emergence of a new non-binary, decolonizing multilingual discourse (Concilio 2016). Memoirs are also at the centre of research presented in this volume conducted by Emily Rose (2016). Starting from the assumption that translation also means 'manipulation and the power to re-present certain gender identities' (Rose 2016: 485), Rose argues that the translation of transgender identity can demonstrate how all translations can be multilayered and queer. Two more matters are discussed in this volume. One of these relates to the rooted gendered rules of some Nordic languages such as Icelandic (Josephson and Einarsdottir 2016) and Finnish (Leino 2016). The authors of the first study conclude that Icelandic is problematic when addressing transgender identities and see no easy solution to this problem. The latter explores the compromises of Finnish language toward a more inclusive definition of transgender identities in Finland. The other issue discussed is concerned with the untranslatability of certain transgender identities. More specifically, Kay Gabriel (2016) addresses a collection of poems by a Canadian author, concluding that translation can be, in the case of the poetry under scrutiny, a way to make transgender identity readable and understandable through binary categories. Similarly, Alvaro Jarrin (2016) analyses the way anglophone discourse is used in the Brazilian medical context to delegitimize transsexual and transgender people's access to health care by representing them as unauthentic women. Jarrin concludes that it is up to academic scholars to create a new framework of analysis in order to de-pathologize transgender people.

The last article of this volume serves as an opening act for the discussion of a different scenario in transgender studies, one that is becoming more and more popular recently. Helen Hok-Sze Leung discusses 'the role of audiovisual translation in the cinematic circulation of trans knowledge' (2016: 433). The case study presented by this author is circumscribed to Cantonese and Thai, arguing for the critical role that multilingualism should have in trans cinematic productions.

Cinema and television have taken on an essential role in the dissemination and acknowledgement of transgender identities. As stated in the introduction to this work, transgender people are becoming popular on the big and small screen. Many scholars have been devoting their attention to the representation of transgender identities in this form of media communication. Linda M. Hess (2017) analyses how the ageing of transgender people and, more generally, queer people is represented in *Transparent* (2014). Jamie C. Capuzza and Leland G. Spencer take into consideration nine scripted US TV series which feature transgender character and conclude that the way transgender people have been represented over the years has evolved from a 'wrong body' narrative to a more diverse and inclusive representation of different transgender identities and subjectivities (Capuzza and Spencer 2017: 3). In 2015, Marcus Hartner affirmed that the representation of transgender characters in films tends to realign transgender identity with heteronormative identities, drawing on the notion of love and family. These examples bring forward the diversity in representation of transgender identity in television and the cinema.

The character of Sophia Burset, and the actress who played this role, Laverne Cox, attracted the attention of quite a few scholars. Emilia Di Martino (2017), for example, analyses the representation of transgender identity given by the actress and how it influences the way masculinity and femininity are perceived.

Theodore R. Burnes and Mindy M. Chen (2012) try to shed light on transgender identity by looking at the various definitions and self-representations. Through the use of a mixed methodology, they position transgender identity among multiple identities, proving hypotheses for new approaches to the understanding of trans identity.

Lal Zimman (2009, 2013, 2014) makes a rather important contribution in this field, as he takes an interest in the representation of transgender men's identities. In 2009 Zimman presented a study on the coming out genre. He argues that transgender people's coming out narratives, as a genre, cannot be included in the same category as gay and lesbian coming out stories, in the sense that there is one main difference in coming out for a transgender person. This process can occur before or after the transition in gender role. Furthermore, Zimman underlines that while gay and lesbian coming out stories mostly point to how the coming out happened, transgender people describe more frequently how they 'came out into their new gender role' (2009: 58). In the following years his interest in the identity of trans men was redefined and as he says himself, he '[focuses] on the power of language to redefine the body in the face of compulsory gender and sexual normativity' (Zimman 2014: 14). In 2013, Zimman published a work that falls into the framework of sociophonetics, analysing how the pitch of the voice changed in trans men after the use of testosterone. His study reveals that, although trans men are generally described as 'gay-sounding', a closer analysis highlights that there are many differences between the speech of a transgender man and that of a gay man, leading to the conclusion that gay-sounding speech cannot be considered as one single speech style, but it encompasses many variations from the hegemonic norm (Zimman 2013). A more recent study from Zimman (2014) focuses on the linguistic representation of the gendered body on behalf of transgender men in online communities. The most important contribution made by Zimman (2012, 2014) in the field of linguistics within transgender studies is the conceptualization of the idea of the 'true transsexual', through which he argues that more and more trans people are forced to fit themselves into specific categories that are recognizable in society in order to be acknowledged. This concept is at the heart of studies on the representation of trans identities as it encompasses the fundamental explanation behind many of the different representational understandings we have of trans identities. Rodrigo Borba (2019) draws on the concept of the 'true transsexual' as he considers interactions between patients and clinicians in a gender identity clinic in Brazil. He suggests that this idea of the 'true transsexual' dominates the conversations between patients and clinicians and is the overarching aim of both parties. The patients want to fulfil the requirements of being 'a true' transgender person in order to get the assistance they need from the national health system and the clinicians are so keen to help their patients that they go as far as suggesting which answers are right and which are wrong when representing themselves as trans people.

These very different and at the same time similar studies are a clear example of the varieties of linguistic research that can be carried out on the relation between language use and transgender identity. Language can be analysed from the point of view of how transgender people use it to communicate, create their own identity and talk about themselves. It can also be analysed to investigate how cisgender people use it to talk about and represent transgender identities in order to put forward their understanding of trans identities. For the purpose of the research presented in this book, the second approach is adopted on the grounds of its relevance in relation to the data analysed.

An influential work for this research has been a study from Paul Baker (2014a). In this work, Baker collected a corpus of newspaper articles from the year 2012 and through the use of Corpus Linguistics tools he analysed the way the British press depicted transgender people in that year. As it will become clear in later chapters, the research presented here takes Baker's study as a starting point and develops along similar lines, though considering a different time span. Among his findings, Baker highlights that:

> the analysis did find a great deal of evidence to support the view that trans people are regularly represented in reasonably large sections of the press as receiving special treatment lest they be offended, as victims or villains, as involved in transient relationships or sex scandals, as the objects of jokes about their appearance or sexual organs and as attention seeking freakish objects. (2014a: 233)

Baker also adds that some positive representations were retrieved but were less frequent.

The media have become one important source for the analysis of the representation of transgender people. So far, we dealt with the investigation of identity represented in television, cinema, and the press, although the internet has also given researcher a lot of material to discuss. Lexi Webster analysed self-identification of transgender people on the social media platform Twitter and the identity performance by transgender people on web-based fora, demonstrating the non-homogeneity of transgender identities (Webster 2019, 2018, respectively). Laura Horak (2014) looked at the consumption of vlogs made by transgender individuals on YouTube, and how these productions at the same time serve their creators as forms of acceptance and acknowledgement of their own identities. Lucy Jones (2019) investigated the identity construction by two transgender vloggers, concluding that they actively use normative discourses to perform their identities, referring again to the idea of the 'true transsexual'.

More specifically on the newspaper representation of trans identities, Kat Gupta (2019) explores the case of the Lucy Meadows in the British press. The teacher was found dead in her apartment after transitioning and coming out as a trans woman in the school where she worked. Gupta analyses how newspapers use pronouns when covering the story, in the author's own words: 'within a journalistic context, pronouns are one of several strategies that are used to question, undermine or validate a transgender person's gender identity' (2019: 32). The author concludes that misgendering is the most common practice when referring to the case of Meadows. More on the press, and its lexical choices for the representation of transgender people, has been written by Adriano Ferraresi (2018), who focuses on citizen journalism and investigates the extent to which those negative stereotypes about transgender people are reversed in citizen journalism.

Thomas J. Billard (2016) investigates the representations of trans individuals in the US press. In the study, Billard aims to determine the extent to which the transgender community is legitimized or delegitimized by news media in the United States. Billard (2016) concludes that the mainstream newspaper's coverage of the transgender community is very limited and uses linguistic strategies which delegitimize trans identities more often. Billard also points to a set of strategies commonly put in place in the press when representing transgender identities. These can be grouped into four main categories which include misgendering and misnaming; misrepresentation (through pathologization) of trans identities; use of puns and mockery; and the sexualization of the transgender body (Billard 2016: 4196).

Before this, a case study on the representation of the murder of trans teen Gwen Araujo in the United States was carried out by Barker-Plummer (2013). Here, the author identifies two main patterns of representation, one is the 'wrong body' narrative, and the other is the use of 'fixing' strategies, retracing instances of misgendering and use of the name assigned at birth.

Studies on the representation of transgender individuals in the press are also found in adjacent fields of study, such as communication and journalism studies (see among others Willox 2003; Capuzza 2015; Spencer 2015). In Billard's words, 'news media coverage disciplines and stereotypes transgender identity' through a number of linguistic patterns recurring in the representation of transgender identities in the press (2016: 4196).

The study presented in this book can be positioned among the studies listed above, as a step forward in the understanding of language with reference to transgender people. The results retrieved in this study expand on a larger time span compared to the above-mentioned study by Baker (2014a) and were able to pinpoint a change in the use of terminology related to transgender identities. Moreover, the analysis presented in this book puts forward different semantic patterns of representation that will be further discussed in Chapters 4 and 5.

The role of the press in the representation of gender identities

As Lia Litosseliti argues, 'newspapers are a prime public site for moral arguments and for constructing values and ideologies' (2002: 136). For this reason, News Discourse is a valuable source for the analysis of how ideologies, power relations and the cultural values of a society are actualized and represented through language. Analysing the language of the media is useful to identify those discourses that pervade, influence and shape the way people see and understand society, its beliefs and values. In this sense, the representational value of gender and sexual identities in News Discourse has increasingly become of interest to language scholars. Similar to the general evolution of the study of gender and language, some of the first issues about gender and language in relation to News Discourse analysed by linguists are concerned with the representation of women in the press, and with the percentage of women actually working and using this means of communication. Cynthia Carter, Gill Branston and Stuart Allan wrote *News, Gender and Power* (1998), a volume that retraces the role of women in the press from different perspectives, starting from the actual contribution of women in the press to how these subjects are represented and why. Some years later, Carolyn Byerly and Karen Ross published *Women and Media: A Critical Introduction* (2006), extending the study from journalism to the media as a more general field of inquiry.

All in all, while the linguistic representation of women and men in news stories has come a long way (see also Clarke 1992; Adampa 1999), that of sexual orientation and gender identities in the press has become scholarly worthy only more recently.

At the beginning of the twenty-first century, several linguists showed their interest in looking at how language is used in the representation of non-binary definitions of gender identities. Elisabeth Morrish and Helen Sauntson (2007) investigated the representation of Peter Mandelson, a British politician, in British broadsheets concluding that he was not only represented as effeminate but also in a negative way through negative stereotypes generally associated, at the time, to gay men. In 2005, Baker looked at discourse prosodies in British tabloids in relation to the representation of homosexuality and gay men. Baker argues that several different discourse prosodies can be retrieved in the corpus collected from the *Daily Mail* and the *Mirror*. Gay people are defined as a minority group, homosexuality as a behaviour, and the articles are written in relation to violent crimes, shame and secrecy, shamelessness, promiscuity, and the gay lobby. Baker concludes that while both newspapers relate gay identity to more negative discourses, one main difference lies in the fact that the *Mirror* does not frequently discuss politically based discourses in relation to homosexuality. In contrast, the *Daily Mail* focuses more on equality and on how gay 'propaganda' influences children. Additionally, similar to the patterns used in the 1980s when AIDS was strongly associated with homosexuality, Baker traces a renewed attempt at relating a sort of homophobic representation to gay men.

If we turn our sight away from the UK, the search becomes even harder. Some studies appear relating to Ireland, following the issuing of the law recognizing same-sex marriage. Leanne Bartley and Encarnacion Hidalgo-Tenorio (2015, 2016) conducted two different studies on a corpus of newspaper articles collected from the Irish press following the release of the above-mentioned law. Their first study, published in 2015, focuses on the verbal processes associated with the terms *gay**, *homo**, *lesbian** and *queer**, that is to say, the authors focused on transitivity processes and how these were used to represent queer identities. The study concludes that the most frequent verbal process used in this case is 'material'.[2] To put it simply, queer people are mostly represented as active participants. The corpus also shows a robust homophobic discourse, and while gay men are demonized, victimized and represented as curable patients, lesbians seemed to be generally more accepted by society. In their second study, the aim was to look at how the perception of homosexuality was filtered through the press (Bartley and Hidalgo-Tenorio 2016: 9). Among other results, the study highlights that gay people were mostly represented as a community, a group of people working together.

Similarly, Carlos Alberto M. Gouveia (2005) analysed the representation of gay and lesbian people in a Portuguese newspaper in a set of articles published across one week with the heading 'gay power' in 2001. Gouveia argues that homosexuality is a topic rarely mentioned in the Portuguese press and is still considered a taboo. Thus, it is notable that the newspaper under investigation in the study centres its attention on gay people as the main actors in the articles published in that week. The articles mirror the discussion about civil unions of the Portuguese parliament from a few weeks earlier. Despite the clear intention not to discriminate gay people, 'at the same time there is also the construction of a sense of fear associated with homosexuality, via the assertion that gays and lesbians have more social and political power than one would expect' (Gouveia 2005: 247), bringing forward again, as in the study by Baker (2005), the idea of a 'gay lobby'.

Similar studies have focused on the press in Slovenia (Kuhar 2003) and in Turkey (Hoskan 2006). In the first case, the analysis focuses not only on the press but more generally on the representation of homosexuality in the Slovenian media. In contrast, the second looks at the representation of homosexuality in the Turkish press.

The studies presented so far discuss lesbian and gay identity. In fact, as I mentioned above, transgender identities, as much as intersex identities, are entirely cut out from most studies that consider gender identities. As stated previously, it is only recently, and in a few instances, that the representation of transgender identities in the press have been investigated from a linguistic scholarly perspective.

The TransCor: UK vs Canada

In this section we move from discussing the literature relevant to the main topic of the book to that related to the data taken into account: the Transgender Corpus.

Corpus Linguistics, the methodological approach adopted in this book, uses the term *corpus* to refer to a set of machine-readable texts collected with a specific aim in mind and being representative of a type of language (McEnery and Wilson [1996] 2001).

One crucial aspect of corpus building is that, whether it comprises written texts or spoken transcribed interactions, it must be representative of the sample of language collected. The question of representativeness is crucial for many scholars in Corpus Linguistics (Leech 1992; McEnery and Wilson [1996] 2001; Sinclair 1996; McEnery, Xiao and Tono 2006). One of the first harsh critiques raised to corpus use in language analysis was from Chomsky (1965), and in a sense, it was related to the question of representativeness. Chomsky affirms that:

> a record of natural speech will show numerous false starts, deviations from rules, changes of plan in mid-course, and so on. The problem for the linguist, as well as for the child learning the language, is to determine from the data of performance the underlying system of rules that have been mastered by the speaker-hearer and that he puts to use in actual performance. (1965: 4)

Thus, following this line of thinking, the use of corpus, by its nature, would produce misleading results. This criticism influenced the field of linguistic analysis for a long time, and as a consequence, for many years, the use of corpora was put aside. Chomsky argued that corpora would always generate 'skewed' results (McEnery and Wilson [1996] 2001: 30) as infrequent utterances would be excluded because of their rarity, whilst other common ones still would have a chance of being omitted. This criticism must be contextualized to the time in which it was made when computer assistance was not as developed as it is nowadays. Thus, the probability of these criticisms being not entirely unacceptable is high. The issue raised by Chomsky is potentially a valid basis for discussion on representativeness. The criteria behind corpus building should always be definite and clear (McEnery and Wilson [1996] 2001). Corpora are generally large, therefore they can be considered as 'representative samples of a particular type of naturally occurring language [...] as a standard reference with which claims about language can be measured' (Baker 2006: 2). The use of corpus methodologies for language analysis has been considered more quantitative, although the numerous relatively recent combinations with discourse analysis and other approaches have been changing this orientation toward a mixed quantitative/qualitative methodology.

The language included in corpora can be of various provenances. Corpora of written language are the ones that come to mind first as they are also the easiest to collect, though many corpora of spoken language are available as well. Some corpora of sign language have been built more recently, as well as corpora made of video recordings that encode paralinguistic features such as gestures and hyperlinks to video or sound (McCarthy and O'Keeffe 2010; McEnery and Hardie 2012; Ferraresi and Bernardini 2019). The use of corpora makes Corpus Linguistics an 'evidence-driven' type of analysis (Partington, Duguid and Taylor 2013: 5).

It is possible to divide existing corpora into two major categories: monitor corpora and balanced or sample corpora (McEnery and Hardie 2012). The monitor corpus approach was first proposed by John Sinclair (1991). These types of corpora are different from the other category in two respects: their collection never ends as they continue to be updated as time goes by, and they include a variety of language materials in them. Distinctly, balanced or sampled corpora, initially conceived by Douglas Biber (1993) and Geoffrey Leech (2007), are specialized corpora collected in order to represent an exact type of language in a given time span. These corpora have an exact size that can vary from as small as under one hundred thousand words to billions of words. An example of sample corpora can be the Lancaster/Oslo/Bergen (LOB) corpus (Stig, Leech and Goodluck 1978), which is a sample of written modern British English from the 1960s, or the International Corpus of Learner English (ICLE) (Granger, Dagneaux and Meunier 2002), which contains essays written by learners of English. One famous example of monitor corpus is the Bank of English (BoE) (Järvinen 1994), started at the University of Birmingham in the 1980s, which is divided into two sections, one of general English and one specialized on language pedagogy. Similarly, the Corpus of Contemporary American English (COCA) (Davies 2008–) contains texts written in American English; the COCA is an example of both a sample corpus and a monitor corpus. The corpus collected for the present study is a sample corpus, it represents a specific type of language, the one used in newspapers in the UK and Canada, on a specific topic, transgender identity.

Corpora can also be distinguished between synchronic and diachronic corpora. The former, like the LOB, are representative of a limited span of time, while the latter stretch on longer time spans in order to analyse language change in the passing of time (Partington, Duguid and Taylor 2013).

Currently, corpora and Corpus Linguistics are being used in a variety of fields, from lexicography to language acquisition to discourse analysis (McCarthy and O'Keeffe 2010). Corpus Linguistics has also become a useful resource in the study of gender and sexuality (Motschenbacher 2010; Baker 2014b) as it allows for shifting the aims of this field of research from the details of qualitative research on a specific community or type of language to more extensive and more general research that discusses the way language is used in relation to gender identities and the expression of sexuality.

Corpus Linguistics has been defined as 'a *tool*, a *method*, a *methodology*, a *methodological approach*, a *discipline*, a *theory*, a *theoretical approach*, a *paradigm* (theoretical or methodological), or a combination of these' (Taylor 2008: 180, emphasis in the original), but so far the question remains open to discussion in terms of finding a definition upon which all scholars can agree upon. For this research, and in light of this definition, Corpus Linguistics will mostly be used as a methodology in combination with other theoretical frameworks. Among the many definitions of Corpus Linguistics, Baker and McEnery suggest that it 'is a powerful methodology' for the analysis of discourse, language of the media and gender identity (2015: 1). Against this backdrop, Corpus Linguistics is used in this book to analyse the language used to represent transgender people in the British and the Canadian press in a specific time span. To do so, a corpus of newspaper articles, which contained references to transgender identities, was built: the Transgender Corpus (hereafter TransCor). The corpus has two parts: TransCorUK (TCUK) and TransCorCan (TCC). The following sections explain in greater details how the TransCor was designed and collected and provide a brief introduction to Corpus Linguistics.

Frequency lists, concordances, collocations and keywords

The tools offered by Corpus Linguistic have been very useful for this study. This section describes, step by step, the procedures adopted in order to analyse the TransCor.

The first step in the analysis of the corpus was to look at the frequencies of occurrence of the search words used to retrieve the articles from LexisNexis, and in some cases also at their morphological variations. Some of the terms were searched by adding an * which is a function used in corpus analysis defined as *wild card*. Both pieces of software used in this study employ the asterisk in order to apply the wild card function. The use of this function can be seen as an alternative to searching for different word-forms of the same term, Tribble defines it as 'a symbol which can be used to stand for one or many alphanumeric characters' (2010: 173). This type of search, while useful for making the search faster, may present some issues, as it may include in the results unwanted terms, according to the search parameters of the software used. The *wild card* function is most likely to be used in concordance searches, as it is discussed more extensively in Chapter 3.

The first tool used to analyse these terms is the frequency list tool. A frequency list is basically the list of all the words occurring in the corpus under investigation displayed in an orderly fashion; either according to their frequency (most occurring to least occurring or *vice versa*) or in alphabetical order. Occurrences can be displayed as raw numbers (i.e. plain number of occurrences) or as a percentage in comparison with the whole corpus (Baker 2014b: 12). Frequencies can also be visualized in their normalized (or relative) score. That is to say, by calculating their presence in the corpus by million words (usually the preferred parameter, but lower parameters can be used as well, namely 10,000, depending on the size of the original corpus). This type of visualization is advantageous when comparing results from corpora that are not similar in size (McEnery and Hardie 2012: 49–50). The analysis of the frequencies of the terms considered key in this corpus makes it possible to have a clear view of the presence and distribution of these terms throughout the data collected, and highlights which newspapers were talking about transgender people in the time span considered, how frequently and which terms each newspaper prefers. These terms are considered key as the aim of this work is to look at the representation of transgender people, these being the search terms from which the corpus was generated and are the most relevant to the topic as well. Frequency must always be considered in relation to the corpus it belongs to and not in 'an absolute sense' (48). This overview of the corpus was a first attempt at giving some context to the answer to the first research question guiding this work, on how trans people are represented in the British and Canadian press. As Stefan T. Gries points out, 'the most frequently used statistic in corpus linguistics is the frequency of occurrence of some linguistic variable' (2008: 403). He continues that this approach can, at times, be misleading (404), in line with other scholars who define frequency searches as a potential reductive method of analysis (Baker 2006; Taylor 2013). Therefore, 'the significance of word frequency also demands qualitative interpretation depending on context' (Kirk 2009: 33). For this reason, the terms identified as the most frequent in the TransCor, according to the criteria considered, were then investigated through a concordance analysis.

Concordance analysis plays a key role in addressing the second research question that I try to answer in this book, unveiling the context in which these terms are inserted, and thus the type of linguistic patterns which accompany these words.

A concordance analysis is carried out through the creation of a concordance list. We can define it as 'a list of all the occurrences of a particular search term in a corpus, presented within the context they occur in' (Baker 2006: 71). This type of visualization of the term investigated allows for an in-depth analysis of the context in which the term is presented. Concordances are also referred to as KWIC (key words in context) (Tribble 2010). In fact, that is exactly what a concordance list does: it visualizes the given terms searched for in its context. Concordances can be visualized according to different settings, in the order they occur in the corpus or sorted. The software used for the analysis allows the researcher to sort the concordances alphabetically, or by highlighting the words that occur on the left or the right of the terms searched for. The researchers can indicate their own preference for the visualization. If the corpus is tagged,[3] the concordances can also be sorted by text or tag. Another very useful technique, of the utmost importance in this study, is the use of sampling. When the concordance lists generate hundreds of concordance lines, it is possible, but extremely time-consuming, to analyse each and every one of them. An alternative for this is to make a randomized selection of the results and use that selection as a sample valid for the whole corpus. Some pieces of software have this function integrated, and the researcher can choose to view a specific number or percentage of results randomly selected (Tribble 2010; McEnery and Hardie 2012). The software used for this study both allowed for this function to be used, as will be explained in Chapter 3. Finally, concordances can also be investigated through the use of a restricted search. In this case, the researcher can narrow down the search to a very specific realization of the term. For this option, a tagged corpus would be the best choice, as it allows searching the corpus according to the specific part of speech one is looking for. When the tagged corpus is not available, the researchers can generate simple algorithms that might help to solve this problem and conduct a restricted search (Tribble 2010). For the study presented in this book, the TransCor was investigated untagged, and the random sample search was employed.

Keyword analysis is also among the option tools of Corpus Linguistics. This consists of generating a list of words that occur more frequently in the corpus under scrutiny when compared to another corpus. In order to generate a keyword list, the main corpus must be compared against a reference corpus. The software will then generate a frequency list from the main corpus, one from the reference corpus, compare the results and highlight those words which, in comparison to the reference corpus, seem to be more frequent. This practice eliminates from the analysis all those words that generally carry no semantic meaning, such as function words. In a written corpus, the determiner *the* is usually one of the most frequent terms, and thus it will be unlikely to find it in a keyword list. This technique is very useful for highlighting those terms that are most relevant in a corpus, and that could unveil a linguistic pattern (Scott 2010). As Costas Gabrielatos and Baker point out 'keyword analyses can reveal statistically more frequent terms in different newspaper types, individual newspapers, or text types and genres within or across newspapers' (2008: 7). This technique was not used in the analyses presented in this book. Instead, Chapters 4 and 5 present the results emerging from a collocation analysis.

McEnery and Hardie maintain that the concept of collocation stems from the hypothesis that:

> important aspects of the meaning of a word (or another linguistic unit) are not contained within the word itself, considered in isolation, but rather subsist in the characteristic associations that the word participates in, alongside other words or structure with which it frequently co-occurs. (2012: 122–123)

First introduced by John R. Firth (1957), collocations can be defined as those words that regularly co-occur with other words, in a way that it is statistically relevant. Collocations are calculated according to specific statistical measures, such as MI (mutual information), T-score, Log-Likelihood and LogDice. Each type of test will give different results as it favours different types of words in the calculation (Partington 1998; Baker 2006; McEnery, Xiao and Tono 2006; Jaworska 2017). For this study, the first 50 collocates generated for each term investigated were considered, and the statistical measure used was MI, with a threshold of 6 and a word span of ± 5 when using AntConc and ± 3 when using CQPweb (more about the software will be said later). MI calculates collocations based on the relative frequency and the overall size of the corpus (Baker 2006:

101), whereas the threshold indicates the minimum times of occurrences that a term displays to be considered in the statistical calculation. Although Susan Hunston (2002) suggests that a threshold of three is ideal for calculating collocates, in this case, due to the size of the corpus under investigation, it felt necessary to raise the threshold in order make the collocates even more relevant (Durrant and Doherty 2010; Baker 2014b). In the two pieces of software used, the word span was predetermined and left unchanged. The collocation analysis was limited to the three terms which resulted as the most frequent among the search terms used for data collection, namely *transgender**, *transsexual** and *trans*. In accordance with the interest expressed in research question one – to address the different representations given by the press – and opposite to the choice of analysing each newspaper on its own. At this stage, the two parts which compose the TransCor were analysed separately. The Canadian data was analysed as a whole. The British data was further divided into the PopCor and the QualCor, this was done to consider an additional division between the quality and the popular press. Each search resulted in a different list of collocates for each term; these were then further analysed through concordance analysis to highlight the main topics surrounding the terms under investigation. In the list, only the first fifty terms were considered for the analysis, except for the term *trans* in the PopCor which did not produce fifty collocates but only twenty-nine.

A more in-depth investigation of the topics, through a qualitative analysis of concordance lines, and more generally the text itself, lead to the identification of discourses about transgender people that news producers are trying to convey or undermine. By carrying out a close reading of concordance lines, I was able to gain a clear impression regarding the functional use of each collocational pair, in which context and what general type of evaluation it carries.

Although Corpus Linguistics methodologies also offer other tools for the investigation of corpora, the ones presented so far are the most commonly used among researchers which employ corpus-based approaches and have been discussed to give the reader a more complete overview.

The TransCorUK

The TransCorUK is a corpus of news articles collected from the British press. This section of the TransCor was built first, and the TransCorCan was later added, compiled mirroring the criteria used for the TransCorUK. All the articles included in the corpus have at least one reference to transgender people. The time span in which the corpus was collected stretches from January 2013 to December 2015. This specific time span was selected for different reasons. The starting point was dictated by the fact that similar research was previously conducted on the year 2012 (Baker 2014a). In 2013 we also witnessed the unveiling of the Chelsea Manning case, which supplied much attention toward the trans community. Chelsea, a trans woman, and a former soldier of the US army, was accused of leaking sealed documents to WikiLeaks,[4] and was convicted and sent to a male prison, opening the debate regarding the placement of transgender people in gender-appropriate prisons. These two reasons led to the decision to start the data collection from 2013. Extending data compiling for the TransCor until 2015 was also due to two factors. Firstly, 2015 is the year in which the project presented in this book was conceived, and secondly, a three-year span allowed me to create a corpus that was large and representative enough to provide a more general idea of the semantic patterns surrounding the discourses about transgender people and retrieve any changes across these years, therefore, establishing if the discourses emerging from the analysis are stable and well rooted or rapidly changing and adapting to societal and news demands.

The newspaper articles were downloaded from the online platform LexisNexis (n.d.), an electronic database containing legal and journalistic documents in different languages, covering many contexts, and downloadable in various formats. The following search terms were used to download the articles: *transgender, transsexual, transvestite, trans, trannie, cross-dresser, sex change, shemale, gender reassignment,* and *dysphoria*. This list was created through various steps. As a starting point, I first referred to the search terms used by Baker (2014a), who compiled a corpus on the representation of transgender people in the British press in the year 2012. The search terms used by Baker to retrieve articles from LexisNexis are the following:

> transsexual OR transgender OR trans OR transgendered OR trannie OR tranny OR mtf OR ftm OR cross-dresser OR transvestite OR intersex OR intersexed OR sex change OR shemale OR genderbender. (2014a: 215)

From this list, the terms *intersex* and *intersexed* were excluded as I believe that they are not relevant to my own RQs, also in line with the guidelines on terminology related to trans identity used as a reference for this analysis.

A pilot study on a sample corpus compiled on the first six months of 2015 was then conducted in order to test the relevance of the search words (Zottola 2018a). This pilot study highlighted the necessity to produce some changes in the search list. In fact, the original search included the terms: *transgendered, mtf, ftm* and *genderbender*. These terms were deleted from the search term list due to their extremely low, at times null, frequency in the pilot corpus. Whereas, two terms that resulted in being consistently present in the articles collected for the case study were added to the final search list, namely *gender reassignment* and *dysphoria*, thus finalizing the list of search terms used to download the final version of the TransCorUK.

Eight national British newspapers were chosen for the collection of the TransCorUK. Due to the peculiarity of the British press which can be divided into different categories according to political preference, publication frequency, topics and other features of the newspapers, for the purpose of the creation of the TransCorUK I decided to include: *The Guardian*, the *i*, *The Daily Telegraph* and *The Times* as representative of the quality press, and the *Daily Express*, the *Daily Mail*, the *Daily Mirror* and *The Sun* as representative of the popular press.

The choice of these newspapers was also dictated by the figures of circulation available through the Audit Bureau of Circulation referring to the year 2013. Table 2.1 shows the average circulation of each newspaper in the month of

Table 2.1 Newspaper circulation rates in the UK.

Newspaper	2013	2014	2015
The Sun	2,409,811	2,213,659	1,978,702
Daily Mail	1,863,151	1,780,565	1,688,727
Daily Mirror	1,058,488	992,256	922,235
Evening Standard	695,645	805,309	877,532
Daily Telegraph	555,817	544,546	494,675
Daily Star	535,957	489,067	425,246
Daily Express	529,648	500,473	457,914
The Times	399,339	384,304	396,621
i	293,946	298,266	280,351
Financial Times	275,375	234,193	219,444
Daily Record	251,535	227,639	203,725
The Guardian	204,440	207,958	185,429

Source: Data from Audit Bureau of Circulation.

January of each year, which can be considered representative of the situation of the whole year.

Having decided to choose eight newspapers, four representative of the quality press and four of the popular press, a further criterion observed when choosing the newspapers was the political preference expressed by the newspaper. In fact, it was challenging to find a balance of 50 per cent conservative and 50 per cent liberal, but I tried to be as close as possible by choosing five more conservative (*The Daily Telegraph*, *The Times*, the *Daily Express*, the *Daily Mail* and *The Sun*) and three more liberal newspapers (*The Guardian*, the *I* and the *Daily Mirror*). When available, Sunday editions were included as well.

The last criterion considered was that the newspapers had to be national editions. For these reasons, some newspapers were excluded from the list below. The *Evening Standard*, which according to the figures results to be the fourth most circulated newspaper, was excluded due to the fact that it is distributed only in London; moreover, being a free newspaper, its distribution figures could be unrealistic. The second newspaper excluded from the ones used in the research is the *Daily Star*, which according to the Audit Bureau of Circulation was the sixth most distributed newspaper in the UK. The reason for the exclusion is that LexisNexis only provided its Sunday edition to download. The *Financial Times* was excluded as well, as unlike the other newspapers it only reports on financial and business news, while the *Daily Record* was excluded as it is only distributed in Scotland. Generally speaking, the circulation figures do not change drastically across the three years, making the data collecting criteria consistent throughout the time span of the research. The newspapers chosen for the TransCorUK are highlighted in bold in Table 2.1.

The corpus collected comprises 3,138 articles, for a total of 2,012,598 million tokens.[5] The articles are divided as follows: 885 articles in 2013, 901 in 2014, and 1,352 articles in 2015, as shown in more detail in Table 2.2.

For the purpose of the analysis, the TransCorUK was divided into two sub-corpora: the QualCor (the name is an abbreviation of Quality Corpus; this sub-corpus is made of all articles collected from the quality press) and the PopCor (the name is an abbreviation of Popular Corpus; this sub-corpus is made of all articles belonging to the popular press). The two sub-corpora are respectively made of 1,923 articles (1,488,352 word tokens) and 1,215 articles (712,873 word tokens). Table 2.3 illustrates in more detail the distribution of articles in the two sub-corpora.

Once all the articles had been downloaded, the corpus was cleaned from irrelevant articles, repetition and other information embedded in the downloaded files and prepared for analysis through Corpus Linguistics tools.

Table 2.2 Distribution of articles across newspapers and years in the TCUK.

Newspaper	2013	2014	2015	Total
The Guardian	245	199	526	970
i	60	85	139	284
The Telegraph	103	80	125	308
The Times	119	113	129	361
Quality Press Total	527	477	919	1,923
The Express	42	42	43	127
Daily Mail	85	93	139	317
Daily Mirror	79	124	105	308
The Sun	152	165	146	463
Popular Press Total	358	424	433	1,215
Total	885	901	1,352	3,138

Table 2.3 Distribution of articles and word tokens across sub-corpora and years in the TCUK.

	2013		2014		2015	
	Number of Articles	Word Tokens	Number of Articles	Word Tokens	Number of Articles	Word Tokens
QualCor	527	383,846	477	360,750	919	743,756
PopCor	358	197,387	424	252,943	433	262,543
Total	885	581,233	901	613,693	1,352	1,006,299

A manual check of the corpus was done in order to ensure the relevance of each article with the topic under investigation. This resulted in the removal of several articles. For example, I discovered that one of the journalists who works for *The Guardian* is named Mark Tran. His articles mostly deal with foreign politics and economics, but his last name is similar to one of the search terms used for data collection. Therefore, all of his articles included in the corpus had to be deleted. A similar problem emerged with words like 'trans-pennine', 'trans-atlantic' and any other word starting with the term 'trans' which did not refer to transgender people. LexisNexis gives the user the possibility to exclude some words. Thus, when recurrent ones were identified, like the examples above, the parameter of exclusion was activated in the search. Although these types of modifications were included, each article had to be manually checked before it was included in the corpus, not being able to predict every term which could result in unwanted articles.

Another issue concerned the selection of articles. As well as regular news stories, the search initially resulted in editorials, opinion columns, sports news, Sunday editions, economic news and weekly schedules. I decided to keep all of the different genres of articles except for the weekly television, radio and theatre schedules. From the point of view of content, these articles were merely a list of television programmes, films and other audiovisual products; no information about the representation of transgender identity could be retrieved through these articles, and they would only add unnecessary word tokens to the corpus. The other genres of news articles were included because I believe that each article, despite the topic it discusses, in the way it does it, adheres to the point of view of the newspaper and therefore contributes to the externalization of the newspaper's stance on specific issues. More than any other type of articles, opinion columns are relatively common in newspapers and are the most explicit sources of the stance of the newspaper. Opinion columns draw the line between what a newspaper is or is not allowed to say and to what extent it relates to the press guidelines when it comes to specific topics (Baker, Gabrielatos and McEnery 2013a). In light of this, it is fundamental to include opinion columns when the aim of the analysis is to uncover hidden or overt ideologies and stances a specific newspaper is looking to put forward, as will become clear in Chapters 4 and 5.

The last choice to consider was regarding the type of edition. Some of the newspapers had different editions for the same article, for example, Irish edition, Northern Ireland edition, Scottish edition or national edition. Keeping all of these editions would result in four or five versions of the same article and skew the analysis, which sees its starting point in the frequency of given terms. The Irish editions were all excluded since the aim of the research was to focus on British news. The national editions were kept when available; in other cases, I considered first the Scottish edition and last the Northern Ireland ones; this edition was considered only when there was no other edition available. For some articles, there was also a choice between a first and a second edition. The first edition was kept when available otherwise second editions were included. LexisNexis included in the download both printed and online versions, and both were included. For those articles which appeared in both editions, the printed version was preferred to the online one, as it is considered to be a more stable version of the article, not subjected to changes and updates.

The software used for the analysis of the TransCorUK is AntConc (Anthony 2014), the version used for the analysis is 3.4.4m.[6]

AntConc allows the user to search the corpus through the use of seven tools. Firstly, through the File View tool, the user can view the contents of one or more files, in order to investigate the data in more detail. The Word List tool counts the tokens in the corpus and displays them in a list sorted alphabetically, by frequency or by word, according to the user's preference. The Concordance Tool creates concordance lists that can also be viewed according to the tokens' position in the text through the use of the Concordance Plot Tool. The Cluster/N-Grams Tool shows a summary of the results generated by the Concordance Tool, looking for clusters of one or more words that occur together. In addition to these tools, collocation analysis is possible through the Collocates Tool. AntConc also gives the possibility to generate keyword lists, through the Keyword List Tool by uploading a reference corpus. Once both corpora are uploaded, the user has the possibility to select the statistical measure that they prefer and the software produces the output in a separate window, the results can be saved in a .txt file. The corpus must be saved as a plain-text file in order to be uploaded onto the software.

The TransCorCan

The corpus of Canadian newspaper articles was compiled following, when possible, the criteria established for the collection of the TransCorUK. News Media Canada,[7] the main outlet in Canada which monitors circulation of newspapers was consulted in order to identify the most relevant newspapers. The circulation rate in 2015 was taken into account, as for the UK corpus. Table 2.4[8] shows the first forty-one newspapers listed by highest circulation figure in 2015. The statistics relevant to the average weekday circulation were taken into account. The first criteria taken into account in the choice for the UK newspaper is that these should be national newspaper. Canada has only two newspapers which are published nationwide, *The Globe and Mail* and the *National Post*, which were both included despite their circulation figures (which are nonetheless very high). The rest of the newspapers are province based, for this reason, I decided to include one newspaper per province with the highest circulation rate excluding those which are distributed for free or are published in French, the other official language of Canada. The corpus, thus, includes *The*

Table 2.4 Newspaper circulation rates in Canada (2015).

Rank	Newspaper	Headquarters	Daily Average
1	**The Globe and Mail**	**Toronto (National)**	323,133
2	**The Toronto Star**	**Toronto (Ontario)**	308,881
3	La Presse	Montreal	279,731
4	Le Journal de Montréal	Montreal	231,332
5	24 Hours Toronto	Toronto (circulates for free)	213,143
6	Metro Toronto	Toronto (circulates for free)	204,840
7	**National Post**	**Toronto (National)**	186,343
8	Journal Metro	Montreal (circulates for free)	172,002
9	Le Journal de Québec	Quebec City	150,248
10	Montreal 24 heures	Montreal (circulates for free)	150,239
11	**Vancouver Sun**	**Vancouver (British Columbia)**	133,329
12	Toronto Sun	Toronto	119,048
13	Metro Vancouver	Vancouver (circulates for free)	113,500
14	The Hamilton Spectator	Hamilton	113,052
15	The Province	Vancouver	112,115
16	**Calgary Herald**	**Calgary (Alberta)**	107,954
17	Winnipeg Free Press	Winnipeg	101,229
18	Ottawa Citizen	Ottawa	93,277
19	Edmonton Journal	Edmonton	91,776
20	The Chronicle Herald	Halifax	91,152
21	**Montreal Gazette**	**Montreal (Québec)**	78,797
22	Le Soleil	Quebec City	74,899
23	Metro Edmonton	Edmonton (circulates for free)	60,779
24	Metro Calgary	Calgary (circulates for free)	60,654
25	London Free Press	London	59,841
26	Times Colonist	Victoria	58,335

Rank	Newspaper	Headquarters	Daily Average
27	*Waterloo Region Record*	Kitchener	53,403
28	*Windsor Star*	Windsor	49,312
29	*Winnipeg Sun*	Winnipeg (Manitoba)	48,767
30	*Metro Ottawa*	Ottawa (circulates for free)	48,319
31	*Metro Halifax*	Halifax	47,210
32	*Calgary Sun*	Calgary	41,675
33	*Le Nouvelliste*	Trois-Rivières	41,475
34	*Le Devoir*	Montreal	39,686
35	***StarPhoenix***	**Saskatoon (Saskatchewan)**	38,763
36	The Edmonton Sun	Edmonton	36,566
37	Metro Winnipeg	Winnipeg (circulates for free)	35,212
38	Ottawa Sun	Ottawa	34,704
39	Ottawa Citizen	Ottawa	34,846
40	The Leader-Post	Regina	34,047
41	***Times & Transcript***	**Moncton (New Brunswick)**	28,404

Source: Data from News Media Canada 2018.

Toronto Star as a representative of newspapers in Ontario, the *Vancouver Sun* for British Columbia, and the *Calgary Herald* for Alberta. The *Winnipeg Free Press*, which is the most circulated paper in the province of Manitoba, was not available on LexisNexis, for this reason it could not be included in the corpus. The next most circulated paper is the *Winnipeg Sun* which was also not included in the corpus as it did not produce any results, leaving no newspapers representing the Province of Manitoba. Representative of Québec is the *Montreal Gazette*, and the *StarPhoenix* was included for the Province of Saskatchewan. The *Times & Transcript* was included to represent New Brunswick. Having reached the same amount of newspapers considered for the UK press, no further newspapers were included in the corpus despite the fact the provinces and territories of Nova Scotia, Prince Edward Island, and Newfoundland and Labrador were not represented by any specific newspaper.

The corpus collected from the Canadian press comprises 2,730 articles, for a total of 2,495,371 million tokens. The articles are divided as follows: 823 articles in 2013, 943 in 2014, and 964 articles in 2015. As for the number of tokens we have: 795,097 in 2013, 789,044 in 2014 and 911,230 in 2015. Tables 2.5 and 2.6 show the figures in more detail.

Table 2.5 Distribution of articles across newspapers and years in the TCC.

Newspaper	2013	2014	2015	Total
The Globe and Mail	85	132	127	344
National Post	131	140	139	410
The Toronto Star	93	140	147	380
Vancouver Sun	127	131	101	359
Calgary Herald	160	131	119	410
Montreal Gazette	137	140	160	437
StarPhoenix	73	88	82	243
Times & Transcript	17	41	89	147
Total	823	943	964	2,730

Table 2.6 Distribution of word tokens across newspapers and years in the TCC.

Newspaper	2013	2014	2015	Total
The Globe and Mail	77,581	124,673	130,326	332,580
National Post	101,437	130,229	136,708	368,374
The Toronto Star	79,239	108,860	135,163	323,262
Vancouver Sun	117,028	124,393	90,307	331,728
Calgary Herald	210,478	83,381	90,304	384,163
Montreal Gazette	143,100	119,906	190,269	453,275
StarPhoenix	49,109	59,426	66,337	174,872
Times & Transcript	17,125	38,176	71,816	127,117
Total	795,097	789,044	911,230	2,495,371

The same search terms identified for the UK corpus were used to collect the articles for the Canadian corpus. As pointed out for the UK corpus, some issue with data collection emerged for the Canadian article collection as well. For example, the surname *Tran* appeared to be a very popular one for citizens in Canada. This meant that a number of articles including it were downloaded. Once this pattern was identified, all those articles were discarded. Other words which created some difficulties and allowed for non-relevant articles to be downloaded were: *trans fats* and *trans mountain pipeline*, articles including these phrases or similar were discarded.

The tool used to analyse the TransCorCan is CQPweb (Hardie 2012).[9] Differently from AntConc (Anthony 2014), which is computer-based, CQPweb is a web-based corpus analysis system. The software's interface emulates the BNCweb system (Lehmann, Schneider and Hoffmann 2000). Another difference between the two pieces of software is that in order to upload a corpus into CQPweb, it needs to not only be stored in a plain-text file but also organized in vertical format, which means that there will be one word-token per line. Additional annotation can be added by tab separation into columns, for example, POS tags, semantic tags and other similar metadata information (for more details on corpus compilation with CQPweb see Hardie 2012). The TransCorCan was annotated using CLAWS POS tagger (Garside, Leech and Sampson 1987) and the USAS semantic tagger (Rayson et al. 2004). CQPweb includes a list of available corpora that can be used. The main tools available through CQPweb allow the users to analyse concordances, collocations, distribution of tokens and texts, random sorting of queries and keyword analysis.

The following chapters will discuss results emerging from the analysis of the two sets of data through the two different pieces of software. The main reason behind the use of different tools was due primarily to the fact that this would allow me to explore different ways of carrying out the analysis as the two pieces of software offer different types of distribution and statistical tools.

3

A matter of choices: Identity labels in English

To use or not use? Choices of gender identity labels in English

Before considering the use of labels regarding transgender identities in English, some discussion on the theoretical and methodological framework that allowed me to draw conclusions on the language under analysis is necessary.

To begin with, identity representation of minority social groups is considered here as being part of a specific type of discourse. Discourse is, from a linguistic perspective, any unit of language beyond the sentence level (Stubbs 1983) that is used to create meaning in relation to a social context. In this sense, a first definition of discourse entailing social implications was suggested by Michel Foucault (1972). The French social theorist explains discourse as a system of beliefs, ideas, attitudes and notions that systematically come together to produce the objects of discussion. The various components are biased by the speakers' background knowledge and in return, shaped by social and cultural surroundings. Therefore, discourse has its own implications in a wider social process of power and legitimation, as it contributes, like a circular system, to the shaping of society. Discourse is realized in and through language. Mary Talbot (1995) defines language as the 'fabric' that constitutes discourse, 'the words spoken or written as the linguistic traces of how a text was reproduced and cues for its interpretation' (Talbot quoted in Polese 2004: 37). This research is based on this very understanding of the concept of discourse, in fact, we believe that the way language is used shapes society's understanding of the world.

Norman Fairclough and Ruth Wodak (1997) define discourse as the way we use language in order to convey both spoken and written communication and as a form of 'meaning-making in the social process' which shapes and creates society. As a consequence of social implications in discourse, we must acknowledge the many different types of discourse, as many 'as there are social settings and purposes' (Partington, Duguid and Taylor 2013: 3). Discourses are constructed socially and are internalized by specific groups of individuals recognized as communities of practice since they all agree upon certain discourses (Hidalgo-Tenorio 2011: 186).

An aspect that should be considered when analysing discourse is not only textual presences but also absences (Baker 2006; Duguid and Partington 2018). Paul Baker takes discourses of heterosexuality as an example suggesting that the 'absence of explicit references to heterosexuality in speech and writing, [functions as] effectively normalizing or unproblematizing the concept' (2006: 5). This aspect is particularly relevant for this research, as it was one of the starting points for it. It was observed, in fact, that the topic of transgender identity was first completely absent in discourses and then suddenly present. This study aims to discover the reasons behind this change. It focuses on the way that language is used in a specific context, that of the media. The data collected was analysed through an approach that stems from Discourse Studies, namely Critical Discourse Analysis (CDA), used in combination with the tools of Corpus Linguistics (introduced in Chapter 2). From the combination of these two approaches, a new framework defined as Corpus-based Discourse Analysis has been suggested.

More specifically, Critical Discourse Analysis advocates for the researchers' intervention in highlighting given ideologies in discourse (Fairclough 1992; Fairclough, Mulderrig and Wodak 2011), and is considered 'a form of academic enquiry which aims to achieve a better understanding of how societies work' (Baker 2006: 73). CDA can be defined as a type of critical social research with the goal of uncovering the power relations and ideologies hidden in specific communicative modes. In CDA, discourse is thought of as a form of social action that is 'socially shaped' but most importantly 'socially constitutive' (Fairclough and Wodak 1997). It not only represents and reproduces society, but it also contributes to change by uncovering power relations and ideologies. The critical point of view that is used in CDA is what differentiates this approach from traditional discourse analysis.

Among the most popular approaches to CDA is the dialectical-relational approach by Fairclough (1989, 1992, 1995, 2005). In order to investigate language, ideology and power, Fairclough has developed a three-dimensional model of analysis in which he considers language as text, discourse and social practice. This model strongly relates to the meta-functions of language at the base of systemic functional linguistics. In the analysis of discourses that I hypothesize to find in this study, this approach seems to be the most relevant one, since it is necessary to analyse discourse taking into account the context in which it is produced and the audience for which it was meant. As it is in the scope of this research to look exactly at how the social context is influenced by the way discourse surrounding trans people is created, this approach fully responds to the necessity of the present investigation.

A number of scholars including Michael Stubbs (1997), Henry Widdowson (1998, 2005) and Jef Verschueren (2001) have raised strong criticism toward the CDA approach, condemning the qualitative perspective, the possible biased standpoints of the analysts and the reliability of the interpretation. Stubbs (1997) raises one main concern regarding the accuracy of results based on the analysis of one single text, suggesting that the use of Corpus Linguistics (i.e. large amounts of data) could be a solution to this problem. However, he does not disregard CDA in its entirety. This criticism is considered to be legitimate and agreed upon in the study presented here. In fact, the analysis presented in this book is carried out using a mixed methodology, which combines the use of CDA and Corpus Linguistics.

The claim brought forward by Verschueren (2001) is linked to a certain extent to the concept of cherry-picking. The scholar recriminates critical discourse analysts for their tendency to exclude from the language under investigation those aspects that might compromise the methodological framework. For this reason, I believe, Corpus Linguistics can be once again the answer. When considering large amounts of data, it becomes difficult for the researcher to find specific examples or exclude others that are inevitably highlighted by the tools used.

Widdowson (1998, 2005), on the other hand, focuses his criticism on the methodological aspects of CDA, questioning the absence of impartiality in the application of specific methodologies. Widdowson believes that focusing on a given lexical item or grammatical feature is not enough to draw conclusions that can be generalized. In order to circumvent these criticisms, that here are judged as grounded, I have no expectation of claiming my findings relevant for all newspapers or periods. My primary focus is to analyse the way language is used in the data under investigation considering the ideologies and beliefs affecting the use of language.

CDA has mostly been a qualitative approach, although, in the past decade, Corpus Linguistics has become increasingly adopted by scholars of CDA as a way to triangulate quantitative and qualitative analyses and consider large amounts of data.

Scholars started to mention Corpus Linguistics as early as 1982 with works by Jan Aarts and Theo van Heuvel (1982) and Aarts and Willem Meijs (1984). The approach became popular in the early 1990s; it was used by scholars such as Leech, Sinclair and Stubbs (Taylor 2008: 179–180). Aside from trying to put Corpus Linguistics into a category, various definitions have been suggested by many scholars. Drawing from McEnery and Hardie, we can define Corpus Linguistics as a 'not monolithic, consensually agreed set of methods and procedures for the exploration of language' (McEnery and Hardie 2012: 1) mainly 'based on examples of real language use' (McEnery and Wilson 1996: 1).

Corpus Linguistics can also be defined as a combination of quantitative and qualitative approaches. In fact, the results of the investigations that can be carried out through the use of various tools provided by Corpus Linguistics, such as collocation analysis or keyword analysis (discussed in more detail in Chapter 2), generally need to be interpreted through qualitative analysis.

Against this backdrop, Corpus Linguistics can be defined as a heterogeneous and versatile field of inquiry, and it encompasses a variety of methods and procedures of analysis.

One of the most common distinctions in Corpus Linguistics is between corpus-based and corpus-driven approaches (Tognini-Bonelli 2001). The main difference between the two approaches is that while the former uses corpora to test, prove or exemplify a given hypothesis or theory, the latter is centred on a corpus, does not seek to prove anything, but the corpus itself 'embodies its own theory of language' (McEnery and Hardie 2012: 6). Both approaches have limitations. Scholars who prefer the first approach could be blamed for not being fully committed to the corpus, as it might be easy to build a set of data selecting what to include according to what is needed. However, for those who consider the second approach as more valid, one accusation could fall on the fact that one can never be fully unbiased, and that just by creating a corpus, language is being sampled thus choices are being made (Tognini-Bonelli 2001).

The choice of using Corpus Linguistics for the purpose of this study is due to the main aim of the research. Since my aim is to uncover more general patterns in the representation of transgender people, the corpus-based approach, which allows me to concentrate on a large set of data, is combined with a CDA perspective. This approach is also known as corpus-based discourse analysis (CBDA). This systematic top-down framework of analysis, which moves from qualitative to quantitative analysis and back and includes nine steps, was first theorized by Baker et al. (2008).

The first step suggests a context-based analysis of the topic under investigation from a historical, political, cultural and etymological point of view, which enables the identification of any existing topics, discourses or strategies thanks to an in-depth reading of the text and reference to other CDA studies. This first step leads to the establishment of research questions and allows the researcher to set out the parameters for the building of the corpus, which is the second step of the process. The third step focuses on the analysis of the corpus collected through frequencies, clusters, keywords, dispersion and other corpus tools. These procedures will highlight potential sites of interest in the corpus and could also uncover possible discourses. A way to discover possible strategies is to relate to previous analyses existing in the literature. The fourth step goes back to qualitative analysis, taking a break from the overall corpus compiled for the research and looking at a smaller, representative set of data taken from the overall corpus. This step involves an in-depth investigation of the data and operates as a magnifying glass on a sample of the data. This more detailed analysis might lead to new findings and possibly to the formulation of new hypotheses or research questions, the fifth step. These new hypotheses then need to be tested through further corpus analysis in order to identify new patterns or discourses, the sixth step. The seventh step of this framework includes the analysis of intertextuality or interdiscursivity based on the findings emerging from the corpus analysis. The further investigation from step seven leads to the formulation of new and final hypotheses, the eighth step. The ninth and final step of this framework is a further corpus analysis, which could lead to additional findings in terms of discourses or strategies that can be identified in the corpus. This framework proposes a circular type of investigation and a new formulation of hypotheses and further investigation of the data collected could go on and on (Baker et al. 2008; Baker, Gabrielatos and McEnery 2013b). In the study presented in this book, a previous investigation of the context regarding transgender identity produced a better understanding of the matter and cleared any doubts about the use of terminology and the issues related to this topic more generally. A first reading of the corpus through the frequencies and collocations highlighted discourses that had not been hypothesized to find, for example, that some newspapers associated transgender people with immigrants in order to depict a collective representation of minority identities, as we will see in more detail in Chapter 5. Lastly, a more flexible framework allowed me to integrate the research questions with additional aspects, such as sociological implications of the use of language, or a more in-depth look at the juridical aspect of gender reassignment and transgender identity.

The flexibility of this approach and its ability to critically consider large amounts of data has made it possible for CBDA to be applied in many different fields of language research. As in this study, newspaper articles are commonly used as a source for CBDA studies. These studies include not only the British press but also newspapers from other geographic areas, for instance, the investigation conducted by Kyung Hie Kim in 2014. In this work, the author focuses on the construction of North Korea by the US media. The analysis focuses on newspaper articles published from *CNN*, *Newsweek* and *The New York Times* in order to identify any specific discursive practices relating to North Korea as well as revealing how specific media discourses are constructed and disseminated in the press (Kim 2014: 222). Kim discovered, through a collocation analysis, that one of the most recurrent patterns was the proximity of North Korea with names of other countries or cities. Some of these collocations were expected, but others were not, for example 'Iran'. The results point to the fact that all those countries which were unexpectedly present as collocates of North Korea have in common an unfavourable relationship with the United States. Therefore, the type of pattern constructed revealed a tendency of putting together countries which are pro and against the United States, constructing similar representations of each country according to the political significance and leaning of the same. The study also highlighted that the US news media have a preference for classifying countries into certain groups related to historical or political reasons.

Other scholars have used CBDA to analyse other fields of discourse. Giuseppe Balirano and Maria Cristina Nisco (2016) considered EU legal texts to seek the discursive strategies employed by the EU to linguistically represent refugees, through a combination of keyword and collocation analysis. The corpus under scrutiny comprised two different sub-corpora, the *EU-Progr* and the *EU-Lex*. The first sub-corpus includes the Tampere Programme and the Hague Programme, whilst the second is a collection of 258 legal texts taken from the EU official websites. The analysis conducted on the collected corpus highlighted the frequent use of spatial deixis associated with the term 'refugee'. This collocational pattern 'insinuates the idea that refugees can only be temporarily accepted within EU borders' (Balirano and Nisco 2016: 119). Another sequence emerging from the analysis of the collocational patters was a number of lexical items dealing with the financial and economic implications of the arrival of refugees in Europe, underlining a shift from the humanitarian dimension of this phenomenon.

Jane Mulderrig (2011) employed CBDA to investigate the construction of social identity in UK education policy discourse from a diachronic point of view. In fact, the corpus collected includes texts from 1972 to 2005. Frequency lists and concordance searches were the main corpus tools used in the study, which highlighted two prominent trends in New Labour's education policy rhetoric which the author identified as 'personalisation' and 'managerialisation'.

The first pattern pointed toward a more inclusive identity representation for the government, while the second brought evidence of a growing tendency of constructing the government's identity as managerial (Mulderrig 2011: 564).

Keyword analysis was the focus of a study by Ibrahim Efe and Omer Ozer (2015). The two authors, considering both positive and negative keywords, analysed mission and vision statements of 171 universities in Turkey for a total of 272 texts collected in December 2013 and updated in April 2014. The study aimed to look at the differences between public and private universities and the discursive practices utilized by Turkish universities to discuss education policies. The first analysis resulted in the fact that there were not many differences between the private and public universities in terms of lexical and discursive choices. The two authors then turned to frequency lists and a more in-depth analysis of the most frequent lexemes, which highlighted that universities in Turkey tend to construct their legitimacy through the use of impersonal authorization and abstraction with an abundance of value-related terms and references to Ataturk's Principles (Efe and Ozer 2015: 1120).

Amanda Potts and Anne Lise Kjaer (2015) employed CBDA to analyse legal texts. More specifically the authors focused on texts, mainly Trials and Appeals Chambers, produced by the International Criminal Tribunal for the Former Yugoslavia, a special tribunal established by the United Nations with the aim of prosecuting those responsible for war crimes in that country during the Second World War. The study had two main aims, a methodological and a practical one. The authors addressed both the extent to which CBDA could contribute to the examination of the language of the law but also investigated how achievements were discursively constructed and manifested in the corpus collected (Potts and Kjaer 2015: 52–78). The study made use of a variety of corpus tools and methods. In fact, through the use of SketchEngine and of Wmatrix, the authors used frequency, collocation, concordance and key semantic tag analysis. With regards to the contribution of Corpus Linguistics to the fields of language and law, the results pointed to some limitations due to the fact that sometimes details such as the position of the word in a legal text is fundamental. Thus, the homogenization of the text was not always useful; moreover, the lack of knowledge regarding terminology related to this issue on the part of the court (being the first criminal court established after the Second World War) also emerged from the analysis. From the point of view of content, and the way achievements were discursively constructed, the analysis highlighted a tendency toward the pivotal importance of giving witnesses a voice and a frequent recourse to the truth-telling function of the court.

Apart from the diverse contexts explored so far, CBDA was extensively adopted in studies which focus on topics related to the representation of gender and sexual identities. In this sense, Paul Baker, for example, carried out a number of studies (see the one mentioned in the previous section [2014a]) based on this approach to examine different gender and sexual identites in various contexts. One among many is a work published in 2003, where he investigates the representation of masculinity in *Gay News* and *The Times* (Baker 2003).

Carmen Rosa Caldas-Coulthard and Rosamund Moon (2010) also used CBDA to investigate the discourse of the media in relation to gender identities. In their work, the authors claim that pre-modification in two different British newspapers is used to create different judgemental stances that result in different representations of women. The study aimed to target the choice of labels which categorize women in the British press, addressing the broadsheet vs tabloid distinction. Caldas-Coulthard and Moon conclude that the choice of specific adjectives such as 'curvy', 'kinky' and 'hunky', which are generally used in other contexts (i.e. curvy is frequently used in relation to cars), are employed in tabloids to sexualize women's and girls' bodies. This type of representation of women appears to be the most frequent in tabloids.

More recently, Tommaso Milani (2013) used CBDA to investigate *meetmarket*, a South African online website for encounters which mainly targets men seeking other men. The main aim of Milani's work is to map the 'libidinal economy' in social networks (Milani 2013: 616). From a strictly lexical perspective, among other findings, Milani concluded that the different nouns used to define the person; mainly 'guy' and 'man' were used in relation to racial connotations. Moreover, to answer the main research question he poses in this investigation, the author finds that the website 'follow[s] a well-known hegemonic system of gender "normality" in which masculinity is the most valuable currency and femininity is rejected as worthless and undesirable' (630).

The examples presented above are proof of the versatility of the CBDA approach through which it is possible to analyse diverse and distinct types of texts belonging to a number of contexts. Despite the relatively new development, CBDA has been already employed in many different studies, which prove the effectiveness of the combination of Corpus Linguistics and CDA. This approach was chosen for the study presented here because the circular analysis, the investigation of a large data set and the critical eye in the analysis, proved to be a productive approach in terms of highlighting different discourses used in the representation of transgender people.

The present study focuses on News Discourse as a source of data collection for the analysis of the representation of transgender identity. As Fairclough points out, media discourse has a hidden power, shared by power-holders who

> exercise this power [through] systematic tendencies in news reporting and other media activities [...] The effects of media power are cumulative, working through the repetition of particular ways of handling causality and agency, particular ways of positioning the reader and so forth. (1989: 54)

This power influences and shapes our understanding of transgender identities.

News Discourse and the press

This section gives an overview of the field of News Discourse, highlighting some of the primary studies conducted by scholars in this field. This aspect of the theoretical framework is fundamental in this study as the corpus under investigation is a collection of newspaper articles. This section will also try to address the strong link between language and power and how the media serves as an effective platform for this purpose. More specifically, following this introduction, the first part will focus on the British press while the second part will discuss in more detail the Canadian newspaper industry, as these are the two sources for corpus collection.

Two good reasons for studying the language of the media can be found in the fact that (1) it is widely and readily available, and (2) it is not subject to the 'observer's paradox'[1] since it is created with the intention of being consumed by an audience (Bell 1991). The language used in the media reveals a lot about the media's structure itself. It affects attitudes and affairs in society and creates stereotypes and biases in culture (Bell 1991: 3–5). Newspaper articles are the main objects of this investigation; therefore, it is necessary to describe the specificities of this medium.

The collective noun *media* is an umbrella term that includes every means through which data or information is communicated to an audience through language, images and sounds. Thus, the press, television, radio, cinema and the internet can all be considered media platforms. In this book, I consider only one branch of the media: the press, both in its printed and online format.

Some of the first studies on News Discourse focused on the style of news language, looking at the genre, the register and the style of newspapers (see

Crystal and Davy [1969], Carter [1988] and Ghadessy [1988] which focused on the lexical choices in news articles to define the language of newspaper discourse). Through a sociolinguistic perspective, Allan Bell (1991) and Andreas H. Jucker (1992) addressed the link between linguistic structures and the social context in news articles. The same approach, but with a diachronic perspective, was chosen by Martin Conboy (2010). Other scholars, such as Monika Bednarek (2006) and Colleen Cotter (2010), chose to focus on news values. These scholars chose to combine the study of evaluation with the use of Corpus Linguistics. The latter approach has increasingly become popular in the analysis of News Discourse. As mentioned in previous chapters, Corpus Linguistics techniques have also been increasingly implemented to uncover linguistic patterns across large sets of news texts.[2] The use of Critical Discourse Analysis as a framework for the analysis of News Discourse, as done by Teun van Dijk (1988a, b), Roger Fowler (1991), Norman Fairclough (1995) and Paul Baker (2006), has also been implemented and combined in different ways (e.g. Baker, Gabrielatos and McEnery [2013b] who combine Corpus Linguistics and CDA). This overview does not intend to be exhaustive but is intended to highlight the most important and popular approaches used in the study of News Discourse with a particular focus on gender identities.

The investigation of News Discourse, through the use of different theoretical and methodological frameworks, has proved to be an effective instrument to uncover various patterns in the representation of minorities, of different social groups and ethnicities, as used by Van Dijk (1988b) for his analysis of racism and the press, or in the study by Baker, Gabrielatos and McEnery (2013b) on the representation of Islam and the research by Alan S. Partington (2015) on the representation of the Arab world. These three studies can be considered as key examples in relation to the analysis that is presented in this book. In essence, they have in common the press as a source of data and the aim to investigate the representation of specific identities.

The following subsection explores the British categorization of the press in more detail. In fact, the British press has been labelled and categorized in many different ways according to the register used, the audience to which it is targeted and the format.

The British press

According to Jane Stokes and Anne Reading, in 1999, the United Kingdom published over a thousand different newspapers (Stokes and Reading 1999: 42), making the newspaper market a competitive one. Twenty years later this is still true, due to the great variety of newspaper productions available on the market. At the same time, it must be noted that generally speaking newspaper purchasing is in decline, taken over by the ever-increasing use of online formats available for the majority of newspapers.[3] When thinking about the UK, we must also bear in mind that many newspapers are local editions; and thus, are consumed locally rather than at a national level.

The publication of written news in Great Britain dates back to the seventeenth century when the first pamphlets started coming out with the primary function of reporting on recent events. The written press can be considered as an evolution of different forms of spoken news such as gossip, sermons, tales and ballads, which were used to communicate important issues (Brownlees 2016). The first newspaper in Great Britain appeared in 1702, at the time known as The *Daily Courant* (Allan 1999: 8–11). Since then, the press has seen many changes, but one feature has been present throughout the centuries: the British press has always had its own internal categorization. From the 'broadsheet' vs 'tabloid' classification, to the 'quality' vs 'popular' dichotomy, moving to the 'up-', 'mid-' and 'down-market' newspaper distinction, the British press has had many labels attached to it. Newspapers in the UK have also been classified according to their political sympathy (left- and right-leaning), based on the frequency of appearance (daily, weekly, Sunday editions) or the geographical area they cover (nationals and locals). Categorization has 'roughly corresponded both to the nature of the contents and design (including the length of articles and size of headlines) and to the social distribution of their readers' (Seymour-Ure 1996: 27). It is possible to argue that reporting news is not the most important goal for newspapers. Colin Sparks (1999: 45–46) points out that newspapers 'do not exist to report the news […] They exist to make money'. Therefore, advertising plays a pivotal role due to its economic relevance for a newspaper's survival (Brownlees 2017). Additionally, many studies (i.e. Stokes and Reading 1999: 53) confirm that by a ratio of approximately four to one, the newspaper reading population of the UK prefers articles that are concerned with sport, celebrity scandals and popular entertainment rather than politics and economics.

Focusing on the last century, Colin Seymour-Ure (1996: 16) points out that by 1920 local editions were still more popular than nationals, which quickly expanded and outdistanced local newspapers by the beginning of the Second World War. While the aim of all categories, and newspapers in general, is more or less similar, to inform and entertain their audience, the various newspapers assign different priorities to the two aims (Jucker 1992: 2). Generally speaking, those newspapers falling under the quality press categorization, such as *The Guardian* or *The Daily Telegraph*, focus more on the informative function of the press; whilst newspapers categorized as belonging to the popular press, such as the *Daily Mail* or *The Sun*, give much more importance to the entertainment function.

Despite the many categorizations of the British press, and the different topics addressed by each newspaper – i.e. the different sections and genres they cover – the main structure of a news article can be said to be similar for all newspapers.

Among the categorization of newspapers, the 'broadsheet' vs 'tabloid' dichotomy was inspired by the size and format of the various newspapers. Put simply, tabloids are those newspapers of a smaller size while broadsheets are larger (Jucker 1992: 48). This distinction generally corresponds to the difference between 'quality' and 'popular' newspapers, in the sense that the same newspapers belonging to the tabloid group also belong to the popular press. The language used in the two categories of newspapers can similarly be described. The main characteristic of tabloids is that they 'employ specific rhetorical features to create a tone that appeals to a particular group of readers' as pointed out by Conboy (2006: 45). This point applies to broadsheets too. Among the characteristics proper of the genre, it is possible to highlight that tabloids usually have shorter articles, focus more on national stories, prefer to cover news stories that deal with gossip and the lives of celebrities and use, from a native speakers' perspective, a more informal style which includes puns, more simplified language and basic sentence structures.

Broadsheets have a larger area of coverage. Articles in this type of newspapers generally include news stories related to foreign politics, business and economics as well as updates from all over the world; the style of writing is more formal, using specialized terminology and complex sentence structure. However, it is worth noting that, nowadays, this definition no longer applies to all newspapers since those falling under the category of broadsheets have in recent years, in many cases, changed their format to a smaller size, for instance, *The Independent* and *The Times*,[4] while some tabloids have modified the length of their articles and opened up to international news (Baker, Gabrielatos and McEnery 2013b: 6–7).

In 1983, Harry Henry proposed a different classification, that of up-, mid- and down-market newspapers. This categorization is based explicitly on the socio-economic status of the readership. To make a parallelism, up-market refers to the same newspapers defined by other scholars as broadsheets or qualities, while mid- and down-markets fall into the category of tabloids or popular press, as discussed below. In fact, according to his study on the readership of the different newspapers, Henry divides newspapers based on the social class of the expected reader. He estimated that two-thirds of the readers of down-markets belonged to the working class, half of the readership of mid-markets to the lower-middle class and the skilled working class and more than half of the readership of the up-markets were members of the middle-middle class and upper-middle class, although, it must be pointed out that, generally speaking, today more than ever, all newspapers are read by all social classes (Jucker 1992: 48–58).

The categorization system that was found to be more suitable for this study is the dichotomy between 'popular' and 'quality' newspapers.

As remarked by Seymour-Ure, 'the quality-popular distinction was sharply drawn by 1945' (1996: 27), although since then the line has blurred, especially after the success of the *Daily Mirror* in 1935, which soon became the first massively distributed popular newspaper. This distinction is mainly based on the different ways adopted by the newspapers in choosing which news to prioritize on the basis of the target readers, and on the linguistic style employed.

According to Jucker (1992), newspapers such as *The Times* or *The Guardian* can be defined as being part of the category of qualities as they observe high standards of news reporting, whereas newspapers such as the *Daily Mirror* or *The Sun* can be said to fall under the category of popular press as they appeal to a much wider readership.

The distinction between 'popular' and 'quality' press seems to have always existed; many scholars use these two words to define the British press. Conboy (2002) claims that the definition 'popular' for the press walks side by side with the definition of popular culture. He refers to the definition of popular given by Raymond Williams, who points to the origin of the word used to indicate something "'belonging to the people" but also [*carrying*] implications of "base or low"' (1976: 5). Conboy posits that the popular press is 'a set of discourses which establish elements of authenticity in part through its rhetoric and is thus able to establish an inclusivity based on its appeal to wide sections of ordinary people' (2007: 7). The popular press owes its large number of followers to the fact that it was able to attract a 'largely working-class readership because of its commitment to delivering a form of journalism these readers wanted to see at a price that they could afford' (Allan 1999: 13). According to Fowler, generally speaking, the popular press uses 'colloquialisms, incomplete sentences, questions and a varied typography suggesting variations of emphasis, the written text mimics a speaking voice, as of a person talking informally but with passionate indignation', whilst the quality press has a more formal type of language (1991: 39).

The rhetoric of the quality press can be described as

> concentrating on a system rather than individuals, on an embryonic understanding of social class rather than the simple dichotomies of the virtuous and the wicked, appeared to refract much wider communities through its pages rather than simply aligning popular discontent through the prism of one outraged commentator. (Conboy 2002: 71)

The eight newspapers chosen for the present investigation – *The Guardian*, the *i*, *The Daily Telegraph* and *The Times* for the quality press, and the *Daily Express*, the *Daily Mail*, the *Daily Mirror* and *The Sun* for the popular press – are clear examples of the two different categories, as is demonstrated in the analysis in Chapters 4 and 5.

The topics discussed, the length and size of articles and the readership are not the only differences between the quality and the popular press. In fact, language usage, as pointed out for all the categorizations presented above, also plays an important role (Jucker 1992).

So far, I have briefly outlined the stylistic development and changes of the British press, however, there is one last aspect that still needs to be discussed. In recent decades, the press, which was initially only paper printed, has faced increasing technological developments. In order to challenge ways of news reporting (e.g. social networking systems, etc.), it has used online formats, which are becoming more and more common among all types of newspapers.

To keep track of all newspaper publications and rates of distribution it is safe to rely on the Audit Bureau of Circulation (ABC n.d.). This body collects all information about media dissemination and from which the data presented in Table 2.1 (Chapter 2) was retrieved from.

The Canadian press

The lengthy and detailed description of the British press does not apply to the case of the Canadian press, which despite having its peculiarities has not, in the past, been very popular among linguists. While the field of journalism and media studies have produced as many scholarly analyses as we find for the British counterpart, the same cannot be said in the field of linguistics. At the same time, many features of the press can be considered as global rather than specific and for this reason will not be repeated.

One of the main differences between the Canadian and the British press is related to the bilingual status of the first country, which consequently reflects the great number of newspapers which publish in French or are bilingual. Another component, peculiar to the internal characterization of Canada, is the existence of a part of the newspaper industry completely managed by indigenous people. In this study, neither French nor indigenous press will be considered, but as it plays such an important role in Canada, I cannot refrain from mentioning it. The colonial history of Canada also significantly influenced the development of the press industry in the country, as well as its proximity to the United States.

Local printed news media in Canada dates back to the mid-seventeenth century with the Halifax *Gazette* and the Quebec *Gazette*, published respectively in Halifax and in Quebec City. The latter was initially published in both English and French. At the beginning of the first decade of the 1920s there were 143 daily newspaper in Canada and a robust indigenous newspaper industry (Vipond 2012).[5] Although newspapers in Canada have never held such an important status as in countries such as the UK, for example, they have had a pivotal role in defining Canadian identity in contrast to colonial parentage and the country's vicinity to the United States (Vessay 2016: 97). Despite this, Mary Vipond (2012) notes that the Canadian newspaper system in English relies strongly on the United States. This concept is reiterated throughout her whole book, *The Mass Media in Canada* (2012), to the point that she asserts that the Americanization of the Canadian English media is threatening their national identity 'by filling our minds with foreign ideas and crowding out our attempts to speak to one another' (9).

In the beginning, newspapers in Canada mainly originated from small, politically oriented environments and continued to be politically affiliated until the middle of the eighteenth century (Vipond 2012: 15). Nowadays, following the American heritage described above, newspapers in Canada tend to be independent of political parties and use a more informal style (Vessay 2016: 40). The growth of the printed press in Canada goes hand in hand with the development of the railway system and of the telegraphs which facilitated not only the distribution of newspapers but also the circulation of news itself (Vipond 2012). The Toronto *Globe*, founded in 1844, can be seen as Canada's first modern newspaper, and while it was initially affiliated to the Reform movement, its founder soon sought to expand its readership beyond party loyalties. It remained conservative in style, mainly discussing issues related to politics, and while a step toward modernity was taken then, we will have to wait until the next generation to truly boost mass distribution (Vipond 2012: 22). Popular daily newspapers began to exist in Canada in the late eighteenth century with the Montreal *Star* at the forefront. These were very different from the old party-affiliated newspapers which continued to exist in relation to a more traditional middle-class readership, and it was at this stage that the Canadian press began to adapt to the very successful American formula. The significant change brought by this new wave of dailies was their independence from any political party. Additionally, many of these newspapers were not only published in evening editions but also sold in the streets or in newsstands (previously newspapers were only available by annual subscription), more convenient for the working class. Lastly, the style of these newspapers was simple, direct, much more informal and definitely more attractive to the population of Canada as a whole, introducing more headlines, illustrations and moving advertisements from the front page to the centre of the publications. The number of pages per publication started to grow from four to eventually twelve, and slowly, increasing space was dedicated to news related to sport and leisure. In time, the more traditional newspapers were forced to adapt to this new and fresh style not to die out completely, and by the turn of the century, the newspaper industry could be defined as quite homogeneous. Canadians began to consume newspapers daily and regularly (Vipond 2012).

Similar to the UK, newspapers in Canada today can be classified in different ways. There are publications in English language only, while others are published in French. As mentioned earlier, a whole section of the industry is owned by the indigenous press. As pointed out in the data collection section (Chapter 2), there are only two national newspapers in Canada *The Globe and Mail* and the *National Post*. All other newspapers are circulated and printed within each province and territory. Another relevant categorization in the Canadian press is between paid and free newspapers. While this distinction applies to the UK as well, most of the newspapers are paid in this country, and free ones are less in number than Canada (at least if we consider national newspapers, which are the most common and distributed in the UK). There is a growing number of newspapers belonging to the indigenous newspaper industry.

According to the advocacy group Newspaper Canada, one of the most popular categorizations is based on the geographic areas in which newspapers are published: Atlantic Canada,[6] Ontario, the Prairies,[7] British Columbia and the Yukon and Quebec (Vessay 2016).

The newspapers included in the analysis presented in this book try to represent the national opinion as well as that of the different provinces.

The language of newspapers

Scholars of News Discourse and language tend to agree on the fact that 'news is socially constructed. What events are reported is not a reflection of the intrinsic importance of those events but reveals the operation of a complex and artificial set of criteria for selection' (Fowler 1991: 2). The construction of news is realized through the use of language, which is never neutral, or a casual choice, but always a highly constructed and elaborated conveyer of significance.

In light of this, newspapers have a language of their own, with specific rules, peculiar features and a defined structure. As far as the structure is concerned, generally speaking, the first element of a news article is the headline, which can be defined as the title of the news article and has the function of framing the event narrated in the article, summarizing the story, and above all attracting readers. The headline has the function of maximizing newsworthiness and giving a first glance at the perspective taken in the article, including the stance of the newspaper and its evaluation of the event reported. Headlines have specific stylistic features that are followed in order to achieve their function (Van Dijk 1991; Jucker 1992; Polese 2004; Isani 2011). Headlines are, in most cases, followed by the lead paragraph. The lead is, together with the headline, called the nucleus of the news article. The lead paragraph has a similar function to the headline, but it presents information in a more expanded format and sometimes represents the beginning of the story that is being narrated. The lead is followed by the body copy, also known as lead development, or body of the article (Bednarek and Caple 2012: 94–104).

Many scholars have dedicated their work to the analysis of newspapers' language in the last century. Among the milestones of the studies about the language of newspapers, we can include, as mentioned before, the qualitative study by David Crystal and Derek Davy (1969), who focus on a comparison of two newspaper articles. Through the analysis of those articles, they draw some conclusions that can be extended, more generally, to the style of the newspaper to which they belong. For example, they show that *The Times*, compared to the *Daily Express*, has more extended and more numerous sentences per paragraph, speech verbs were usually moved from their original position and inverted with the subject, and a high number of adverbials appeared in emphatic clause-initial position.

Similarly, W.R. O'Donnell and Loreto Todd (1980) carried out a study comparing *The Guardian* and the *Daily Mirror*. Looking at headlines, they noted that *The Guardian* has a tendency to avoid finite verbs while the *Daily*

Mirror tends to avoid verbs altogether. O'Donnell and Todd also compiled a list of lexical items which were more likely to appear in the *Daily Mirror* rather than *The Guardian*.

In 1988 Ronald Carter, on news reports, and Mohsen Ghadessy, looking at sports articles, focus their research on lexical choices. More specifically, Carter presents a theory about the use of lexical choices related to their 'coreness'. According to Carter 'lexical choices are as significant as syntactic patterns and, indeed, tend to be the items which attract most attention' (1988: 9). He, thus, identifies a pattern recurring in his data, that is the presence of a core vocabulary, more specifically, 'elements in the lexical network of a language which are unmarked' (9), that is to say, those lexical items which constitute the base, the most simple and basic words used, the ones that we use the most in spoken language. His proposal can be helpful to understand the lexical choices being made and to isolate non-neutral vocabulary that can be described as ideologically connoted.

There are three more names worth mentioning when it comes to the language of the press who contributed extensively in understanding the stylistics behind this genre. Bell (1991) focused on the notion of news story, the importance of the processes which contribute to the production of the language of the media and the role of the target readers, in the frameworks of discourse analysis and sociolinguistics. Fowler (1991), from the perspective of critical linguistics, starts from the assumption that news making is a social practice and product of the political and social context in which it is produced and looks at news values and the processes of selection of the news, moreover he analyses news in relation to gender, power and law discussing the way they influence stereotypes offered by the news. More recently, Bednarek (2006), and Bednarek with Caple (2012), carried out a more quantitative study using corpora. Adhering to the broadsheet vs tabloids dichotomy they address not only a comparison of the language used in the two groups but also focus on news values and evaluation in news articles.

Turning to the language of newspapers, generally speaking, we can start from the results of the study conducted by Bednarek (2008). From this research, she concludes that the most used nouns in the UK press refer to cities, countries and people, while personal pronouns are uncommon. In this study, she also highlights that noun phrases are commonly used to indicate time, or function to label news actors and sources. Moreover, as far as verbs are concerned, she finds that modal verbs are infrequent, and among these, journalists are more likely to use *will* and *would*. Finally, she finds that verbs tend to occur more in the present tense rather than the past; this is to emphasize the recency and relevance of the event in the body of the articles. Passives can be generally used to obscure agency, whilst adverbials are generally used to link or to express time and space. Another feature of newspaper language is the use of figures and numbers, enabling a story to be more objective, thus newsworthy, by providing facts. As we will see later in this subsection, newsworthiness has a pivotal role in news making. One more linguistic strategy retraceable in news articles is the use of evidentiality and intertextuality, that is to say, the embedding of other linguistic materials such as laws, quotes and reported speech inside the news article (Bednarek and Caple 2010: 84–94).

Newspapers are not only about the language used in the articles but also about the content, which is also chosen according to specific criteria.

In fact, as pointed out by Fowler,

> the news media select events for reporting according to a complex set of criteria of newsworthiness; so news is not simply that which happens, but that which can be regarded and presented as newsworthy. These criteria, which are probably more or less unconscious in editorial practice are known as 'news values'. (1991: 13)

A first categorization of news values, reconsidered by a number of scholars, was proposed by Johan Galtung and Mari H. Ruge (1973).

News values have a different definition, aside from the one discussed above by Fowler (1991). In the same year, Bell defined news values as the criteria or rules that news workers apply to determine what is 'news' (1991: 155), whilst Cotter has defined them as 'the qualities/elements that are necessary to make a story newsworthy' (2010: 68).

Bell (1991) divides news values into three categories: (1) values in the news text; (2) values in the press process; and (3) values in news actors and events. In the first group, he includes brevity, clarity and colour. In the second group, we find continuity, competition (among news institutions and among news stories), co-option (association of one story with another one which is more newsworthy), composition (mix of different stories), predictability (scheduling of events), and prefabrication (already made input sources). The third group of news values identified by Bell is more complex and includes a larger set of values, which is a readaptation of the categorization proposed by Galtung and Ruge (1973). The news values included by Bell (1991) in this last category are:

- negativity: news stories concern dreadful events such as conflicts, accidents and disasters;

- timeliness: the event is more newsworthy if it is more recent;
- proximity: this value concerns the geographical and cultural nearness of an event;
- prominence/eliteness: the news stories which respond to this values are about high status individuals;
- consonance: the extent to which aspects of a story fit in with stereotypes that people may hold about events and people;
- impact: the effects or consequences of an event makes the story newsworthy;
- novelty: unexpected news stories are more newsworthy;
- superlativeness: the maximization and intensification of an event; and
- personalization: the process of humanizing and making an event more personal to increase newsworthy.

Classifications around news values tend to be similar to each other, and in many cases, some values overlap. What can be concluded is that the choice of topic must take many factors into account, of which the most relevant is to what extent it will interest the readers since 'the aim of a news story is first of all to catch the readers' attention' (Polese 2004: 64). In light of this, many studies have been conducted on the language of newspaper and more specifically on the ways that language is used and what are the consequences of that precise use. Newspaper articles have been a resourceful fount for the analysis of the way topics and issues are presented and represented in society, stretching from political to more social issues.

Maria Cristina Nisco (2016) analysed a corpus of newspaper articles, with the aim of investigating the way the press constructed the riots that happened in the UK in 2011, with a specific focus on the linguistic representation of the main actors involved in the riots and their agency. The corpus collected for this study includes six British national newspapers (the *Daily Mail*, the *Daily Mirror*, *The Sun*, *The Guardian*, *The Times*, and *The Daily Telegraph*) over a time span of five months starting from August 2011, the date signalling the beginning of the riots. Nisco combined a qualitative and quantitative analysis, following a CBDA approach. The first phase of the investigation (qualitative) served as a way to identify the most referred to actors and their linguistic construal, whilst the second phase (quantitative) allowed for the semantic categorization of the lexis used to define the rioters relying on frequency information. The author, then, focused on evaluative strategies in the texts with regard to the social actors involved. The main results of the analysis point to a common pattern which relates rioters to matters of race and ethnicity, reinforcing the stereotype about people who are diverse from Caucasian being violent and deviant individuals.

Similarly, Gabrielatos and Baker (2008) focus on the discursive representation of refugees and asylum seekers in the British press. The authors took a more diachronic approach, looking at data collected in the time span stretching from 1996 to 2005 for nineteen UK newspapers. The research question guiding the study related to the linguistic representation of refugees and asylum seekers (the authors use the acronym RASIM: refugees, asylum seekers, immigrants and migrants) lead to the identification of the most frequent topics discussed in relation to RASIMs and to determine the extent to which the tabloid vs broadsheet dichotomy was reflected in terms of political stance when addressing this topic. From a methodological and theoretical point of view, the authors considered the notions of keyness and collocation and of semantic preference and discourse prosody. Several patterns emerged from this study. A first look at frequencies highlighted that the interest in RASIM on the part of the media is characterized by a more occasional/seasonal attraction (Gabrielatos and Baker 2008: 17) due to the sociopolitical situation in the country. The stance taken by the newspaper in dealing with RASIM confirmed previous investigations on the same topic, and the authors retraced a rather negative representation of these social actors, with continuous reference to aspects such as numbers (i.e. large quantities of people invading the UK). The study also proves that the media use the terms 'refugees', 'asylum seekers', 'migrants' and 'immigrants' overlapping their meanings in the time span under investigation. Lastly, as expected, the results point to a different representation given from tabloids (*The Sun, Daily Star, People, Daily Mirror, Daily Express, Daily Mail* and their available Sunday editions) and broadsheets (*Business, The Guardian, Herald, The Independent, The Daily Telegraph* and their available Sunday editions) with only one overlapping related topic.

Analysis on newspaper articles can consider numerous newspapers and a varied time span but can also concentrate on only one newspaper as the case presented by Kieran O'Halloran (2009) who focuses on *The Sun* over a period of six weeks. Following the decision in 2004 by the EU to expand to more countries, including a large part of Eastern Europe, O'Halloran analysed the quasi-campaign put forward by *The Sun*, before the enacting of the law in May, against the free migration of people from Eastern Europe to the UK. The main aim of the study was to address the way that the use of specific repeated linguistic features can influence cultural reproductions. The author argues that 'regular exposure to those strategies positions the readers to reproduce a set of inferences in relation to Eastern European migration in subsequent reading of related texts from the same newspaper' (O'Halloran 2009: 22). The author makes use of CBDA to address the research questions and more specifically of keyword analysis and collocational patterns.

Newspapers articles have been used not only to discuss topics linked to politics-related issues but also to investigate how identities are constructed in the press.

Bartley and Hidalgo-Tenorio (2015) investigated the Irish press to observe the discursive construction of homosexuality and more generally of sexual orientation by looking at transitivity patterns in the texts. The authors collected texts from three Irish newspapers from 2008 to 2012 for a total of more than 2,300 articles through a search query of sexual-orientation related terms. Some of the results of this investigation point to the fact that 'sexual identity still remains a problem for the individual and the society which is not ready to accept it yet', whilst homosexuality is seen 'as an unnatural choice, a disease similar to cancer, a deviation' (Bartley and Hidalgo-Tenorio 2015: 24).

Issues related to gender, as seen in the study previously examined, have been widely investigated through the analysis of newspaper articles and Corpus Linguistics. In 2012 Sylvia Jaworska and Ramesh Krishnamurthy, for example, widened their horizons looking at both the British and the German press for the representation of feminism in a twenty-year time span. The authors compiled two different corpora, one of articles taken from the major national British newspapers and another one of articles taken from the German newspapers available on Nexis UK through the search term *feminism* in English and *Feminismus* in German. Results highlighted, for the British corpus, three main patterns of representation. These are: a strong historicalization of the topic, the treatment of feminism as a commodity and lastly a tendency for the term to occur with others which recall a negative evaluation. In the German corpus, the term *Feminismus* was often accompanied by negative attributes, and when the attributes were positive, they were being questioned.

Once again, the extensive literature that pays attention to newspapers is further corroboration of the strong relevance this media has in society, and how it is a never-ending source of analysis.

This section has provided a general overview of the theories on which the investigation presented in the following chapters is based by means of exploring studies that fall under this same framework of analysis.

Identity labels in the press

The labels we choose to identify ourselves are 'outward manifestations of our multiple identity roles, each of which comes to the fore depending on the situation we find ourselves in. Clearly, identity is a much more complex construct than immediately apparent' (Leigh 2009: 22). In light of this, the identity we choose to identify with and those chosen by others cannot be taken for granted. These labels help us understand who our interlocutors are and cannot be chosen lightly.

In each type of communication that involves a verbal process, there is always an agent and a patient, one who performs an action and one who receives this action. These can be defined as social actors. Social actors can be interpreted here as either individuals or collectives (e.g. political parties, communities of practice, social movements, minority groups) who exercise agency as opposed to constraining social structures that determine and bind individual or collective identities. In discourse analysis, agency is fundamental as it sets the action in a context, which in return determines the nature of the agent and of the patient. From a linguistic point of view, this can be realized through a variety of grammatical items (Van Leeuwen 2005), among which are naming strategies (Richardson 2007) and the use of identity labels.

The UK[8] vs Canada

This section introduces the frequency of occurrence of the search terms used to collect the corpus under investigation. This preliminary analysis of the data will help us to understand the choices related to naming strategies and the use of labels in the press. This first step sets the basis for the results and analyses presented in the following chapters. In fact, the combined use of frequency lists and concordance analysis proved to be a useful method to highlight linguistic patterns in the use of language in relation to transgender identities. Tables 3.1 and 3.2 report the frequency of use of the search terms in the two sub-corpora in each year of collection. The frequency of each term is presented as raw data and normalized by category by 100,000 words. This means that each category was normalized taking into account the total amount of tokens in the category itself (year).

The most common among the search words under investigation to appear in both the TransCorUK (hereafter TCUK) and the TransCorCan (hereafter TCC) is the term *transgender**. The following most common terms used

Table 3.1 Frequency of search words in the TransCorUK by year.

Transgender*	TransCorUK						TOTAL	
	2013		2014		2015			
	Raw Frequency	Norm. by Category	Raw Frequency	Norm. by Category	Raw Frequency	Norm. by Category	Raw Frequency	Norm. by Category
transgender*[9]	603	103.74	748	121.88	2,189	217.53	3,549	176.34
trans	68	11.70	34	5.54	858	85.26	960	47.70
transsexual*[10]	261	44.90	221	36.01	194	19.28	676	33.59
sex change*[11]	247	42.49	189	30.80	174	17.29	610	30.31
transvestite*[12]	185	31.83	193	31.45	103	10.23	481	23.90
gender reassignment*[13]	74	12.73	81	13.20	172	17.09	327	16.25
dysphoria	42	7.23	29	4.72	69	6.86	140	6.96
cross-dresser*[14]	44	7.57	30	4.89	27	2.68	101	5.02
trann*[15]	18	3.10	29	4.72	20	1.99	67	3.33
shemale*[16]	4	0.69	2	0.32	4	0.40	10	0.50

Table 3.2 Frequency of search words in the TransCorCan by year.

Transgender*	TransCorCan						TOTAL	
	2013		2014		2015			
	Raw Frequency	Norm. by Category	Raw Frequency	Norm. by Category	Raw Frequency	Norm. by Category	Raw Frequency	Norm. by Category
transgender**	632	79.49	1,100	139.41	1,518	166.59	3,250	130.24
trans	131	16.48	229	29.00	611	67.00	971	38.90
transsexual*	113	14.09	125	15.59	70	7.57	308	12.18
sex change*	32	4.02	40	5.07	11	1.21	83	3.33
transvestite*	47	5.91	47	5.96	20	2.19	114	4.57
gender reassignment	9	1.13	26	3.29	70	7.68	105	4.21
dysphoria	9	1.13	27	3.42	48	5.27	84	3.37
cross-dresser*	8	1.13	10	1.26	11	1.20	29	1.20
tranny*	4	0.50	11	1.39	2	0.21	17	0.68
shemale*	0	–	0	–	0	–	0	–

in the two sub-corpora are slightly different, in fact, for the TCUK we find *trans* followed by *transsexual** and *sex change**, while in the TCC we find *trans* followed by *transsexual**, *transvestite** and *gender reassignment**. This indicates that with reference to the use of the more general umbrella terms the Canadian and British press present similar patterns (this is also confirmed by the normalized frequency which shows the relevance/frequency in relation to the size of the sub-corpora), while when it comes to more specific terms the results are different. The third most common term in both of the sub-corpora is *transsexual**, an adjective (more about its use will be said in the following chapters) that while not being used by all members of the transgender community because of the specificity of its meaning which tends to be used to refer to people who have undergone gender reassignment surgery, it still falls within those terms that are used to refer to transgender identities. The fourth most popular term in the TCUK is *sex change** while for the TCC we find *transvestite**. At this superficial descriptive level of analysis, which takes into account the presence of the terms under investigation, this is where the two sub-corpora begin to diverge from one another. The British papers continue using a term that, despite being considered derogatory, still refers specifically to transgender identities, while the Canadian press uses a term *transvestite**, which – has been recently replaced by the term cross-dresser (which also appears in the corpus in a very small percentage of cases) – does not refer to transgender identities at all, as it indicates a person who likes to use clothes, styles and accessories stereotypically and culturally associated to the opposite gender but who do not wish to transition to a gender that does not align to the sex assigned at birth.[17] It must be noted that the TCC reports very low frequencies of all terms after *trans* which appear less than fifteen times each (considering the normalized frequencies). In a similar work conducted by Baker on the year 2012 in the UK press, comparable patterns were found (Baker 2014a: 217). The author highlights that the most frequent term in his data was *transgender**, followed by *transsexual** and *transvestite**. These results mirror, almost perfectly, those found in the Canadian data and the British data as well, with only one major difference in the presence of the term *trans*, which in the frequency list presented in that research occurred in sixth place while it is in the second and third position in the data presented here. Baker also notes that *transsexual** is preferred over *transgender** by *The Sun* in 2012 (218). If we consider the TCUK we can see that this pattern changes in the following years (32[18] vs 47 in 2012, 99 vs 51 in 2013, 118 vs 37 in 2014, and 147 vs 35 in 2015) when the use of *transgender* becomes more prominent. Some organizations and groups[19] whose aim is to support and advocate for trans people consider the term *transsexual** to be derogatory as it puts an accent on the sexual/physical and not on the identity aspect of being a transgender person. We can note here that the frequency of given terms bursts in specific years and is more frequent in one sub-corpora over the other. If we look at the TCUK, for example, the more inclusive general/umbrella term *trans* starts to be massively used only in 2015 (858 occurrences), while it occurs less frequently in the previous two years (102 occurrences in total). A similar pattern is found in the TCC, but the term is more common in 2013 and 2014 as well. The most used term, among the search terms, in the TransCor is *transgender** but the use of the term was already rising in frequency in 2014 in Canada where it doubled the presence that it had in 2013, almost reaching the same frequency registered for 2015, while in the UK it was only in 2015 that a boost in the presence of the term in the press was recorded.

Another aspect pointed out by the above-mentioned groups and associations is that *transgender*, *trans* and *transsexual* should never be used with a nominal function but only with an adjectival one. Regarding this aspect, the TransCor reveals an interesting pattern. In fact, considering 10 per cent of the overall occurrences[20] of each term in the two sub-corpora, 80.3 per cent of the time the term *transgender** was used as an adjective in the TCUK while it had this function in the TCC 89.6 per cent of the time. *Trans* occurs as an adjective in the TCUK 82.3 per cent of the time and 96.9 per cent of the time in the TCC. *Transsexual** was found as an adjective 58.8 per cent of the time in the TCUK and 48.39 per cent of the time in the TCC. This pattern highlights the term that is used more frequently as a noun is *transsexual*. The meaning carried by this term, in a way, facilitates its nominal use, which reinforces the representation related to the biological rather than the identifying gender and suggests a preference of the representation related to the physical/external aspects that are connected to the representation of transgender identity.

The stress on the more physical aspects of transgender identity is displayed not only through the use of *transsexual* but through another search term as well: *sex change** (610 occurrences in the TCUK and 83 in the TCC). First, it is notable that this phrase occurs over seven times more frequently in the TCUK than in the TCC, this seems to be pointing to the different types of representations in the British and Canadian press. Whereas, the British press is giving more importance/space to the sexual and physical aspects of transgender identity, as opposed to other aspects of identity such as feelings. This figure is also reinforced by the normalized frequency which is ten times more frequent in the TCUK as opposed to the TCC, and by the fact that this term is the fourth most frequent in the British data, while it is in seventh place in the Canadian data.

Back in 2015, the phrase that was most commonly being used to replace sex change and was considered more inclusive was gender reassignment surgery (today substituted in many cases by gender confirmation surgery). This phrase was used among the search terms to collect the data and appears 327 times in the TCUK and 105 in the TCC, respectively the sixth and fifth places in order of frequency. A term that is more closely related to the medical area, used to collect the data, is dysphoria, which occurs less in both corpora (140 in the TCUK and 84 in the TCC) and is also less relevant in the sub-corpora as a whole if we consider the normalized frequencies.

Among the search terms used to collect the corpus, in addition to the terms described so far, others were relevant to this analysis. These terms are *trann**, *shemale* and *cross dresser**. As pointed out by GLAAD (n.d.-b), some of these terms (i.e. *trann** and *shemale*) have more recently been labelled as derogatory by some people belonging to the LGBTIQ+, although they were more commonly used in earlier decades.

When it comes to these last three search terms, results in the two sets of data become radically different. The term *trann** occurs a total of sixty-seven times in the TCUK, while it occurs only seventeen times in the TCC. It turns out that in the Canadian corpus the terms occurs eleven times in a completely unrelated context (three times it refers to the parts of a car 'variable tranny' referring to a type of transmission in an automobile, and eight times it refers to the character in a Canadian production called *Toronah* [2015]), the remaining six occurrences are reported speech in articles mainly related to trans people describing episodes of discrimination. In the TCUK the number of occurrences is much higher, and by analysing the examples in more detail it is possible to highlight two different patterns in the use of this term, as exemplified below:

> (1) You might be surprised at how much the transgender community would agree with you. Because being trans (not a '**tranny**',[21] please that's just rude) has far less to do with sex swaps or changes or striving to be a real' anything than you might imagine. (*Daily Mail*, 9 May 2013)

> (2) The dress is only one element of the psycho-sexual process. Just because you don't have a dress on doesn't stop you being a **tranny**, in the same way as, if you're not in bed with a man, it doesn't stop you being gay. (*The Guardian*, 4 October 2014)

Example (1) is representative of the first pattern, which occurs 19 times. In these cases, *trann** is used to underline the fact that this term is considered a derogatory and offensive word and should never be used to refer to transgender people (relevant might be the fact that this excerpt is from an article written by a transgender woman, Jane Fae). The other pattern retrieved is exemplified in example (2). This pattern occurs 48 times. In these cases, *trann** is used as an informal synonym of *transgender* or *transsexual* or even of *cross-dresser* and *transvestite* at times (see example 3).

> (3) **TRANNY** FURY AT BRIDE-SHOP BAN
> A **CROSSDRESSER** was left fuming after being turfed out of a bridal shop for asking to try on a wedding dress. (*The Sun*, 12 February 2015)

There are some main differences that need to be highlighted with regards to this pattern: many occurrences are, similarly to the TCC, from reported speech, but here we also find a few examples from the reporters' text (see example 3).

These kinds of representation of *tranny* in a negative context, associating these people with negative events and behaviours, contribute to a more negative representation, or prosody, of transgender identity. This concept of negative and positive prosody, further explained in Chapter 4, will be referred to throughout Chapters 4 and 5. This representation builds up though the examples examined and contributes to the final image that the newspapers offer to the reader.

Another term that can be considered as derogatory is *shemale*. This term never occurs in the TCC and only occurs ten times in the TCUK. Here, it is generally associated with *tranny* or with *gender reassignment*. Thus, the context usually uncritically relates the term to the transgender community, except for the following examples:

> (4) Grammar pedantry aside, what would be the social impact of this addition to the language? The feminist argument is as obvious as it is compelling. And in the case of gender-nonbinary people, how do they get around the problem? Minding your language is important here. Shim and **shemale** are pejorative portmanteaus, sometimes lazily applied to trans people. (*The Guardian*, 30 January 2015)

> (5) Almas Bobby, president of the Pakistan **Shemale** Foundation, an advocacy group, said she knew of at least five. (*The Guardian*, 10 May 2013)

Example (4) is the only case in which *shemale* is mentioned to explain why it should not be used. Example (5) shows its use in the name of an association that occurs twice in the QualCor, where the term *shemale* has been reclaimed and used in the name of an advocacy group. The representation cannot be considered negative in these cases. This last example indicates that it is unwise to make blank judgements with regards to certain terms as being always good or always bad since there is a process of reclaiming and reappropriation of these terms by some members of the LGBTIQ+ community.

The last term considered as more problematic, and close in terms of meaning to *transvestite**, which was analysed previously, is *cross-dresser**. This term occurs 104 times in the TCUK and 29 times in the TCC. The definition of problematic here is not to attribute to the term per se, but to the use made of the term in the press. In the British data, the term is associated with the transgender community nine times in the whole corpus, highlighting that, although in terms of meaning it is close to *transvestite*, it does not have the same pattern associated with this word. An example of the way in which *cross-dresser** is used in articles in relation to the transgender community is the following:

> (6) I'm **transgender** and have been for many years. I love to dress as my two alter egos and love all the things that go with being a woman – wearing make-up and high heels and so on. What's really getting me down is that I can't get a girlfriend, which is what I want.
>
> **Cross-dressing** has ended relationships with girls in the past, so I've tried not to dress as a woman and to act more like a boy, but it just depresses me more because my ultimate dream is to be a woman. (*Daily Mirror*, 20 March 2013)

Example (6) suggests that these two collocates are used in contexts in which their meaning is associated as part of the same identity, making reference to a generalization that does not always apply.

The Canadian press shows a very different pattern, in fact, nineteen times the term occurs in a context where it stands for its meaning, and it is not associated to any other gender or sexual identity. In two examples the term actually refers to a car, so it is unrelated. The other eight times the term is associated with being transgender (twice), gay (three times), transvestite (once) and to the world of drag queens (twice). In all 8 cases the terms were associated one with the other by appearing within the same article but were never used as loose synonyms as we see in the TCUK.

In this last section, I presented a general overview of naming strategies and the way the search terms were used across the TransCor, focusing primarily on the frequency of occurrence and presence in the two sub-corpora. The representation of trans people in the British and the Canadian press has many different facets. Therefore, the analysis presented in this work called for the use of different tools of Corpus Linguistics. The results presented so far are all outcomes of the analysis of frequencies combined in some cases with concordance analysis.

The following chapters will investigate further the use of the terms *transgender*, transsexual** and *trans*.

4

Semantic prosodies in the press

Understanding a word 'by the company it keeps': Semantic prosodies in the press

As highlighted in Chapter 2, discourses are always set in a context which influences our understanding of the specific topic discussed, in the same way, lexical items are accompanied by patterns of meaning that influence our understanding of the issue. In other words, one word repeatedly accompanied by others that carry a specific connotation will be included in that semantic domain of signification. This linguistic behaviour is defined as 'semantic prosody' (Firth 1957; Sinclair 1987; Louw 1993; Stubbs 1995; Partington 1998; Hunston 2007).

The different theories on semantic prosody became more popular in the late 1950s, the time when John Firth wrote probably his most famous quote: 'you shall know a word by the company it keeps' (Firth 1957: 11). The definition of semantic prosody as unitary and agreed upon is still under discussion in the linguistic community. Following is a discussion on the main ideas about it, focusing on the approach that best fits the purpose of this study.

Firth initially used the term to refer to the phonological behaviour of specific sounds, which assimilate with others when put in a specific position. Later, he suggested that lexical items could share the same type of pattern, in the sense that the words could assimilate the same semantic meaning of the other lexical items they were surrounded by.

One of the first scholars to pick up on this theory was John Sinclair (1987). He noticed that this type of pattern mainly manifested in the collocational behaviour of lexical items. As was underlined in Chapter 2, a term can be said to have a collocational relationship with another when they co-occur together a number of times that can be considered statistically relevant in their context. Sinclair's point of view implies that this co-occurrence is not casual. Functionality is one of the most important features of communication, which includes, apart from grammatical choices necessary for the structure of the sentence, lexical choices as well. These lexical choices rely on a sort of preference relevant to the aim of the communication. Thus, the semantic prosody carried by the words is fundamental to express the speaker/writer's attitude and evaluation of the sentence produced (Sinclair 1996). Sinclair was not the one to coin the phrase semantic prosody, but he did describe this phenomenon as the tendency of many phrases and words to evolve 'in a certain semantic environment' (Sinclair 1991: 112). In later works, he also adopted this terminology, although one of the peculiarities of Sinclarian semantic prosody is a non-classification between positive and negative or good and bad prosody. Sinclair does not regard semantic prosody as gradable, as it is hard to categorize the various units of meaning that semantic prosody involves. Sinclair also identified a difference between semantic preference and semantic prosody, the first strictly related to the collocational pattern, while the latter goes beyond the collocation to the intrinsic meaning of the term. Other scholars have elaborated this concept further.

The first to coin the phrase 'semantic prosody', later used by many others, was Bill Louw (1993). Semantic prosody is defined by Louw as 'a consistent aura of meaning with which a form is imbued by its collocates' (1993: 157). Louw suggests that we have been using semantic prosodies for centuries, but our perception and intuition had no access to it, until now (173). Additionally, he suggests that semantic prosodies can be defined as positive or negative, or 'bad' and 'good' (170) in the way they influence our understanding of communication, although we are much more likely to use bad prosodies rather than good ones.

Michael Stubbs (1995) proposed an alternative definition to this behaviour of lexical items. He claims that there is a difference that must be underlined between semantic preference and discourse prosody, which he defines as the relation between a 'lemma or word-form' and a set of 'semantically related' terms (Stubbs 2002: 65). Stubbs (1995) identifies three types of discourse prosodies, strictly related to the collocational pattern, positive and negative, similar to Sinclair and others, but also a neutral type of preference, mainly sentences with an informative function. In drawing a distinction between discourse prosody and semantic preference, Stubbs defines the latter as a set of lexical items which frequently occur together and have some semantic features in common (Stubbs 2002). To put it simply, the first definition points to an evaluation of the context of use, while the second focuses on similarities in the use of lexical items.

Another perspective on semantic prosody is given by Alan Partington who maintains that '[it] refers to the spreading of connotational colouring beyond single words boundaries' (1998: 68). For example, the term 'water' can be thought of in a 'favourable' way if we find it together with 'sun', 'beach' and 'sea' or in an 'unfavourable' way if it associated to 'drowning', 'hurricane' and 'death' (Partington 1998: 66). In this perspective, semantic prosody works on a binary distinction between good and bad. According to Partington, semantic prosody is the evaluative meaning carried by a unit of language, that goes beyond what is 'visible by the naked eye' (2004: 132). Semantic prosody is the way in which we express our evaluation of things.

Susan Hunston (2007) also uses the phrase 'semantic prosody' and suggests that this approach comes 'from corpus linguistics, and in particular from the "phraseological" tradition that focuses on the typical behaviour of individual lexical items' (Hunston 2007: 249). She points out that the immediate context of a lexical item is contingent to the type of semantic prosody it carries, and is not strictly related to the lemma, bringing forward the example of *persistent*. In fact, while the semantic prosody of this term in its adjectival function seems rather negative, this same pattern is not present when the term is used predicatively. Moreover, she adds that the concept of a word having a positive or negative prosody has to be inevitably linked to the point of view; therefore, it is unlikely that a term objectively has a positive or negative semantic prosody of its own (254–257).

At this point, it seems necessary to elaborate further on the dichotomy between semantic preference and semantic prosody, which so far has been described just as a different labelling of the same phenomenon. Monika Bednarek (2008) argues that the difference does not only lie in the nomenclature but also in the meaning. She identifies semantic preference as the collocational patterning, the co-occurrence of a term with others belonging to a same semantic category that influences the meaning of the term itself but does not define the term per se. Semantic preference can be classified as positive or negative (or neutral) according to the context in which it is set. On the contrary, semantic prosody is defined as the meaning that a lexical item has acquired as a consequence of the semantic preference. In this case, the term maintains the positive or negative connotation, as if the meaning now directly implied this evaluation. She argues that a term could have a negative semantic preference but a positive semantic prosody, in line with Partington (2004) who proves this with his research on the term *brook*, and with Sinclair (1991) who suggested this dichotomy earlier as well. Bednarek finally suggests that semantic preference should be used to refer to a particular positive or negative 'collocation' and semantic prosody to identify particular positive or negative 'connotations' (2008: 133). That is to say, while semantic preference is strictly related to the context in which the collocation pair is found, semantic prosody goes beyond the context and refers to a meaning and evaluation that the term has now acquired.

Relatively to this point of view, Partington (2004) had already suggested that semantic prosody becomes inevitably related to the community of speech in which that co-occurrence of lexical items is used.

Against this backdrop, this study seeks to analyse the semantic preference that these terms have in the two different sub-corpora as a way of establishing the semantic prosody that they consecutively acquire and identifying the impact on the perception of the representation of transgender identities offered by the press through the use of specific linguistic strategies and patterns.

As a way to apply this approach and discuss the intrinsic positive or negative meaning that some terms may carry, Richard Xiao and Tony McEnery (2006) investigated English in comparison to Chinese words considered near synonyms, focusing on the collocation analysis and the semantic prosody that the terms carry. The authors intended as near synonyms 'lexical pairs that have very similar cognitive or denotational meaning, but which may differ in collocational or prosodic behaviour' (Xiao and McEnery 2006: 108). They concluded that semantic prosody is observably a cross-cultural phenomenon both in Chinese and in English, although the semantic prosody of near synonyms is different and cannot be interchanged in either language. Furthermore, while the two languages are completely different, the semantic prosody of the near synonyms was revealed to be similar.

A similar cross-cultural study was conducted by Tony Berber Sardinha (2000) on the semantic prosody of words in English and Portuguese. In this case, the results differ from the previous case study presented. Sardinha found that semantic prosody varies in English and Portuguese. Through the study of semantic prosody associated with specific terms, Sardinha was also able to point out that frequently the results of contemporary dictionaries are inadequate for the study of languages.

A further study, which aimed to demonstrate that the semantic prosody of a term is not monolithically positive or negative, is the one conducted by Bill Louw and Carmela Chateau (2010). They analysed semantic prosody in specialized corpora and concluded that the semantic prosody in those texts is influenced by the impersonal scientific context.

Finally, Costas Gabrielatos and Paul Baker (2008) explored through the use of semantic prosody the attitudes and evaluations that newspapers have toward RASIM, similar in scope to the present research where the representation of identity is at stake.

As it has been pointed out in this section, the definition of semantic prosody is not always as straightforward as it seems. For the purpose of this analysis, semantic prosody will be considered in the way conceived by Partington (2004). The terms under investigation will be analysed in relation to the ones with which they consistently co-occur in the corpus. The context will then be analysed in order to establish if the lexical choices mirror a specific ideology and if the meaning and relevance they carry are represented as positive or negative, thus how the newspaper is evaluating the topic bearing in mind that:

> evaluation is the engine of persuasion. Speakers employ it to convince an audience of what should be seen as right and proper and what not and that therefore the audience should conduct itself in a manner appropriate to the goal of achieving the former and eschewing the latter. Thus, as well reflect, it can impose, overtly or covertly, a value system. (Partington, Duguid and Taylor 2013)

Prosody will be considered as a way to communicate evaluation on the part of the newspapers and will be tackled as 'the "invisible" non-obvious cohesive glue' (Partington 2017: 202) that holds the texts together and expresses evaluation. In this study, semantic prosody is employed from a discourse analysis perspective, and the occurrence and function of terms will be considered from a textual perspective (Morley and Partington 2009). In the first case, lexical items will be looked at as the textual phenomenon that carry the evaluative intent of the speaker/writer. In the latter perspective, the terms will be analysed considering their relevance in the corpus. In order to do so, a collocation analysis will be carried out taking into account specifically the terms *transgender**, *transsexual** and *trans*.

Semantic categories of representation in the British and Canadian press

Picking up from the analysis presented in Chapter 3, I then conducted a collocation analysis of the three most frequent terms among the search terms, namely, *transgender**, *transsexual** and *trans*. This tool was useful to continue the initial analysis presented in Chapter 3. It allowed me to establish the semantic prosody patterns expressed in the representation of transgender identities in the press. As explained in Chapter 2, I produced a list of collocates for each search term in each of the sub-corpora. Of this list, I considered the first fifty elements. In terms of results, this tool was the one that was the most effective, highlighting different semantic groups used by the newspapers to represent transgender identities. All collocates considered for the analysis belonging to the terms *transgender**, *transsexual** and *trans* were grouped according to semantic relevance. The results will be presented in the following sections and in Chapter 5. A reminder to the reader, the British press was further investigated to consider the differences between the popular (PopCor) and quality (QualCor) press.

Defining transgender people in the British press

Among the different categories of semantic representation of transgender identities in the British press, two specifically build on the way that trans people are described as individuals. These two categories have been defined as *personal details* and *implying verbs*.

The prosody – the positive or negative representation – surrounding transgender people is strongly influenced by the use of pre- and post-modifiers, which contribute to the building of the representation of transgender identity that each newspaper chooses to give. This section addresses the use of pre- and post-modifiers, in reference to transgender people, which emerged from the analysis of the TCUK, through the analysis of the two semantic categories of representation mentioned previously.

Personal details

The first category considered is that of *personal details*. This group of collocates contains pre- and post-modifiers (*color, openly* and *Catholics*) that refer to personal details of the social actor discussed in the article, such as race or religious faith. Table 4.1 summarizes all the collocates retrieved that fit this category.

As we can see from Table 4.1, this pattern is mainly present for the term *transsexual**. Despite the fact that the number of terms in each category seems to be apparently low, it is worth looking at the collocates retrieved for *transgender** and *trans* as well. Starting from the collocates of *transgender**, in the QualCor this category only occupies 6 per cent of the words in the collocation list, whilst it never occurs in the PopCor.

A closer look into the use of these terms allows us to understand how they add further information when writing about transgender people. The first collocate that we will focus on is *color*, which occurs eighteen times in the QualCor. The use of this noun is narrowed down to one pattern, as in eleven out of eighteen

Table 4.1 *Personal details* in the TCUK.

	QualCor[1]	Terms Occurring in Both Sub-corpora	PopCor
*transgender**	color (18), openly (42), Catholics (8)		
*transsexual**	Brazilian (12),	first (14/14), male (10/12) female (11/11), old (7/9), sex (8/11), year (6/13)	pre (12), op (11), surgery (6), women (7), woman (13)
trans	color (8), colour (8), youth (7), students (10)		

Note: Numbers in brackets equal the frequency of the collocates. Double numbers in the third column indicate first the frequency in the QualCor and then the frequency of the collocate in the PopCor.

times it refers to the phrase *transgender women of color*. The repeated use of this phrase points to a similar pattern that will be found again in Chapter 5 when discussing the relationship between *transgender* and *migrant*. There is an implicit acknowledgement of intersectionality in the use of this phrase, where a minority and discriminated identity (*transgender*, therefore gender identity) is represented within another minority and discriminated identity (*people color*, hence race) that are then associated to *woman*, which can also be considered a discriminated identity on its own.

Focusing on the more general discourse, the patterns surrounding these social actors shows that such a phrase carries a discourse preference for violence, as we can observe from example (7):

(7) Three **transgender women of color** have been **murdered** in America less than one month into this new year: Lamia Beard in Virginia, Ty Underwood in Texas, and Goddess Edwards in Kentucky. (*The Guardian*, 29 January 2015)

The following terms and phrases are found in the sentences under scrutiny: *victims, tears, abuse, faced record-breaking amount of violence, homicide, systemic violence, epidemic of violence, murdered, face physical risks, high risk of murder, hate crimes*. All these terms are reporting on stories involving trans women of colour who are currently facing extreme struggle and violence. In this case, we can observe that newspapers are functioning as a platform to inform readers about the tragic situation transgender people are facing and at the same time pointing to the fact that there is a minority within a social group that is considered a minority, and that is struggling even more. This linguistic strategy, intersectionality (about a similar topic see Crenshaw 1991), will be discussed further in Chapter 5, where more examples of it will be displayed. In this case, we can see the collocate associated to a heavy pattern of violence, which creates an aura of negativity connected to transgender people of colour and at the same time acknowledges the difficulties these people are faced with.

The second collocate of this group, *openly*, presents a slightly different pattern, which will be analysed below. The term occurs forty-two times in the QualCor, where it appears to have two different functions. The first refers to the fact that a transgender person is living their identity freely while the other relates to the military environment, pointing to the fact that it is now possible for transgender people to serve in the military without needing to disguise their gender identity in the UK. In the examples where the pre-modifier is used with this first meaning, the articles are usually narrating the story of a transgender person, as in the following examples:

> (8) The Liberal Democrat Sarah Brown, who was the **only openly transgender** politician in the UK for a time, was listed in the transgender rather than politics category, but Paris Lees, a prominent trans rights activist and writer, was placed in the influencers category. (*The Guardian*, 26 June 2015)

> (9) Those horrific comments about Fallon Fox, the **first openly transgender** fighter in MMA [Mixed Martial Arts] history which she never fully backed off from when given the opportunity. (*The Guardian*, 13 November 2015)

The articles in which the pre-modifier is used with its second meaning, mostly describe the situation bringing forward the fact that this is a new right achieved for transgender people in the UK, as in the following example:

> (10) Flight Lieutenant Ayla Holdom, 34, is the **first** and currently the **only openly transgender** military pilot in Britain. (*i*, 22 December 2014)

As example (10) shows, in most cases, the adverb *openly* is pre-modified by adjectives, mainly *first* and *only*. These two terms serve to underline novelty, in the sense that the overall prosody of the examples and more generally of the occurrences of the adverb imply that the subject or topic of discussion is relatively new, or uncommon. Through this construction, the newspapers seem to be acknowledging that transgender people are for the first time feeling that they can be truthful to their identity, and more importantly, that laws are changing to allow them to do this. In fact, the last legislative document issued to regulate transgender identity dates back to 2010 (Polese and Zottola 2019). Looking forward, this type of representation can be considered to be positive. All the examples taken into consideration do not show any sign of disagreement with this change in direction from the military service and from transgender people in general. Writing this at a moment in which society seems to be taking a step back after the declaration made by current US president Donald Trump (2017), banning all transgender people from serving in the US military force, gives hope for the future that other countries, such as the UK, are still going to acknowledge this right despite the general political leaning of the major economic and political forces today.

This category of collocates has one more term that is worth considering in more detail, *Catholics*. This term occurs only eight times and is mainly used as a noun, as reported in the following examples:

(11) Father Bernard Lynch, an openly gay priest who helped found Soho Masses but has not been involved in the group for a number of years, told *i*: "I believe it will be devastating on the soul life of lesbian, gay, bisexual and **transgendered Catholics**." (*i*, 3 January 2013)

(12) Early next month that very same church – the Church of the Immaculate Conception, Farm Street, as it is formally known – will open its doors to dozens of lesbian, gay, bisexual and **transgender** Roman **Catholics** who have been exiled from a West End church where they have attended mass for the past six years. (*The Guardian*, 15 February 2013)

As the reading of the present study advances, we will see that the prosody surrounding this term, and the linguistic strategies for which it is used, relates to a type of discourse that will be introduced in more detail in Chapter 5, that of a collective representation of transgender people. In all occurrences transgender people are described in a list that also includes gay and lesbian people, creating a sort of a macro group that includes different communities of practice associated for a specific reason. Similar to the function of the term *color* mentioned in example (7), or of *migrant*, as we will see in Chapter 5, we find occurrences of intersectionality between different social groups. Among the social group of Catholic people, there is another group (minority within minority discourse), which is different as it has been, on some occasions stigmatized by the church itself.

This leads to another finding that has emerged from the examples analysed, that is, the discourse related to this term finds similarities to the conclusion drawn from the prosody surrounding the term *openly*. Some of the articles, as in example (12), acknowledge the fact that also the church is making an effort to open up to a more inclusive behaviour toward transgender people.

It can be pointed out that in three cases, as in example (11), the term *transgendered* is used to refer to transgender people. This term has been used 113 times throughout the TCUK, and according to websites such as GLAAD, not all transgender people feel comfortable when this term is used. The poor accuracy in the choice of terminology on the part of the journalist comes as a discordant note in a more positive and inclusive type of discourse identified here.

So far, we have looked at collocates resulting from the collocation analysis of the term *transgender**. We will now move on to look at the results emerging from the collocation analysis of the term *transsexual** with regards to this semantic category of representation. When it comes to *transsexual**, the collocation analysis reveals a different pattern in comparison to the term *transgender** analysed above. The first difference lies in the fact that collocates that fit this category were retrieved from both sub-corpora, while in the case of *transgender** they were only found to occur in the QualCor. Moreover, the percentage of terms in this category is greater than for *transgender**. The terms belonging to the *personal details* category here cover 22 per cent of the collocates considered in the analysis. Some of the terms in this category are not new, but others such as *pre*, *op* or *surgery* relate to a specific aspect of the transsexual identity, namely the gender reassignment operation. The collocates for *transsexual** relating to this category can be grouped according to their meaning. There are collocates which refer to age (*old* [6/9], *year* [6/13]) occurring in both sub-corpora. Retrieved from both sub-corpora are also collocates which refer to gender more generally (*male* [10/12], *female* [11/11], *women* [7 PopCor], *woman* [13 PopCor]). *Brazilian* (12) occurs as the strongest collocate in the QualCor, and it refers to the geographical origins of the individuals mentioned in the articles. Terms that relate to transition and gender reassignment were found only in the PopCor (*pre* [12], *op* [11], *surgery* [6]). Other collocates retrieved are *first* (14/14) and *sex* (8/11). Some of these collocates are going to be analysed in more details in the following paragraphs. From this preliminary information it is possible to say that this type of occurrence among the collocates mirrors the results presented in Chapter 3 which highlights the presence in the TCUK of representation related to the physical or medical aspects of transgender identities.

Altering the order in which the collocates were presented so far, the term *pre* occurs as the third strongest collocate in the PopCor while the collocate *op* occurs in the sixth position, indicating that both collocates are strong in this set of data. The two terms occur together nine times, seven of which were in

The Sun. In seven (once in 2013, three times in 2014 and three times in 2015) of the occurrences under investigation, the term was found in contexts like the following:

> (13) You would have thought they would have been outraged that Mr Sheen, knowing he was infected with HIV, would have continued to have unprotected sex with girlfriends, hookers and **pre-op transsexuals.** (*The Sun*, 20 November 2015)

> (14) I'm too beautiful to work; Says **pre-op transsexual** Tiffany Davies, who relies on rich men 'I BUY TWO NEW FROCKS A WEEK.' (*The Sun*, 5 June 2014)

As in examples (13) and (14), *pre-op transsexuals* are either represented as prostitutes or as opportunists who rely on other people to live a wealthy and easy life. This last description is particularly explicit in the description in example (14). The pattern exemplified in example (14) was found in four other articles. This type of construction can be defined, from the perspective of social actor representations, as a form of determination, more specifically of 'Categorisation' (Van Leeuwen 1996: 52–54). I would also add that this is an imprecise type of categorization, as these people in the examples under investigation are represented 'in terms of an identity and function they share with others' (Van Leeuwen 2005: 52), but that does not represent their identity as a whole. The type of prosody that emerges from this representation is negative, as pre-op transsexual people are associated with roles that in our society are still stereotypically and culturally constructed as not positive, similar to that of a prostitute. The other three occurrences of *post* are followed by *operative* (twice) and *operation*, the extended version of *op*. These cases do not reveal any additional elements that contribute to a specific representation.

These two collocates, together with *surgery*, which was also included in this group of terms related to gender reassignment and transition, all contribute to the type of representation of these social actors presented above: categorization. As I will explain in more detail below this class is divided into functionalization, appraisement and identification, which is again subdivided into classification, relational identification and physical identification. This last category, physical identification, fully defines the linguistic strategies used in these articles. Moreover, according to GLAAD – the guidelines for the use of the terminology related to transgender identities followed throughout this study – these terms should be avoided in favour of the term 'transition', as some transgender people could find their use uncomfortable. In fact, some individuals could feel that it is inappropriate to continuously refer to the transition surgery. The reference to gender reassignment puts an accent, as pointed out in the previous chapter when discussing the use of the term *transsexual*, on the physical characteristics of the person rather than their identity. In the case of these pre- and post-modifiers, the pattern was found exclusively in the popular press.

A similar conclusion, in terms of a representation focused on physical appearance, can be drawn from the examples included in another group of collocates: *old* and *year*. Both in the PopCor and in the QualCor, *old* always occurs together with *year*.

In the examples related to these collocates, the specification of the age does not really add any important information to the piece of news described in the article, instead, it seems to satisfy more a need of sensationalism to meet newsworthiness criteria imposed by journalistic standards.

Retrieved in both sub-corpora are also collocates which refer to gender (*male* [10/12], *female* [11/11], *women* [7 PopCor], *woman* [13 PopCor]). Among these collocates, it can be noted that there is a focus on the terms *male* and *female*, which out of context could give the idea of a sort of impersonalization (Van Leeuwen 2005: 59). The two collocates (10 times in the QualCor and 6 times in the PopCor) were found to co-occur in the phrase 'male-to female' or 'female-to-male' (sometimes also found in the acronym form MTF and FTM[2]), and refer to the transition from the sex assigned at birth to the identifying gender. These phrases were found in contexts such as the following:

> (15) Is it easier to change ones voice as a **male-to-female** or as a **female-to-male**?
> Easy or hard isn't exactly the thought here. Both groups of people require different things, but essentially, **male-to-female** trans people have more work ahead of them. **Female-to-male** trans people don't seem to be as fundamentally unhappy with their voices. (*The Guardian*, 2 June 2015)

In the case of these collocates, we can say that in both sub-corpora the prosody surrounding them is positive. They are used in contexts where they have an informative function and cannot be seen as having any underlying negative evaluative purpose.

The collocates taken into consideration in the following analysis are both peculiar for different reasons. *Brazilian* (12) occurs as the strongest collocate in the QualCor, and the only adjective retrieved referring to geographical origins. This collocate occurs only in the QualCor. On a preliminary note, we could say that the use of this adjective reinforces the stereotype present in Europe that many sex workers who come to European countries are from Brazil, are transsexual and are particularly renowned for their beauty. If we look at the data, it is possible to see that in reality, the phrase is used in a completely different context, for instance:

> (16) In January Burchill used a column in the Observer to launch an attack on critics of her friend and fellow writer Suzanne Moore, who had written a magazine article that claimed women were expected to have the body shape of a '**Brazilian transsexual**'. (*Daily Telegraph*, 27 March 2013)

The occurrences all refer to the case of *The Observer*'s columnist Julie Burchill (Baker 2014b: 212), who wrote a defamatory article on transgender people in 2013. The article received strong criticism to the point that it was removed from the online newspaper. It seems that she only wrote the article in defence of her colleague journalist Suzanne Moore, a columnist for *The Guardian*, who days before had written an article in which she represented women as struggling because they were expected to have the body of a 'Brazilian transsexual'. Needless to say, this article also received numerous complaints and was at the centre of intense criticism. The collocates, except for one, are all related to articles that appeared in 2013 in relation to this event. The four newspapers considered in this sub-corpus all talked about this event, in rather different ways. While *The Times* and *The Guardian* presented the issue and described it in a rather objective way, underlining in different parts of the article that both Moore and Burchill were strongly criticized and encouraged to leave their jobs, the *i* and *The Daily Telegraph* had different behaviours.

Example (17) is an excerpt from the *i*. Here the writer uses the phrase 'claimed *offence*' in explaining why the article was considered misleading and inappropriate by the readers. As I will argue later in this chapter when analysing *implying verbs*, the metapropositional verb 'to claim' is controversial since it suggests that what is being said might not be true, especially when being followed by a term in italics, as in the case of *offence* in example (17):

> (17) Suzanne Moore, also a fine columnist of long standing, wrote a magazine article in which she railed against the pressure for women to look like, as she put it, 'Brazilian transsexuals'. Cue uproar on Twitter, where Moore was subjected to a barrage of insults from transsexuals, who **claimed *offence***. Burchill stepped in to defend her friend and, as is her way, went that little bit further, describing transsexuals as 'a bunch of bed-wetters in bad wigs'. (*i*, 16 January 2013)

Much more explicit is the stance taken by *The Daily Telegraph*, through the words of columnist Allison Pearson. The journalist states that Moore 'meant no offence'; on the contrary, it should be considered as a compliment to be a model, to set the standard, clearly undermining the offensive statement and in a way aligning to it.

The last collocate examined in this group is *first* (14/14). This collocate is relevant because it has a similar function as one of the collocates analysed for the term *transgender**: *openly*. As we concluded for the collocate *openly,* the use of these pre-modifiers introduces a discourse of novelty, again a sort of inclusive and open discussion toward transgender identities, which are now at a point where transgender people feel less constrained by society's judgement.

The collocate analysis, as anticipated at the beginning of this chapter, was conducted for the terms *transgender**, *transsexual** and *trans*. So far, we have discussed the collocation analysis that emerged from the first two terms. For the term *trans* only a few collocates were retrieved that can be included in the category being described here: *color* (8), *colour* (8), *youth* (7) and *students* (10). All of the collocates were retrieved from the QualCor.

Color and *colour* are respectively the third and the eleventh strongest collocates. The use of these pre- or post-modifiers, in this case, is identical as for *transgender**, with an intersectional function. This could hint at the fact that the QualCor uses *trans* as a synonym of *transgender* or as an umbrella term.

The second collocate we are going to look at from this category is the noun *youth*, which occurs in the sub-corpus seven times, in contexts such as the following:

> (18) We do have to, as a movement, give hope to these kids, and especially **young trans youth** like Leelah Alcorn, who committed suicide last year after leaving a devastating indictment of the world that she experienced, or Islan Nettles, who was murdered on the streets of New York in 2013. (*The Guardian*, 30 June 2015)

This noun, although similar in terms of meaning to the post-modifiers found for the term *transgender** (*years*) as it puts an accent on the aspect of age, does not have the same function. The use of this term, together with the other collocates retrieved for the term *trans*, namely *students*, occurring ten times in the PopCor, introduces a new topic, that of young transgender people. The specific example presented above (example 18) refers to an unfortunate event that happened in the United States in 2015 when a teenage transgender girl committed suicide in Ohio. An in-depth analysis of all the examples reveals a similar type of context. The examples referring to transgender youth deal with the description of problematic situations, in which suicide rates or the unfortunate circumstances in which young transgender people find themselves are discussed. Although representing a rather sad reality, in this case, newspapers should once again be praised for acknowledging and giving space to young transgender people. Talking about it means acknowledging and endorsing the fact that cases such as these exist and society should make an effort in supporting these adolescents. The same pattern was found to occur for the collocate *students*. The articles containing this collocate mostly describe the harsh situations with which transgender students are confronted every day. These identities are, at the same time, acknowledged in articles, for instance:

> (19) It's important to honour students' choices of name – for **trans students**, this sends the important message that you accept their identities unfailingly. (*The Guardian*, 2 June 2015)

This example (19) stresses the necessity to respect transgender students' identities starting from their name and pronoun choices. This last section of the analysis highlights an attempt on the part of the quality press considered in this study to introduce a more inclusive discourse in relation to transgender people, with the inclusion not only of new topics such as transgender youth identity but of a collaborative and non-discriminatory behaviour toward transgender people.

Implying verbs

As I explained in the introduction to this section, I would like to address here two different categories that emerged from the collocation analysis. These two groups have in common the fact that the terms included function as pre- or post-modifiers of the terms under investigation. The second category of collocates that will be analysed here has been defined as *implying verbs*. This category only includes three collocates and is found only for the term *transsexual** in the British popular press. Despite the fact that this category is narrowed down to just one sub-corpus and one search term, it will be discussed here as we believe that it strongly reinforces the pattern related to the problematic use of the term *transsexual* highlighted in the PopCor. It can be noticed that some of the verbs that were collocates of *transsexual* can contribute to the creation of a specific pattern; I defined this category as *implying verbs*. These are verbs that, in this context, carry a negative connotation and give a rather controversial representation of transsexual people as they imply something in their meaning. The collocates found relating to this pattern are: *cheated*, *claims* and *called*.

Cheated is the strongest collocate for *transsexual* and occurs six times, five of which are in 2014 and one in 2015. The term was found in contexts similar to the following example:

> (20) Kendra recently split from her husband Hank Baskett after he allegedly **cheated** on her with a transsexual escort. (*Daily Mirror*, 15 November 2014)

This kind of construction depicts a situation in which transsexual people are represented as homewreckers and as doing unconventional jobs, for instance, being an escort. When in this construction, the term *transsexual* is either nominalized or followed by *model* or *escort* as in example (20).

The second verb that contributes to the negative representation of *transsexual** people is *claims*. This collocate is the seventh strongest for *transsexual** (8 occurrences), and it is found in contexts such as the following:

> (21) What actually happened was that he was placed in a women's prison because, dontcha know, he **claims** to be a transsexual and is waiting for that all important op. (*The Express*, 19 December 2013)

Here, the verb *claims* implies that what is being said might not be true. Additionally, the choice of the pronoun (*he*) reiterates that the person under discussion is not really a woman but a man who claims, or allegedly says, to be female. This type of pattern might create in the mind of the reader an image of transsexual people as liars, and although this specific example only relates to the person who is being discussed in this specific article, like all the other examples relate to the case presented in that article, this repeated pattern, associated to transsexual people, could create a link between transsexual people more generally speaking and the possibility that they are liars. This assumption follows the idea that semantic prosody influences the way the reader/hearer perceives the meaning of specific words according to the context these are generally set in, thus the meaning this context associates to these terms. The repeated presentation of the term *transsexual* in relation to verbs that have a negative connotation automatically affiliates this term to that meaning and evaluation.

The last term that can be included in this category is *called*, occurring nine times. In all occurrences it was found in the phrase 'a transsexual called + *first name*', as in the following example:

> (22) Manson, who is now a transsexual **called** Kyran Lee, wooed Carol with a fake Facebook account using photos of a man. (*Daily Mail*, 28 November 2015)

This type of construction implies that the name with which the person is addressed is akin to a pseudonym, and not their actual name. This pattern is only found in relation to the term *transsexual** and could be critically interpreted as particularly problematic because it gives a negative representation of transsexual people, as they were not 'real' people. This type of representation is similar to the

Semantic prosodies in the press 93

discourse presented when discussing examples (7) and (8), where transgender people are represented as 'living as' a woman or man. Similarly, here the verb *called* implies that this name is not always the real one. As pointed out above, the occurrences of the specific terms analysed might not seem relevant in terms of quantity. Nonetheless, they all have a similar function that builds up on a specific pattern of representation.

Defining trans identities in the Canadian press

In the definition of transgender people, the Canadian press differs from the British press in a number of ways. The two categories identified in the British press as defining trans identities were retrieved in the TCC as well, and again the *personal details* category was more prominent. The category of *implying verbs* was found in the TCC as well, but differently from the British corpus, in the Canadian data, this category was associated to the term *trans* only rather than *transsexual**, as discussed in the previous section.

Personal details

We will first examine the category of *personal details*, the collocates are summarized in Table 4.2.

Of the three terms researched *transgender** is the one that offers five collocates that relate to the semantic category of *personal details*. Looking in more detail at these collocates we can see that two of them concentrate the attention on a specific group of transgender people, youth, these collocates are teen (21 occurrences) and 12-year-old (8). Starting with the latter, of the eight collocates of 12-year-old, six relate to the story of a 12-year-old transgender boy in Alberta. The story of this boy from Edmonton, reached the press in 2014 as a victory and one of the first achievement in trans rights. In fact, it refers to the alteration of the law in the province of Alberta that regulates the issuing of birth certificate

Table 4.2 *Personal details* in the TCC.

transgender*	transsexual*	trans
12-year-old (8), teen (21), patients (28), competitor (7), contestant (6)	male-to-female (6), Belgian (7), German (6)	youth (39), kids (8)

for trans people. Until then it was a requirement to have gender confirmation surgery in order to have a birth certificate issued indicating one's identifying gender, this feature of the law was dropped, and the boy was able to receive his birth certificate indicating his identifying gender without having to undergo surgery. In the next chapter we will see that this event is also related to other collocates and was a highly popular topic in the news in Canada.

One of the collocates refers to a teen, Olie Pullen, who was awarded an anti-bullying award for their work to promote the change of law on gender description on provincial IDs before the National Assembly committee. Other articles within the TCC discuss this event, again as a celebration of the victory achieved and the bravery of such young individuals to fight for their rights. The last example, reiterating the discourse of relevance of trans issues in the press, highlights the increasing presence of transgender issues in Canada in reference to the appearance of a short film with a 12-year-old transgender character in the Toronto International Film Festival (TIFF) Kids.

Alongside this first collocate, the other one that gravitates around the field of youth is *teen*. Collocates of teen reveal different patterns. One example recalls the same event mentioned above, the TIFF Kids. One example relates to a teen, president of the Queer-Straight Alliance, who expresses their joy for the change of law in Alberta which no longer requires gender surgery for IDs to indicate the identifying gender (the same law mentioned above). Seven collocates refer to two teens who became famous in Canada. One of them is Jazz Jennings, a transgender teenage girl from the United States, who is also a YouTuber and TV personality, who became famous in 2007 as one of the youngest people to identify as trans and who featured in her own show about her journey as a trans teenager. The other celebrity related to this collocate is Hamilton Elliot, the transgender teen contestant on the Canadian reality show *The Amazing Race* (2015). The type of discourses related to these stories, presented partially in relation to the term *teen*, are very different. In the case of Jazz, the detail 'age' about her is seminal in all the articles we find about the topic. If we go beyond the articles in which the collocate is found, we see, as in the example (23) below, that her identity is presented and constructed in relation to her age.

> (23) Jazz Jennings is a cute, precocious teenage girl who plays soccer, likes art and loves hanging out with her friends, possibly even in the well-appointed living room in which she is being interviewed. Then she reveals she's a transgender person. (*The Gazette*, 13 July 2015)

The stories about Jazz are narrated because of this personal detail, and her story became famous, as we mentioned before, exactly for this reason. On the contrary, Elliot's age, as well as his gender identity, are mentioned in the articles but do not acquire a central role. What the articles that include this collocate are mostly interested in describing is the diversity of Canada and this is done through the description of the different contestants on the reality show, from immigrants to working-class people to trans people, all are part of the incredibly diverse Canadian population. In this case, the personal details in relevant but not the main aspect that is considered in the representation.

A pattern that we find in relation to this collocate is that of crimes committed against transgender teenagers. In fact, seven examples point to stories of trans teens being murdered or facing transphobic assaults. In the next chapter, we will see how in the British press this pattern is found in a conspicuous amount, to the extent that it forms a specific semantic category of representation. In the case of the Canadian press, this seems not to be the case, but a close examination of this collocate highlights this pattern. What is interesting here is that all the stories narrated do not happen in Canada, but mostly in the United States, and are reported in the press because of the negativity of the event itself, example (24) is representative of this pattern.

> (24) Police on Tuesday were investigating the physical and sexual assault of a **transgender teen** who said he was attacked in a bathroom at a suburban San Francisco public school where another transgender student had reported being the target of bullying. (*The Calgary Herald*, 5 March 2014)

Related in a way to the topic discussed above, two collocates found in this category are *contestant* (6) and *competitor* (7). Both these collocates, except for one concordance line which is related to the case of Hamilton Elliot outlined above, refer to Jenna Talackova, the first transgender woman to take part in the Miss Universe competition. Jenna is originally Canadian and in 2012 she initiated a legal battle to be admitted as a contestant in the beauty competition. In all the examples related to these two collocates, the articles underline the difficulties in being admitted into the contest and describe the problems she had to overcome and how she now is an icon for trans rights and an activist.

The collocate in this category to present the highest number of co-occurrences is *patient* (28). The two words co-occur in the noun phrase 'transgender patients' in all but one concordance line. This repetition already establishes the creation of this subcategory of trans people, and links trans people with a sort of medical discourse that depicts them as vulnerable but also as sick.

Looking at the collocates in more detail we notice in the first place that the collocates are related to a number of different topics. This differentiation in the topics discussed can be related to the fact that the newspapers included in the TCC differ from those found in TCUK in the fact that they are local to the province rather than national. For this reason, in many cases, they report on more local news that might not be found in papers from other provinces. A variety of articles are found, for example, one article discusses the issue of doctors refraining from giving a diagnosis of gender dysphoria out of fear. Another article discusses the opening of a new, more inclusive clinic welcoming people from the LGBTIQ+ community and with other specific needs. An article explains a doctor's claims that surgery for trans people is not an ideal solution as the still high number of suicides committed by trans people proves that it is not a valid route to pursue for trans people. Among the many different topics that emerge from the concordance analysis of this collocate, three appear to be more frequent.

Four collocates relate to a story which reports on a number of patients who have lamented that doctors have refused to treat them citing moral reasons, that is to say, that doctors refused to take trans patients under their care because they do not agree with the people identifying as trans. The evaluation of this act in the articles is absolutely negative, expressing that this behaviour is against the law and reprimandable.

A different group of articles linked to this collocate (5 occurrences) raises a big issue not only for Canada but for the trans community globally, the fact that doctors do not have formal training to treat transgender patients, thus making it hard both for patients to find a doctor with whom they feel comfortable and at ease, and for the medical staff as well who do not have the skills and the tools to deal with trans patients.

The largest group of occurrences (15) of this collocate is related to a problem that a number of provinces in Canada are facing. In fact, it seems that there are only a few clinics that by law are allowed to refer trans patients for surgery, making it very hard and time or money consuming for people to be referred. In 2015 a new bill was being discussed, put forward by MPP Cheri DiNovo titled Affirming Sexual Orientation and Gender Identity Act, which aimed at changing this and allowing a larger number of practitioners across the country to refer trans people for surgery. Despite the number of different topics that emerge from the concordance analysis of this collocate that was included within the *personal detail* category, I believe it is possible to identify a *file rouge* that runs across all these articles, and it is a discussion on the condition of trans people who are, for one reason or another, patients that need to improve and be taken care of.

Moving on to the analysis of the collocates of *transsexual**, the first we consider here is *male-to-female* (6). This collocate is used in four different articles, two of them refer to characters in a film and a novel, the other two deal with more complex issues. Two collocates are included in an article which presents the candidate to the position of mayor of Montreal in 2013 Melanie Joly and one of her team members who is described as a male-to-female transsexual who had to withdraw from the team because she was accused of being a prostitute. The other article discusses ideas from some strands of the feminist movement which does not recognize trans women as 'true' women and thus argues against sharing safe spaces that are designated for women.

In the first case, this representation of the mayoral candidate's team member as a transsexual prostitute not only is a way to diminish her by putting her into a category that is stereotypically regarded as negative but also superfluous in relation to the main topic discussed in the article which is strictly related to the mayoral candidate's campaign. We can speculate that this type of representation is being used to extend that same derogation onto the candidate as well. Thus, trans identity is being used as a way to shed a negative light on someone who does not even identify as a trans person.

The second article describes more of a scientific discourse in which different theories are being presented, the journalist does not really take a stance, this choice could be a sign of approval, but nothing explicit is written.

The two collocates that refer to nationality, *Belgian* (7) and *German* (6), have very different functions from the nationality collocate *Brazilian*, analysed in the TCUK. In the case of *Belgian*, there are two main topics discussed in the articles in which the collocate was found, a more trivial one and a more serious one. The former articles refer to *Before the Last Curtain Falls* (2015) a feature documentary by Thomas Wallner which recounts the life stories of six Belgian trans and drag queen performers between the age of sixty and seventy. The latter discuss a controversial issue related to euthanasia. The articles use the case of a Belgian transsexual person to argue against the Belgian law that allows people to request assisted death. The journalist hopes that Canada will remain a compassionate country where these type of things do not happen and makes the case for this by saying that the person killed themselves as they were not happy about the results of the gender confirmation surgery. The journalist argues that this problem could have been solved with therapy and help from specialists rather than death. Whether to agree or disagree with the perspective suggested in this article is a subjective matter, what is problematic from a representational point of view is the use of the term transsexual as a noun, whereas it should be used as an adjective, as explained in previous chapters.

For the collocate *German*, all occurrences are related to the German singer Hedwig Robinson and the Broadway show that documents her life *Hedwig and the Angry Inch*. Opposite to what we find for the use of the nationality adjectives in the TCUK, in the Canadian data these are not used to undermine, offend or denigrate the people to which the adjectives refer.

Moving on to the last group of collocates that fall within the *personal details* category, those that collocate with *trans*, only two collocates that fit this category were identified. These recall the pattern discussed for the term *transgender** related to young people: *youth* (39) and *kids* (8). The numerous articles that relate to these two collocates in the TCC discuss a number of different issues, which in some cases overlap.

Above all, the issue of trans youth harming themselves, committing suicide, being abused and facing a number of health challenges is discussed thirteen times in relation to the collocate *youth* and once in relation to the collocate *kids*. These articles aim to be an alarm bell for society, explaining the problem and the consequences that certain views have on trans children. On a similar note, nine collocates of youth relate to the problem of homeless trans youth and invite people to donate and support local organizations who work toward solving this problem. To support what is being discussed in these articles and to demonstrate even further the gravity of the situation, six articles talk about laws regarding trans identity and how they should be changed to favour youth as well. On a more positive note, three articles describe how trans youth are beginning to have more positive and effective role models because more people are coming out as trans thanks to the Canadian society being more accepting and inclusive. Six article which include both collocates narrate positive life stories of trans kids who have successfully transitioned and are living a happy life and three articles discuss a study put forward by the University of British Columbia on the positive effects of having supporting adults in trans youth lives has in terms of their happiness and serenity.

All in all, the articles related to this issue that include the term *trans* seem to be very positive and the use of these details within the articles serves the purpose of constructing a stronger and more relevant narrative.

This is in line with the general discourse put forward by the Canadian press when thinking about the few collocates that make up this category. Differently from the British press, which presents quite a few collocates in this category, language choices in the TCC do not make use of terms which could fall within this description. Additionally, the few words that can be seen as *personal details* are used in a positive way and to discuss issues that can benefit the transgender community. A specific focus on younger generations of trans people and an effort to make life better for trans people from childhood are observed in the articles examined. In this case, we can argue that young trans people are being depicted as beneficialized social actors (Van Leeuwen 1996: 45), they are gaining something from this representation, as they are being discussed as a third party who will gain a better quality of life from the actions of adults, whether its trans children's parents, teachers or policymakers.

Implying verbs

The other category that was interesting to analyse in the British press was that of *implying verbs*. We observed in the TCUK that these verbs were mainly found as collocates of the term *transsexual*, and they generally convey a negative representation of transgender people. In the TCC a small pattern representative of this category was also retrieved, but this time the verbs collocate with the term *trans* rather than *transsexual*. These verbs are summarized in Table 4.3.

There is also another significant difference between these verbs and the ones analysed in the British data, and that relates to what these verbs imply. As mentioned above, the implications in the TCUK are generally negative and point to a representation which reinforces the idea that trans identity is not a 'real' identity. The discourses that we find associated with these verbs in the Canadian press tend to point to the opposite representation. Here we find constructions such as 'help normalize being trans' (*Calgary Herald*, 13 June 2015), where the collocate is used to describe trans identity and to point to a positive discourse. Other articles related to the same collocate reinforce the discourse discussed in the previous section in addressing trans rights and ways to fight discrimination.

The use of the verb 'to identify' that we observe in two collocates in this category is always followed by *as*, these constructions build on a type of representation that acknowledges trans identity and the choice that trans people make to come out as transgender. Differently from the patterns highlighted above of 'verb + as'

Table 4.3 *Implying verbs* in the TCC.

| trans | face (11), identifying (6), being (24), identify (7) |

that pointed to a negative representation of trans identities, here the examples always use language in an inclusive and acknowledging way. The last verb of this category, *face* (11), already carries a negative semantic prosody, the very definition of the verb entails solving a problem. *Issue, threats, problems, risks, barriers, struggle* and *challenges* are what trans people face. This, in fact, is a list of nouns that are found as the objects of the verb to face in the examples that include this collocate. The press becomes a platform to acknowledge these difficulties and becomes a voice, once again, to fight discrimination.

Transgender people as social actors

In each type of communication that involves a verbal process there is always an agent and a patient, one who performs an action and one who receives this action. These can be defined as social actors. As mentioned earlier, social actors can be interpreted here as either individuals or collectives, for example political parties, communities of practice, social movements or minority groups. In discourse analysis agency is fundamental as it sets the action in a context, which in return determines the nature of the agent and of the patient. From a linguistic perspective, this can be realized through a variety of grammatical items (Van Leeuwen 1996). In the previous section instances of categorization have been mentioned a number of times. Here I aim to describe the framework from which this terminology arises in more detail.

In the framework of CDA, Theo van Leeuwen proposed a taxonomy for the representation of social actors, in his words a '*sociosemantic* inventory of the ways in which social actors can be represented' (1996: 32, emphasis in the original), both linguistically and semantically. Each categorization he presents is linked to a specific linguistic and rhetorical construction. I chose to apply this approach to this study, as the way social actors are represented customarily mirrors the social practices diffused in society.

Among categories of representation, Van Leeuwen identifies two major ones: exclusion and inclusion. In line with this, a newspaper can take a stance about a social actor by talking about this social actor, and by doing so in a specific way or by not talking about them at all. Inclusion and exclusion strategies can be considered as a means through which stances are legitimized or delegitimized. For example, while retrieving the articles to build our corpus, I explained earlier that it was necessary to include the term *sex change* among the search terms. Some articles, in fact, despite talking about transition and transgender people, never used the term *transgender* but only referred to it in terms of the pragmatic act of gender reassignment. As will be discussed in greater detail in Chapter 5, this choice entails a strong stance on the part of the newspapers by taking agency away from the individual and putting it onto the medical procedure.

The aim of this section is to illustrate this taxonomy. To do so I will begin by discussing practices of inclusion, which Van Leeuwen (1996) thoroughly categorizes in forty-six different categories, and then we will discuss practices of exclusion, which instead are only subdivided into two different categories.

When it comes to inclusion strategies, the first distinction concerns the way language is used to identify and define the actor or agent in the text in relation to the goal or patient. This is defined through activation or passivation. The former represents social actors as active participants or better, as the promoters of an action; in the latter case, the agent is represented as receiving or undergoing an action. Passivation is further divided into subjection and beneficialization. The subjected social actor is represented as an object. Subjection can be realized through three different practices: (1) participation, if the social actor 'is [the g]oal in a material process, [p]henomenon in a mental process, or [c]arrier in an effective attributive process' (Van Leeuwen 1996: 45); (2) circumstantialization, when the social actor is represented through a prepositional phrase; or (3) possessivation when a prepositional phrase is modifying a nominalization. The beneficialized social actor is represented as a third party which gains something from the action, whether it is in a positive or in a negative way.

So far, we have presented a first set of strategies that are in a way connected to each other in the representation of social actors from the perspective of inclusivity. Now we will discuss another group of strategies for the inclusion of social actors in a text. This set of strategies stems from the distinction between personalization and impersonalization. Personalization strategies are the most detailed ones. These are divided into two macro areas: determination and indetermination. In the first case, the identity of the social actor is in some way specified, whilst in the latter case social actors are represented as 'anonymous' individuals or groups, that is to say, in an unspecified way (Van Leeuwen 1996: 51). Determination is divided into four major groups of strategies. The first group is formed by a binary distinction between association and dissociation. Van Leeuwen identifies association as a way to refer to social actor(s) by never labelling them as one specific group but rather constructing that identity by opposing it to a specific activity that brings the various components of that group together, whereas dissociation is exactly the opposite practice. The practice of association is strongly present in the TransCor, as we will see in Chapter 5.

The second group belonging to determination practices is divided into differentiation and indifferentiation. The first one operates by specifically differentiating the social actor from the group or from similar social actors, mainly expressed through the 'us vs them' dichotomy or through practices of otherness; indifferentiation, instead, works in the opposite way.

The third group of the determination strategies is divided into categorization and nomination. This group of strategies looks at social actors considering in the first case the actor's unique identity; whilst in the second case, the representation focuses on the characteristics that each actor shares with others. Nomination can be realized typically through the use of proper names, which can be formal (surname only), in this case the strategy is known as formalization, semi-formal (name and surname), a strategy known as semi-formalization, or informal (only name), in which case it is referred to as informalization. When other titles are used rather than proper names, the strategy is identified as titulation, realized either through honorification, when honorifics are used, or through affiliation, when the social actor is represented in term of a personal or kinship relation. Nomination can also be realized through detitulation, when the title, in whatever definition we consider it, is absent. This group of strategies lies on a thin line determining the main distinction between nomination and categorization, since by mentioning the title we are also making a reference to the function that the social actor has, therefore we are categorizing them.

Categorization is further divided into: functionalization, appraisement and identification. Functionalized social actors are represented in terms of an activity or a function they have, basically in terms of what they do. Appraisement is realized when social actors are represented through a term which evaluates them. Identification, differently from functionalization, defines social actors in terms of what they are instead of what they do. Van Leeuwen proposes three types of identification: classification, relational identification and physical identification. The first category mirrors the major social classes through which society is classified, namely age, gender, race and education. Classification, in fact, is hard to define, as it is strictly related to the society one lives in when using this strategy and refers to the class the social actors belong to, whether it is related to gender, race or education. Relational identification represents the social actors in terms of the relationship they have with a specific other and is typically possessivized, which differentiates it from affiliation. Physical identification represents the social actors in terms of the physical characteristics that make them unique. We will see in the chapters that discuss the analysis of the TransCor that these strategies are among the most used in the representation of transgender people and express different functions in terms of the construction of the prosody that accompanies the discourse on transgender people in the press.

The fourth group of determination strategies is composed of single determination and overdetermination. The first strategy is opposed to the latter, which can be defined as the representation of social actors as participants in more than one social practice. This strategy can be realized through four different types of effectuations: distillation, which represents social actors through a combination of abstractions and generalizations; connotation, which happens when a nomination or physical identification is used to represent a classified or functionalized social actor; symbolization, which occurs when a fictional social actor in represented in a non-fictional context; and inversion, which represents a social actor connected to two practices of which one is the opposite of the other. This strategy is further divided into anachronism and deviation. Anachronism is used when the text needs to express something that cannot be said in a straightforward way; in this case, the social actor is represented in terms of another social actor who would normally not be involved in that activity, while deviation is realized when social actors are projected into the future. This fourth group of strategies did not occur in the TransCor.

On the other hand, impersonalization strategies are less numerous and can be realized either through abstraction or objectivation. These strategies shift from what we have seen so far, as they no longer represent social actors from a personalized but from an impersonalized perspective. Abstraction is realized when the social actors are associated with a quality which is not intrinsic to the social actors' identity but is assigned to them by the representation or the context in which they are set. Objectivation occurs when the social actor is represented by the use of references to a place or an entity associated with the person or the activity discussed in the text.

As a bridge between personalization and impersonalization we find the distinction between genericization and specification. In this case, the focus is on the 'specific vs generic' representation of social actors. Genericization can be realized through the use of plural forms or mass nouns. In a sense, in the present study, every instance of the phrase 'transgender community' can be defined as such. Specification is further divided into individualization and assimilation. In the latter case, the social actors are represented as groups. Van Leeuwen distinguishes between two different types of assimilation: aggregation and collectivization (1996: 50). In the first case, social actors are quantified and referred to in terms of statistics, whereas in the second case representation is realized mainly by the use of collective pronouns or mass nouns such as 'the community' or terms like 'experts'. When individualization is used, the social actor is referred to as a single individual. Chapter 5 will highlight the different ways in which the strategies just discussed are used in the TransCor when it comes to representing transgender individuals and groups.

So far, we have examined the various inclusion strategies identified by Van Leeuwen (1996); now we will discuss the exclusion strategies.

The practice of exclusion can be completed in two different ways: suppression and backgrounding. In the first case, the social actor is completely omitted from the text; in the latter case, the social actor is only mentioned in the text and usually not in reference to the activity they are being discussed for.

As Van Leeuwen (1996) points out, the different categories and linguistic strategies presented here should not be considered strictly and can be subject to adjustments according to the text under investigation. This framework was useful in the analysis of the TransCor to uncover patterns of representation of the main social actors represented in the dataset, namely transgender people, in the British and the Canadian press. Given the number of categories provided by this approach, some categories were more relevant than others, but the overall methodology resulted in an indispensable tool.

Similar to the analysis presented in this study, this methodology has found many different applications over the years, tackling a number of aspects relevant to the use of language.

Social actors' theory can be used in the field of language teaching, as suggested by Safoura Davari and Mohammad Raouf Moini (2016), who use this approach to analyse the representation of male and female social actors in textbooks to determine the extent to which this representation is influenced by ideology. They conclude, by looking at strategies of deletion, substitution, passivation and activation, that 'positive attitudes were reflected towards males and negative toward females' (Davari and Moini 2016: 79), hiding behind an ideology which depicts male social actors as free and independent individuals compared to female social actors.

Vanda Polese and Stefania D'Avanzo (2012) apply the framework of social actors' representation to analyse the way in which the EU promotes its educational programmes, namely the Erasmus Programme. Among other results, they conclude that nomination is used 'to delete authority, minimise social distance and represent social actors as people with whom we are familiar and with whom we feel closer because their lives appear appealing and imitable' (Polese and D'Avanzo 2012: 241). Other strategies have also been retrieved and analysed by the two authors who use this framework to investigate academic and bureaucratic discourse.

Laleh Dashti and Saeed Mehrpour (2017) use this framework to analyse two speeches by two philosophers, Jiddu Krishnamurti and Alan Watts. They note that both philosophers used backgrounding to represent their audience, whereas humanity was represented through the pronoun 'we' in a collective representation.

Veronika Koller (2009), on the contrary, similar to the study presented here, uses social actors' representation to analyse discourses about gender identity. The author looks at the way lesbian communities discursively construct themselves collectively. Among the findings, the author underlines that one of the social actors mainly involved in the text is the reader, while women and men as social groups are referred to through genericization. She concludes by saying that collective identities are not constructed in a linear way (Koller 2009).

Carmen Rosa Caldas-Coulthard and Theo Van Leeuwen (2002) also look at the representation of gendered social actors by analysing toy advertisements. They conclude that when it comes to toys, social actors representations still follows a binary heteronormative men vs women type of representation, where men are strong and brave and have superior powers, while women are represented as housewives and associated to values such as nurturing and aesthetics.

5

Differences and similarities in the representation of trans identities

In this chapter, I discuss the remaining semantic categories of representation that were identified through the collocation analysis, using the methodological and theoretical tools described in Chapters 3 and 4. The first two categories of representation were discussed in Chapter 4: *personal details* and *implying verbs*. The type of representation that is put forward through those two categories provides a representation of trans people as individuals rather than a community and often address the lives of specific people. Continuing on the semantic categories of representation based on the groups of collocates of the terms *transgender**, *transsexual** and *trans*, introduced in Chapter 4, this chapters presents three different patterns. The semantic categories highlight, first, collective forms of representation, and then crime stories and awareness and transgender rights in the British and Canadian press.

Forms of collective representation

One of the patterns emerging from the collocation analysis suggested that some of the most common collocates associated with the three most frequent search terms under investigation (*transgender**, *trans* and *transsexual**) are related to a sort of collective way of representing trans identities. In other words, I found mention of the three search terms in co-occurrence with terms representative of other social groups or more in general to the LGBTIQ+ community both in the TCUK and in TCC. Two distinct semantic categories of representation are suggested in this section, *LGBTIQ+ group and labels* and *celebrities and entertainment*. The names of these categories are self-explanatory, and they will be discussed in more detail in the following sections. Each section, following the structure of Chapter 4, is divided between the British and the Canadian press.

LGBTIQ+ group and labels

United Kingdom

Table 5.1 illustrates the collocates found for the three terms that indicate a type of collective representation. As explained in Chapter 4, when analysing the TCUK, an extra level of distinction is taken into account, and the analysis is carried out considering two additional sub-corpora division which include the quality press (QualCor) and the popular press (PopCor).

This pattern of representation emerged for both sub-corpora (QualCor and PopCor) and all three of the terms considered, pointing to the fact that it is a recurrent pattern throughout the TCUK. The terms found in this category of representation, defined as *LGBTIQ+ group and labels*, mostly include descriptors of different groups who could be collectively seen as encompassing the LGBTIQ+ community.

Table 5.1 *LGBTIQ+ group and labels* in TCUK.

	QualCor	Terms Occurring in Both Sub-corpora	PopCor
transgender*	intersex (52), persons (16), binary (11), immigrant (8), individuals (28), lesbians (20), LGBTI (14), gays (18), hijras (7)	bisexual (456/100), lesbian (499/115), bi (8/6), questioning (14/6)	community (62), LGBT (15), gay (142), groups (8), group (16), people (102), members (6), trans (6)
transsexual*	gays (10), lesbians (9), bisexual (21), lesbian (25), gender (12), and (123)	transvestite (6/8), gay (38/6), people (19/14), transgender (6/10)	transsexual (6), woman (13)
trans	cisgender (6), trans (35), lesbians (6), person (40), queer (14), feminist (5), bisexual (27), non (9), lesbian (24), men (21)	community (42), women (111), people (232), woman (59)	lobby (6), transgender (6)

The numerous occurrences of these words, both in terms of collocation and observed frequency in the texts, seem to point to a specific pattern in the context of use of the three adjectives, in some cases stronger in one sub-corpus than the other but, nonetheless, present throughout the TCUK.

As it is the most frequent term, we will first focus on *transgender**. Starting with the QualCor, this term often occurs as part of a list made up by the collocates *bisexual, intersex* and *lesbian*. These terms also happen to be its three strongest collocates and comprise some of the words that form the acronym LGBTI. *Transgender** occurs in the QualCor 2,521 times. It is in a list with *lesbian, gay, bisexual, intersex, questioning* 493 times. In 434 of these occurrences, it occupies the last position while for the remaining 59 times it is followed by *intersex* or *questioning*, and never by the other terms. The order of the words that precede *transgender* is not fixed. The term occurs in combination with only one of the words mentioned above ninety-one times (e.g. 'gay and transgender'). What emerges from this analysis is that one of the ways in which we find mention of transgender people in the QualCor is through a more collective representation, as shown in example (25):

(25) Many **gay, lesbian, bisexual** and **transgender** people are sincerely and deeply mourning Margaret Thatcher's passing. (*The Guardian*, 10 April 2013)

In a way, it is possible to relate this type of representation to what Theo Van Leeuwen (1996: 50) defines as association. In his categorization of the various ways in which social actors can be represented, he identifies association as a way to represent social actors as groups. In fact, through this strategy, social actors 'rather than being represented as stable and institutionalised, [are] represented as an alliance which exists only in relation to a specific activity or set of activities' (Van Leeuwen 1996: 50–51). This kind of representation seems to be popular. Paul Baker argues that 'the popularity of this practice of joining together a range of identity groups who are viewed as having minority or diverse sexualities and/or genders is sometimes signified by the acronym LGBT' (2014a: 221). He continues by suggesting that this can be interpreted as a way of inclusivity. However, as he notes in his research as well, the typical positioning of transgender people at the end of the list may also hint at a sort of hierarchical system within the same LGBTIQ+ group.

Widening the perspective, two further ways of representing transgender people emerge from the one just illustrated. This group representation was found in contexts that fall under two different patterns. One is in articles that deal with LGBTIQ+ issues, where it makes sense to find this acronym or the terms written out in full, as in the following example:

(26) Emmerich, who is gay, will tell the story of the 1969 riots at Stonewall Inn, in New York City's Greenwich Village, a mafia-owned bar popular with the **lesbian, gay, bisexual** and **transgender** community. (*The Guardian*, 10 April 2014)

In other cases, the term *transgender* occurs in lists in articles that are not specifically about transgender issues but refer, instead, to a wide range of minority or disempowered groups:

(27) Similarly, women, children and other traditionally marginalised groups such as people with disabilities, older people, people living in rural areas, racial, religious, ethnic, migrant and indigenous minorities, lesbian, gay, bisexual and **transgender** individuals must be enabled to overcome the additional hurdles they face. (*The Guardian*, 21 April 2015)

The repeated use of this pattern may suggest to the reader that all people in the LGBTIQ+ community have homogenous needs and concerns. While this is not the case, by mentioning the term the newspapers underline the fact that this community is considered as an underprivileged minority that is in need of compassion and help by more privileged groups in society. This can be seen as contributing toward an inclusive discourse but at the same time does not fully acknowledge transgender people and perhaps the LGBTIQ+ community as a whole by the frequent practice of associating transgender identities with other groups. Minority groups based on sexual identity (gay, lesbian, bisexual) are thus conflated and collectivized with transgender identities and other groups. In a random sample of 100 concordances, the first pattern described above occurs 69 times while the second only occurs 31 times. Thus, we might summarize by saying that pattern one occurs 70 per cent of the time while pattern two occurs 30 per cent of the time.

Pattern two, described above, is reinforced by the use of another term, which can be included in this category, not specifically for its meaning but for its use: *immigrant*. This collocate occurs in the QualCor only in the section of articles distributed in 2015. In this year, among the articles collected for the QualCor (919), thirty-three articles were about immigration. Bearing in mind that all articles chosen for inclusion in the corpus had to make reference to transgender identity, this means that thirty-three times the topics of immigration and transgender identities occurred in the same article, usually in contexts such as the one presented in the following example:

(28) The Ovarian Psycos Bicycle Brigade combines feminist ideals (it refers to womxn, not women) with advocacy for **immigrant**, indigenous, gay,

transgender, prisoner and other marginalised groups. (*The Guardian*, 5 October 2015)

The general pattern indicates that the tendency is to bring transgender people together with other social groups, who have little in common other than their marginalized status. More specifically, the collocation analysis highlights the eight cases in which the two terms, *immigrant* and *transgender*, are to be considered as collocates. In some cases (four out of eight), the two terms are used according to the second pattern described above, as in the following example:

(29) Having pledged to be the champion of everyday Americans, presidential hopeful Hillary Clinton came out swinging during a speech in New York on Thursday night in which she expanded her personal doctrine – 'women's rights are human rights' – to the plight of mothers, fast food workers, **immigrants,** retirees, students, gay and **transgender** people and victims of sexual abuse. (*The Guardian*, 25 April 2015)

In other cases (four out of eight), instead, there is an intersectional use, in the sense of people holding multiple intersecting or overlapping social identities that are considered oppressed, discriminated and dominated, as shown in example (30):

(30) After the incident Gutiérrez said: 'There is no pride in how LGBTQ and **transgender immigrants** are treated in this country. If the president wants to celebrate with us, he should release the LGBTQ immigrants locked up in detention centres immediately.' LGBTQ stands for lesbian, gay, bisexual, transgender and questioning (or queer). (*The Guardian*, 25 June 2015)

In all of the occurrences of this collocational pairing the meaning being conveyed by the sentence is that immigrants and transgender people are similar as they are both a minority, a group separated from the rest of society, an underprivileged and discriminated group. In example (49) transgender people are thrown into a mix of different groups or people for which Mrs Clinton is willing to fight for. Nonetheless, all these groups – immigrants, transgender people or victims of sexual abuse – have different requests and different needs. Referring to them together mainly helps to build a stronger argument for the presidential candidate. Example (50) highlights the discrimination LGBTIQ+ people face, more so if they are immigrants. In particular, this example puts an accent on transgender people. Despite being already included in the acronym, they are also specifically mentioned.

Again, we find two patterns, one that relates to the second one presented above and the other to a more intersectional use of the collocates. Both patterns point to a vulnerable representation of these identities. The prosody that comes with this linguistic representation seems to be positive although there is stress on three different aspects: (1) the transgender community is a social group which is at great risk; (2) some groups are more privileged than others; and (3) there is a willingness to change this situation.

Looking at the PopCor, for the collocations of *transgender**, it is possible to notice some similarities in the results between the two sub-corpora as well as some differences. Similar to the QualCor, *bisexual* is the strongest collocate also in the PopCor, followed in fourth and fifth position by *lesbian* and *questioning*. The difference is that the discourses surrounding the phrase *gay, lesbian, bisexual and transgender* in the PopCor differs in comparison to the QualCor. There is still a willingness to represent transgender people in a more collective way, but the context in which the phrase is usually found is different. The QualCor examples show that in many cases this phrase is found in articles in which the main topic is not the transgender community nor the wider LGBTIQ+ community, and transgender identities are only mentioned in passing as an example of one of many marginalized groups. In the PopCor, instead, only a few examples of this pattern were retrieved, for instance:

> (31) The night before she announced the breakdown of her marriage, the blonde actress appeared at a gala in Los Angeles titled 'An Evening With Women' a fundraiser for the **lesbian, gay, bisexual** and **transgender** community. (*Daily Mail*, 12 June 2014)

In this case, the article is about the life of Billy Elliot, and the mention of the phrase has no specific relevance to the overall article. What is notable here is that despite the collective representation, most of the articles retrieved are related to LGBTIQ+ issues, as in the following example:

> (32) THE website of former children's minister Sarah Teather boasted last week: 'Previous governments have shied away from taking action on equal marriage but the Liberal Democrats are tackling the inequalities faced by the **gay, lesbian, bisexual** and **transgender** community head on.' (*The Express*, 7 February 2013)

This pattern introduces an inclusive type of discourse, with the aim of informing the readership about rules and other decisions taken in order to fight inequalities, prejudice and homophobia and to raise awareness about LGBTIQ+ issues. The PopCor contains a total of eighty-four articles that use the phrase *lesbian, gay, bisexual and/or transgender*, or a combination of the four terms, fifty-six of which specifically refer to LGBTIQ+ issues, while twenty-eight use the phrase in articles unrelated to such issues. Similar to the second pattern described for the QualCor, the PopCor also presents a share of articles in which the term *transgender** is mostly used to sensationalize the news rather than to actually talk about a related issue.

Furthermore, another type of prosody is also retrieved; in some cases, newspapers made specific linguistic and content choices that could lead to a negative representation of transgender people and the LGBTIQ+ community more in general, as we can see in the following example:

> (33) FIRST, we had all-woman' shortlists for prospective MPs. Now Labour MP David Lammy calls for black and minority ethnic shortlists to boost their number in the Commons.
> At this rate, how long will it be, I wonder, before we have **gay, bisexual** and **transgender** shortlists, too? You read it here first. (*Daily Mail*, 2 August 2014)

It could be argued that example (33) presents a negative representation of transgender people. The opinion columnist Amanda Platell, an Australian journalist, and one of the most established voices of the *Daily Mail*, wrote the article from which this excerpt was taken. In the article, Platell is commenting on various political situations occurring in the UK, also pointing her finger at David Cameron. In the excerpt presented in example (33), she is suggesting how bad it would be to have representatives of the LGBTIQ+ community as MPs, putting them in the last position after a previous series of bad choices, first shortlisting women, then people of colour to become active politicians. Assertions such as this, made by key figures of the newspaper's staff, strongly resonate with the newspaper's point of view about specific issues. As suggested in Chapter 3, the opinion column, like the one presented here, generally expresses the stance related to the general views of the newspaper. The fact that the newspaper lets its journalists speak about transgender people in such terms does not convey solidarity toward the community but the opposite feeling. Articles such as the following support this type of discourse:

> (34) She-o was he-o in Rio
> THIS boy from Brazil is transformed into a catwalk queen at a **transgender** beauty pageant in Rio de Janeiro.
> More than 30 bikini-clad **transsexual** and **transvestite** contestants strutted their stuff before brunette Raika Ferraz, 21, was crowned Miss T Brazil 2013.
> Raika will represent Brazil at Miss International Queen in Thailand next month. (*The Sun*, 23 October 2013)

In this brief article, the term *transgender* seems to be used as a hyponym for *transsexual* and *transvestite*, as the contest is defined as a 'transgender beauty pageant', but then it specifies that it has transsexual and transvestite participants.

Similar to other findings that will be presented later in this chapter, the different terms are used indistinctively, and this behaviour, as mentioned already, can be problematic. The participants to this beauty contest held in Rio de Janeiro are first referred to as *transgender*, then as *transsexual* and finally as *transvestite*. Identity is not something that we can simply define with any word and without paying any attention to the words used, namely, using words that are not synonyms as such – especially when it comes to gender identity. Moreover, while the terms *transgender* and *transsexual* refer to gender identity, *transvestite* refers to a practice some people are keen on and does not account for all transgender people and vice versa. As if this was not enough, to mislead the reader even more, the author of this article also decides to create a pun with pronouns in the headline. Pieces such as this one, even if occurring once in a corpus of 3,000 articles, tell readers that it is right to play, to make jokes, to create puns about someone's gender identity, and reinforces the idea that, after all, if it makes you laugh it is ok to say it, that irony is always justifiable. Articles such as example (34) put newspapers like *The Sun* in that list of media outlets that still have a long way to go in terms of equality and respect for others.

Among the collocates retrieved only in the PopCor, the terms *community* and *groups* were also found to occur. As the nature of these terms suggests, they convey a plural and collective representation. Both collocates were found in most cases (*community* 47/62; *groups* 5/8) in collocation with the adjective *transgender* putting under the spotlight the concept of a 'transgender community', for instance:

(35) Watt insists it is not a gimmick but a genuine effort to help the **transgender community.** (*Daily Mail*, 8 November 2015)

This type of representation, using the term community to indicate a group of people that identify as transgender, does reify the concept of a single transgender community that, in reality, does not exist. As pointed to in the Chapters 1 and 4, transgender identity as much as the transgender community cannot be given one specific definition. The concept of community, in this case, could be read in light of Benedict Anderson's idea of 'imagined community' (1983). If we agree on the fact that transgender identities have many forms of expression and that the term transgender cannot be indicative of one specific identity, the same goes for the transgender community, which in turn can be considered a socially constructed community. Thus, it cannot be referred to as a unit, where all individuals have the same needs and represent themselves according to the same characteristics. If we go back to Van Leeuwen's (1996) taxonomy we can also link this type of representation to a form of genericization, a type of representation of social actors realized through the use of plural forms or mass nouns, specifically, community.

Different newspapers seem to foreground different aspects, but the overall prosody of the articles taken from the *Daily Mail*, the *Daily Mirror* and *The Sun* build on a positive and inclusive representation of transgender people when it comes to articles which talk about 'the community'. Phrases and terms such as *genuine effort to help*, *efforts*, *bigoted vomit* (referring to insults toward transgender people), *cater for*, *loads of support* are frequently used in these articles, which provide a welcoming and caring representation of the transgender community. A different type of representation seems to be conveyed by *The Express*, for example:

> (36) I bet you couldn't screen this in today's mustn't- give- offence world. The notoriously touchy '**transgender community**' would be in uproar. For starters, you can't talk about sex change any longer, you have to call it gender reassignment or some such. (*The Express*, 6 June 2015)

> (37) It is not the first time the Green Party-controlled Brighton council has surprised locals with their proposals. Last year councillors agreed to scrap the words 'men's' and 'ladies' on public toilets in favour of 'gender neutral' facilities so as not to 'alienate the **transgender community**'. (*The Express*, 8 March 2014)

In examples (36) and (37) the transgender community is described negatively, as *notoriously touchy* and exaggerated (*in uproar*) in its (supposed) reactions. Example (36) also complains about language regulation around transgender people and is dismissive of the supposedly correct term ('or some such'). In addition, example (37) starts by mentioning how the city council is helping ex-convicts and finishes by mentioning that the idea of gender-neutral toilets came as a surprise to locals in Brighton. *The Express* seems not to be in line with the other three newspapers included in the PopCor, using more discriminating and non-inclusive language to refer to the transgender community. Similarly, in the findings retraced by Baker, *The Express*, by using these specific wordings 'contributes towards a construction of this community in terms of its propensity for offence [...] over trivialities' (Baker 2014a: 223).

The discussion so far has focused on the collocates of the term *transgender** that belong to the *LGBTIQ+ groups and labels* category. For this category collocates were retrieved for the term *transsexual** as well. Despite the fact that some of these collocates differ from the results found for *transgender**, we can point to the words *transvestite* and *and*, affirming that the representational pattern reflects the one mentioned above. This last term is believed to be part of the collective type of representation because it was used in all the collocates in the phrase 'transsexual and x' where x is one of the other words of this category, adhering to the pattern of collective representation described for *transgender*.

As far as the term *trans* is concerned, the pattern found is comparable to those associated to *transgender** and *transsexual**. The most frequent collocates are the same or similar to the ones found previously except for one: *lobby*. This collocate was found in the phrase 'trans lobby' six times in the PopCor. *Lobby* is the strongest collocate for *trans* an example of its use is in the following excerpt:

> (38) This is where the insanity of the rights' culture leads. And there is no group more militant or vituperative than the minuscule but totalitarian **trans lobby.** (*Daily Mail*, 5 June 2015)

All occurrences are found in the *Daily Mail*, which puts forward the idea of a fundamentalist and militant transgender lobby that is trying to take over from a supposedly now in power gay lobby and instilling provocative ideas in the minds of people. This representation builds on adjectives such as *vituperative*, *totalitarian* and *vociferous* to describe this 'lobby'.

All in all, we can observe a very different pattern from what we saw in the previous chapter, going from focusing on specific individuals to representing trans identities as groups. Within this representation, it is also possible to see how both positive and negative ideas are associated with trans identities. A common pattern in the British press is of not being coherent with the different ideas put forward, this applies to both the quality and the popular press and is found in a mix of positive and negative prosodies.

This section analysed in more details the way in which transgender identities are represented in the TCUK through the use of strategies that build on a collective representation of transgender people. The following section looks at the same category of representation in the TCC.

Canada

The Canadian press also presents a high number of collocates that refer to this category of semantic representation. Table 5.2 summarizes all the collocates retrieved for this category.

The general representational pattern related to the use of labels related to other groups or to the LGBTIQ+ community at large remains a peculiarity in the TCC as well. Again, we are able to relate this type of representation to Van Leeuwen's association category, in which social actors can be represented as groups rather

Table 5.2 *LGBTIQ+ group* and *labels* in TCC.

transgender* 14	*transsexual**	*Trans 19*
queer/questioning (26), bi-sexual (6), bisexual (520), bisexuals (17), questioning (69), gender-variant (19), two-spirited (9), intersex (16), queer (92), persons (17), transsexual (33), communities (31), individuals (39), students (136)	transvestites (6), lesbians (8), bisexual (23), queer (8), transgender (32), men (8), people (9)	genderqueer (6), variant (6), gender-variant (9), intersex (10), queer (21), community (66), bisexual (17), straight (7), within (7), many (25), number (6), folks (10), persons (10), person (37), people (245), woman (49), women (44), men (20), man (14)

than individuals (1996: 50). There are a few major differences between the collocates found for this category in the two sub-corpora. The first one is the number of collocates retrieved, which in the British press was higher for the term *transgender** while here it is higher for the term *trans*. Secondly, the Canadian data presents the culturally specific term *two-spirited*, as well as a higher number of more general terms such as *queer* or *questioning* as opposed to the British press where we found more occurrences of terms that were specific to sexuality, such as *gay* or *lesbian*. Different types of collective nouns are also found in the Canadian press, which once again tend to collectivize the identity but are more targeted to specific groups of the population, such as *folks* or *students* as opposed to more neutral nouns such groups or members retrieved in the TCUK. We will now take a closer look at some of these collocates through a concordance analysis in order to establish the general prosodies that are presented in the Canadian press.

Starting with the collocates of *transgender**, the terms in this category are among the strongest collocates for the term, six out of the ten most closely associated collocates of *transgender** are terms found within this category. Some of the terms are very similar, for example, *bi-sexual* (6), *bisexual* (520) and *bisexuals* (17). The concordance analysis for these three terms reveals a very similar pattern (in the case of *bisexual* given the high number of occurrences a random sample of 100 concordances was analysed in more detail), in line with the results presented in the previous chapter with regards to the Canadian press, the prosody is mostly positive, discussing ways of making life easier, safer and more inclusive for trans people and the group they are associated with. In fact, all occurrences of the two terms are set in lists that also include the terms gay and lesbian. Examples of the main phrases found in the vicinity of these collocates are *create a safe and supportive environment for, support, promoting justice and reconciliation for*, and *prohibit workplace discrimination against*. The main difference between the three terms is in relation to the noun that follows the list of adjectives (in most cases). For *bi-sexual* we find a number of different nouns pre-modified by the collocates (i.e. community, people, athletes), in the examples that include the collocate *bisexuals* the term is always followed by people. It is interesting to point out here that the construction of the sentence in which we find transgender co-occurring with bisexuals could very easily lead to making mistakes and using the adjective as a noun, i.e. gays, lesbians, bisexuals and transgender people. In fact, it would be almost logical to use the term transgender in the plural as well, which only happens once in the seventeen concordance lines. This implies that, differently from the many examples found in the British data, the journalists are likely to be aware of the rules on the use of terms related to trans identity and more generally to terminology related to sexual and gender identity. An interesting pattern is found around the use of the collocate *bisexual*, in the random sample analysed, in 43/100 concordances, the collocates were pre-modifing terms such as *youth, students, young people* or *children*. Once again, we observe that another semantic category of representation highlights this trend in the Canadian press to focus the discussion on the well-being of young transgender individuals.

In line with this finding, one of the collocates of *transgender** is actually *students* (136). The same pattern is retrieved here, where 25 per cent of the concordances include phrases such as: *adopt policies to protect, creation of a policy for* and *to vote [...] on a proposed policy that would support*. Similarly, 35 per cent of the concordances discuss the issue of making schools a safer place by regulating the use of toilets and changing rooms and accommodating students on the use of gender-neutral pronouns or identifying pronouns.

The strongest collocate for the term *transgender** in the TCC is *queer/questioning* (26). This collocate was analysed together with two similar ones *questioning* (69) and *queer* (92). Examples (39) and (40) report the sentences in which the collocates *queer/questioning* and *questioning* were found twenty-three out of twenty-six times (example 39) and sixty out of sixty-nine times (example 40).

(39) PFLAG Montreal offers discussion and support group meetings in a non-judgmental environment for LGBTQ (Lesbian, gay, bisexual, transgender/transsexual, **queer/questioning**) individuals, their parents, family and friends. (*The Gazette*, 10 August 2015)

(40) LGBTQ Support Group for parents of a child who is lesbian, gay, bisexual or **transgender** or **questioning** their sexual identity. A discussion group meets on Thursdays from 7 to 9 p.m. at Beaconsfield United Church, 202 Woodside Rd. Share and discuss your concerns in a safe and confidential environment. (*The Gazette*, 9 January 2013)

Both sentences are retrieved in a correspondent number of articles appeared throughout 2015 in *The Gazette* (Montreal). Both examples sponsor support groups for LGBTQ people, and example (40) is especially targeted at parents of an LGBTQ child. The collocate *queer* has been used in the TCC in a similar way as the one described for the collocate *bisexual*.

A different pattern is found for the collocate *gender-variant* (19). Differently from the other collocates, here the two terms are found in a couple, namely, transgender and gender-variant, and the two adjectives pre-modify a number of different nouns from people to community, but mainly groups, never individuals. The general inclusive pattern described above for the other collocates is found here as well.

The collocate *two-spirited* (9) is a new entry for the TransCor, as this is the first time it is encountered. This term is obviously culturally related, and it makes sense to find it specifically in the Canadian data. It is an umbrella term that refers to indigenous North American people who fulfil a traditional third-gender role in their cultures or identify as gender-variant. The term is found in the TCC a total of twenty-eight times, nine of which occur as a collocate of the term *transgender**. The prosody of this term mirrors what has been said so far of the collocates in this category for the TCC. In terms of use, it is similar to other terms that refer to gender or sexual identities, generally found as part of a list. The rest of the collocates all carry a positive semantic prosody, similar to what has been already said in this section. The collective representation strategy here is useful to the extent that it is true that all these categories of people who identify differently are nonetheless in need of more inclusive policies, safe spaces to express themselves and more of a general acknowledgement of the discriminated status in which they live. An additional positive pattern I found, which reinforces the positive prosody described so far, is related to the use of the collocate *transsexual* (33). In all the occurrences of the collocate this is positioned either in a list with other terms related to gender and sexual identities, including the term transgender or in a phrase such as *transgender and/or transsexual people*. This construction is very positive and inclusive as by specifying that a person can either identify as transgender or as transsexual it acknowledges the fact that the two identities are not the same thing but very different, and that people may wish to identify as one or the other. Furthermore, different to what was observed in the TCUK, the order of the occurrence of the list – i.e. gay, lesbian, bisexual, transgender, while occurring in most cases in this way, is not as strict as was observed in the British data, and many occurrences of the adjectives in different orders are found, highlighting a sort of step forward in the cancellation of the hierarchy of gender and sexual identities that we discussed in the section about the United Kingdom.

Moving on to the collocates of the term *transsexual**, the first thing to note is the small number of these collocates, only seven opposed to twelve retrieved in the TCUK. Despite this, we must note that all collocates in this category are within the first fifteen strongest collocates of *transsexual**. The way these six collocates are used is very peculiar and diverse. When *transsexual** co-occurs with *lesbians* (8), *bisexual* (23), *queer* (8) and *transgender* (32) it is always in a list with other gender and sexual identities, following the pattern described for some of the collocates of *transgender** earlier in this section. What I praised the Canadian press for not doing when discussing the collocates *transgender* and *bisexuals*, namely, not using the plural of transgender, does not, unfortunately, happen for the articles in which we find the collocates *lesbians* and *transsexual**. Despite the general prosody being very positive and the topics discussed in the articles similar to those discussed previously, the use of language, as observed for the TCUK, in reference to *transsexual* is less attentive to being non-discriminatory. Another similarity that we can see with the TCUK is related to finding examples of *transsexual** co-occurring with the collocate *transvestite*. The two terms are found in a couple of articles, but the representation here seems to be less problematic than what was observed in the British data; three of the six concordances refer to the show *Before the Last Curtain Falls* (see Chapter 4). One concordance includes a reference to the *Rocky Horror Picture Show*, and another one is a reference to a book. The last example from this collocate relates to the issuing of a law in Russia banning transvestite and transsexual people from driving. In this article published by the *Toronto Star* on 10 January 2015 the sentence 'New Russian road safety regulations bar transsexuals, transvestites and others with sexual "disorders" from driving, ostensibly for medical reasons' is reported. The article continues by highlighting the absurdity of this law but, nonetheless, decides to quote the sentence and portray transsexual people as being affected by a disease. The article, in fact, does not explicitly contrast the way in which language is used or the fact that being transsexual is not the same as being transvestite, let alone a disease. Instances of this type of linguistic choice are very low, as we have seen so far, but still place a negative effect on the representation of trans identities.

The last group of collocates analysed here are those related to the term *trans*. This group is the most numerous in this semantic category of representation. As for the collocates of *transgender** we see some here that are very similar. Details of the concordance analysis of some of the collocates follows. The collocate *genderqueer* (6) appears five out of six times in one single article, a column in *The Times & Transcript* written by Beth Lyons on 24 April 2014, which is basically an anti-abortion piece that addresses anyone who is able to have a child, including genderqueer people. It is clear here that the author of the piece is not really interested in genderqueer people, but their aim is to reach the largest possible audience and get as much consent as possible on the topic.

We have two recurring patterns for the collocates *variant* (6) which always occurs in the sentence *trans and/or gender variant* or *gender-variant* (9). The first pattern follows the content of the articles, discussing issues related to trans people such as the use of toilets or the creation of safe spaces for trans people. The other pattern, following the collective representation trend, highlights that these collocates always pre-modify collective nouns such as *people, folks, residents* or *population*.

A similar behaviour to the one observed in this and the previous section is that of the collocates *intersex* (10), *queer* (21), *bisexual* (17). These mostly appear in lists with other terms related to sexual and gender identity and are the most explicit example of collective representation and association, using Van Leeuwen's (1996) terminology. What was observed earlier about the order of appearance of the terms is valid here as well. Different examples use different orders of the terms.

An interesting and unexpected collocate is *straight* (7), the concordance analysis reveals different patterns. In four out of seven examples of this collocate the authors refer to the difficulties of pregnancy; they argue that these go beyond the gender and sexual orientation of the pregnant person. It can be argued that these articles have a very positive impact on the representation of trans identities in the press as they include people in the LGBTIQ+ community within a discourse that has historically and socially been reserved for cisgender women only. In two of the articles which contain this collocate, the discussion is related to a bill that was being discussed in 2015 to ban conversion therapy for trans youths. Mentions of this law are discussed with reference to a different collocate but were also found in the TCUK in relation to Barack Obama and his effort to ban conversion therapy in the United States after the suicide of the teenage girl Leelah Alcorn.

Differently from the collocates related to the other two search terms, for *trans* we see a number of collocates which refer to single individuals (*person* [37], *woman* [49] and *man* [14]), while a number of collocates refer to more collective nouns (*community* [66], *folks* [10], *persons* [10], *people* [245], *women* [44], *men* [20]).

The collocates that indicate single individuals present some interesting patterns. Specifically, the use of trans woman and trans man are very similar, twenty-seven out of forty-nine times the collocate *woman* refers to a celebrity, a politician or a fictional character, these articles discuss the increasing prominence of famous trans character but also point out to the fact that this reality they depict is very different from that of non-celebrities who do not have the same financial and social support to go through their own journeys. The rest of the collocates, twenty-two out of forty-nine for *woman* and eight out of fourteen for *men* narrate stories of trans citizen, from activists to simple people who share their positive experiences. One striking element that is common for all articles is the use of pronouns and other inclusive language patterns that are always appropriate and non-discriminatory, differently from what we observed in the TCUK. The collocate *person*, not aligning with the other two, is used in reference to one specific trans person only four times out of the thirty-seven examples. The rest of the examples refer to constructions such as *it's not about one trans person* or *the average trans person*, in other words, to describe possible scenarios for trans people and discuss issues related to laws and policies or the proper behaviour around a trans person, thus, despite using a singular noun, still displaying a collectivization strategy.

The semantic category of *LGBTIQ+ group and labels* in the Canadian press presented some similarities to the British one but also many differences. First of all, the differentiation in the collocates that form the category, as we find cultural-specific terms but also more general terms that can be used with reference to gender and sexual identities rather than the more specific ones found in the TCUK. The TCC displays a more predominant discourse focused on young trans individuals and on laws and policies. The strong pattern of intersectionality recurrent in the TCUK is not present in the Canadian data. Lastly, among the labels that are included in this category, we also find a high presence of terms in the singular, this does not mean that the pattern of collectivization is not as strong in this section of the data, on the contrary, the analysis shows that apart from a small number of examples, even those terms that are in the singular are used to discuss issues related to trans identities in more general terms.

The following section discusses a different category of representation that while being considered a form of collective representation is related to a new semantic pattern, namely, *entertainment and celebrities*.

Entertainment and celebrities

This section deals with a different semantic category from the one examined above, although still defined under the more general category of collective representations. The group of terms emerging from the collocation list included in this category deals with the world of celebrities, famous transgender people or characters on television or in films – this group of collocates is defined as the *entertainment and celebrities* category. In a way, this type of representation, especially in the cases of fictional characters, more generally speaking, recalls what Van Leeuwen (1996) defines as symbolization. This strategy of inclusion in the representation of social actors 'occurs when a "fictional" social actor or group of social actors stands for actors or groups in non-fictional social practices' (Van Leeuwen 1996: 62). This strategy was found to occur when referring to fictional transgender characters, while the representation is different when we are talking about artists who play a character in a film.

United Kingdom

The collocates retrieved for this category in the British data are presented in Table 5.3. As for all sections presenting data from the TCUK, the analysis addresses the distinction between quality and popular press.

Starting from the results retrieved in the QualCor for the term *transgender**, this is the second largest group of collocates among all the categories in the QualCor, as it includes 30 per cent of the terms. Many of the collocates in this category are names of actors and actresses or show business personalities who identify as transgender or that have been involved in playing a transgender character. These include *Jeffrey Tambor* who played the character of Maura in the TV series *Transparent* (2014), or *Laverne Cox* who not only identifies as transgender but also became famous for playing the character of Sophia Burset in the TV series *Orange is the New Black* (2013). *Judy* is the main character of the British TV series *Boy meets Girl* (2015), another example of a transgender character played by a transgender actress. *Pioneer*, *Elbe* and *Lili* all refer to the

Table 5.3 *Entertainment and celebrities* in the TCUK.

	QualCor	Terms Occurring in Both Sub-corpora	PopCor
transgender*	Lees (9), Elbe (16), Rayon (6), Woodlawn (9), Tambor (10), Jeffrey (10), Lili (17), Judy (8), Holly (8), blind (9), superstar (6), Laverne (8), celebrities (8), sitcom (8)	pioneer (13/6)	Lauren (7), Caitlyn (14), artist (11), plays (9), Jenner (12), character (13), soap (7), MP (7), promoter (6), plays (11)
transsexual*	Burchill (6), Moore (6)		Harries (7), Lauren (8), Hayley (18), model (7), Julie (6), Kellie (14), London (6)
trans	Laverne (6), Root (7), Fox (6), Cox (7), actor (12)		

film *The Danish Girl* (2015), and *Rayon* is the transgender character played by Jared Leto in the film *Dallas Buyers Club* (2013). *Paris Lees* is a transgender activist who became famous for her transgender awareness campaign. *Holly Woodlawn* is a transgender actress of Porto Rican origins who worked closely with the singer Lou Reed and was mentioned in many newspapers after the death of the abovementioned artist. The *entertainment and celebrities* category does not only include personalities from the big screen but from politics as well. In fact, the collocate *blind* refers to a British, Labour party MP who is blind and identifies as transgender. The rest of the terms refer more generally to the world of celebrities.

An important point to make in relation to this category is that TV and films are one of the major platforms through which transgender identity is presented to a larger audience. This raises the question about how people perceive transgender individuals in their appearance in entertainment, and what effects this presence has on the audience. The outcome of this representation might, on the one hand, dramatize and fictionalize their identities, making them glamorous, larger than life and exciting; on the other hand, if the portrayals are sensitive, this may help in terms of raising awareness and making people sympathetic. At the same time, this representation could have a negative impact if taken to the extreme. In order to understand the way that references to the world of entertainment and celebrities are used in the British press, and to try and see to which of the hypotheses presented above this representation is closer, a small number of collocates are examined in more detail through a concordance analysis.

One of the cases that holds an important role, especially in 2015, is about Lili Elbe, one of the first people in history who underwent gender reassignment surgery in 1930. Her story was narrated in the film *The Danish Girl*, which came out at the beginning of 2015. The main roles were played by Eddie Redmayne, who interpreted Lili, and Alicia Vikander, who played Gerda Wegener, Lili's wife. From the point of view of collocations, in the QualCor, *Elbe* occurs sixteen times, *Lili* seventeen and *pioneer* eleven times (*pioneer* is a collocate of *transgender** thirteen times but occurs in contexts related to *The Danish Girl* only eleven times). These three collocates all refer to the film. If we look at concordances of the same terms, and of other terms related to this, *Elbe* occurs 56 times, *Lili* 77 times and *pioneer* 13 times, while *Wegener* occurs 48, *Einar* 56, *Eddie* 79, *Redmayne* 154, *Danish Girl* 86, to underline the high number of articles discussing this film, and its relevance in the corpus. The extracts presented below are a representative sample through which it is possible to identify the kind of discourse constructed around this topic. If we consider the three collocates, we can see that *Elbe* always occurs with *Lili*, and *pioneer* occurs with the other two collocates eight times, only once with *Lili*, three of the collocations occur in the same article, and another two are grouped in a different article. Thus, we have a total of sixteen different articles in which the collocates occur. Looking more in detail at the examples taken from the QualCor, it emerges that there are two main patterns used to discuss this topic. The first pattern can be observed in the following example:

(41) Elsewhere in the festival competition, the world premiere of Tom Hooper's *The Danish Girl* will give some indication of whether Eddie Redmayne can hope to win best actor two years in a row. The role is timely – he plays **transgender pioneer Lili Elbe**, an artist who lived in 1920s Copenhagen. (*The Times*, 29 August 2015)

In ten of the articles under investigation, we can see the emergence of this first pattern, as in example (41) above, where the main focus is on the actor and the fact that playing this role gave him a chance to win a prize as best actor twice in a row. This first pattern does not emphasize the film for its content but for the mastery of the actor. Some information about the film is given, and in many cases the information is almost contrasting, considering the different newspapers. The role is defined as *timely*, and the whole article focuses mainly on Redmayne's interpretation. The most important aspect of the film, namely, to narrate the story of one of the first transgender people in Europe, seems to be somehow left behind in these examples. The type of representation recalls what Van Leeuwen (1996: 39) defines as backgrounding, a practice of exclusion in the representation of the social actor who instead of being the primary centre of attention, or excluded *tout court* as it happens for the suppression strategy, is represented in the background, with minor references to them. This type of representation is not in line with any of the hypotheses presented at the beginning of this analysis, so far as it does not really give a strong evaluative stance on transgender identity.

The second pattern emerges in the other six articles under investigation, and the general prosody found in these examples is similar to the following example:

> (42) Having played the **transgender** artist **Lili Elbe** in his latest film project *The Danish Girl*, Eddie Redmayne has said he 'salutes' Caitlyn Jenner's bravery for publicly revealing her new female identity on the cover of *Vanity Fair* in April. [...] Redmayne added that he was so grateful to the transgender community for educating him in such an open way as he prepared for the role. (*i*, 13 August 2015)

In these articles, as in example (42), the topic of transgender identity is dealt with in a more sympathetic way. A supportive and accepting discourse emerges from this example taken from the *i*. Here Redmayne describes Jenner as brave and shows gratitude to the transgender community as he prepared for the role. The example positions Redmayne as collaborating with the transgender community to be ready to interpret the role. This shows him as supporting the community, but most importantly, it also positions the community as supporting him, helping to legitimatize his portrayal of a transgender person. The prosody presented in these articles is positive and responds to one of the hypotheses presented at the beginning of this analysis which suggested that the portrayal of transgender identity in relation to celebrities might help raise awareness and give a more realistic and positive representation of transgender people.

This representation is reinforced by another set of collocations, that is, *Jeffrey* and *Tambor*, which always occur together and refer to the actor who played Maura in the TV series *Transparent*. In the ten articles, except for one case, the focus is on transgender identity and the way this representation is helpful in terms of raising awareness about this topic, in line with the findings highlighted in the second pattern above. In these examples, great emphasis is put on the transition and the struggles Maura and her family go through as she announces her transition. This type of representation again recalls symbolization (Van Leeuwen 1996) as the story of a fictional character is useful in explaining what transgender people go through in real life. The prosody in these examples is again positive, and there are references to the need to talk about the issue and to the reciprocal acknowledgement of the actor and transgender people. The pattern of representation which reinforces the positive prosody about transgender identity described so far is retraceable for the collocate *Judy* as well. In the eight examples in which this collocate is present the main focus is on the groundbreaking BBC TV series *Boy Meets Girl*.

> (43) Boy Meets Girl was commissioned by the BBC after the script, by Elliott Kerrigan, won the Trans Comedy Award in 2013, and will be the first BBC comedy to feature transgender issues prominently, as it follows the developing relationship between 26-year-old Leo and 40-year-old **Judy**, who is a **transgender** woman.
> Judy is to be played by actor and stand-up comedian Rebecca Root, who underwent transition surgery in 2005. While it is still rare to see trans actors playing trans characters on British screens, Root follows in the footsteps of comedian Bethany Black, the first trans woman to play a recurring trans character on TV, Helen in Russell T Davies's Channel 4 comedies Banana and Cucumber. (*The Guardian*, 4 February 2015)

Example (43) explains that the main character of the series, a 40-year-old transgender woman, is played by a transgender actress. The article, which is taken as an example, stresses the importance of having shows like this one, where transgender people are represented in a way that humanizes them and is far from the medical, and at time, artificial type of representations that we could have, especially when it comes to love relationships where everybody has their worries and struggles. Narrating these stories, even in a fictional context, is a way of building up awareness about the topic of transgender identity.

So far, we have examined how the use of *transgender* in the quality press in relation to the entertainment world has a positive prosody and contributes to a discourse of inclusivity and awareness raising. Turning our sight to the popular press, we can see that the category of *entertainment and celebrities* only represents 22 per cent of the collocates in the PopCor. Some of the results are related to the same topics discussed for the QualCor. However, in this sub-corpus we found a mention to *Caitlyn Jenner*, which was not mentioned in the collocation list for the term *transgender** in the QualCor and also to boxer *promoter* Kellie Maloney who underwent gender reassignment in 2014.

Starting with the only term this category has in common with the QualCor, *pioneer*, the topic is not as popular in this sub-corpus as it is in the previous one. This term collocates with *transgender** only seven times. Extending the search to other concordances the results are not much different, *Lili Elbe* was found only eighteen times, which demonstrates that this topic was much less discussed here compared to the QualCor. In all seven occurrences of the collocate *pioneer* the pattern of representation was similar to the first pattern found in the QualCor: the articles are mainly about the actor's experience in the film rather than the topic of the film, and again the issue of transgender identity is backgrounded.

As far as differences in the two lists are concerned, the first one I noticed was that while the QualCor discusses fictional transgender characters more extensively, the PopCor keeps its focus on celebrities who have transitioned from their sex assigned at birth. We will now see what type of prosody is carried in this representation. The analysis that follows addresses two collocates related to each other – *Caitlyn* and *Jenner*, and the collocate related to *Kellie Maloney*. These two celebrities are popular in the PopCor as the two terms *Caitlyn* and *Jenner* occur forty-four times, while the two terms *Kellie* and *Maloney* occur in total ninety times.

The articles (seventeen, considering those in which the two collocates co-occur) which contain the collocates *Caitlyn* and *Jenner*, follow the pattern shown in examples (44) and (45):

> (44) Impressive, but small beer compared with **transgender** woman du jour **Caitlyn Jenner**, who this week bagged a record 1 million followers in four hours. (*Daily Mail*, 4 June 2015)

> (45) In a Q&A session in San Francisco this week, reality TV star Kim Kardashian, 34, who's expecting her second child, a boy, with rapper husband Kanye West, opened up about **transgender** stepdad **Caitlyn**. (*Daily Mirror*, 2 July 2015a[1])

In nine cases, the articles mention the collocates in the pattern shown in example (44). In these cases, the story is not about the celebrity's life, nor about her transition. It seems like the mention is a strategy of sensationalization rather than being used for reasons related to her and her identity. Representations such as this contribute to the glamorization of her identity, as we hypothesized at the beginning of this analysis. The representation builds on her popularity; example (44) emphasizes how many followers she gained in a few hours, and similar comments are made in the other articles, where her popularity is compared to other celebrities, depicting her as a heroine and an example to follow. Although the prosody carried by these articles seems to be positive, it could be argued that this type of representation is a double-sided coin and can be seen as negative for transgender people. In fact, the extreme celebration and dramatization of this identity might create a positive representation of it in the eyes of the readers but also have the opposite effect.

In reference to Caitlyn, another pattern of representation was retrieved in three articles. According to this pattern, Caitlyn is mentioned in articles about her family, the Kardashians. As we can see in example (45), in these articles, she is referred to as *stepdad* or *ex-husband*. Similar to what is found in relation to the pattern exemplified in (44), *Caitlyn Jenner* is only mentioned in these articles as a way to attract attention to the article. Furthermore, while in the first case the prosody that results is positive, these articles refer to a woman through male appellatives, which build a negative representation of her identity, and generate confusion in the reader who is presented with an incoherent representation. We discussed this type of pattern earlier in Chapter 4, these choices point to a misgendering of the person talked about in the article as they rely on the sex assigned at birth, one which Caitlyn Jenner no longer identifies with. In addition, in three of the sixteen articles, the practice of referring to the name assigned at birth was noticed, for instance:

> (46) Anna Wintour, editor-in-chief of American Vogue, was second and Hollywood star Jolie third. **Transgender Caitlyn Jenner,** formerly **Bruce**, was seventh. (*Daily Mirror*, 2 July 2015)

We discussed the practice of using deadnames in the previous chapter, in relation to Chelsea Manning; this new evidence proves that this is a common practice for newspapers.

The other celebrity that will be discussed here, as a consequence of the results of the collocational analysis is Kellie Maloney. The collocate which refers to her is *promoter*, found as a collocate six times. The main pattern used in the representation of Kellie, differently from the representation strategies used for Caitlyn, in four out of the six articles considered here, concentrates on the celebrity's life and transition. It could be argued that this pattern is due to the fact that Kellie is a local celebrity while Caitlyn is an international celebrity. Therefore,

British people might have more interest in learning about local celebrities' life. As already mentioned, the popular press, as one of the peculiarities of its genre, mainly focuses on local (UK, Ireland, Europe) news. Thus, this might influence the way the two celebrities are talked about. As the practice of deadnaming occurred for both celebrities, I believed it was worth looking deeper into the matter. A concordance analysis of the two names was carried out to determine how frequent this practice is.

The collocates *Caitlyn Jenner* occurred in thirty-five different articles (articles in which there was more than one occurrence were counted once), eleven of which contain the reference to the name assigned at birth. The collocates *Kellie Maloney* were found in sixty-seven articles (articles in which there was more than one occurrence were counted once) and in thirty-five of them the reference to the name assigned at birth is present. This brings even more evidence to the fact that this practice is common despite not being preferred by many transgender people. The negative aspect of this practice is that it makes the reader feel that it is acceptable to use the name assigned at birth or refer to the person before the transition, while this is a really subjective issue and each transgender person has different feelings about it. During the analysis, articles in which Caitlyn Jenner was referred to only as Bruce (her name before the transition) were found. This is evidence that the press does not follow clear guidelines when it comes to transgender identity, and it is mostly up to the good sense of the journalist.

So far, this analysis has concentrated on the collocates this category shows for the term *transgender**. We will now move on to the analysis of *trans* and *transsexual**. The collocates retrieved for *trans* that fall under this category are all from the QualCor. A more in-depth analysis reveals that no interesting results emerge from their linguistic environment. *Transsexual** also presents some collocates that fit this category. In the QualCor, this category, in reference to *transsexual**, has only two words (4 per cent of the collocates). These two collocates, *Burchill* and *Moore*, are among the strongest collocates as the former is in second place while the latter is in fifth place in the collocation list. The collocates refer to two journalists, Julie Burchill and Suzanne Moore, who are popular among the LGBTIQ+ community for two articles that they wrote where they used arguable adjectives to define transsexual women. This issue is discussed in Chapter 4, in reference to another category that emerged from the collocational analysis, *personal details*. The article written by Burchill was also discussed by Baker who argues that this case opened up the debate on the representation of transgender people in the press and on what should be considered as freedom of speech and what should be condemned and forbidden in the press (Baker 2014a: 212). The articles which contain the collocates here are not the ones which raised the discussion. These are articles by other journalists and newspapers discussing the issue and are of the utmost importance, in this case, to determine what kind of stance the press is taking following the critiques from the readers of these two journalists.

Most of the collocates co-occur in the articles. However, while Moore's article, as Allison Pearson suggests in her piece published in *The Daily Telegraph* on 17 January 2013 (this article was also discussed in Chapter 4 and is part of the TransCor), meant no harm, Julie Burchill did not even attempt to control her pen, and insulted transsexual people not only through the words she used to describe them (see Baker 2014 and Chapter 4) but also by a generalization on behaviours of transsexual people, generally defined as *transsexuals*. The twelve collocates (six for *Burchill* and six for *Moore*) occur in eight different articles. Different newspapers had different behaviours regarding this issue, and while *The Times* (two articles) and *The Guardian* (one article) maintained a descriptive attitude and limited articles to narrating the events from both points of view without giving any judgement toward the facts themselves, the *i* (two articles) and *The Daily Telegraph* (three articles) had more evaluative opinions on the matter. More evidence to support this statement can be found in example (47) below. The article from the *i* appears in 2013, right after the facts happened. In 2013 (see also example 16, in Chapter 4) the article is an ode to Julie Burchill and her innovative and transgressive style of writing. The article was written by Simon Kelner, a British journalist and newspaper editor. He defines Burchill's work as 'a soundtrack to [his] journalistic life' and goes on by saying that although not always in line with her point of view he 'venerated her as a true original who, through the power of her prose, regularly made you ashamed for following conventional wisdom' and ends the article by implying that freedom of speech also 'includes the freedom to offend' (*i*, 16 January 2013). While Kelner never explicitly states that it was wrong to condemn Burchill for publicly insulting people, he never defines these events as a dark page of the British press.

Freedom of speech and the use of social media is the main focus of the second article that appeared on the *i* and containing these two collocates. In this case, the events are used as an example in which social media platforms can function as a real crucifix, where information spreads quickly and where people are keener to express themselves freely regardless of correctness. The events were not evaluated as negative, rather the newspaper took Burchill's side disagreeing with the violent dislike she received following her article. We have described the *i* as an inclusive and considerate newspaper in other parts of the analysis presented in this study, but this case is a clear exception and proof of the consequences of not having clear guidelines to follow and an informed knowledge of the issues discussed.

Similarly, *The Daily Telegraph* had controversial thoughts about the events:

(47) Given the outrage this month when the columnist Suzanne **Moore** joked about **transsexuals** – and the even noisier outrage when another columnist, Julie Burchill, used the phrase 'chicks with d—' – I doubt such a scene could be written today. (*Daily Telegraph*, 26 January 2013)

While the *i*, despite its beliefs tried in a way to keep the tone down, the story is different for this newspaper, where supposedly 'offended transsexuals' are advised to 'man up!', and the readers' expressions of dislike for these comments are defined as 'even noisier outrage'. The lexical choices in these articles carry a specific prosody, when the journalists choose to use the verb 'to joke' and the adjective 'noisy', or when the term 'offended' is put in inverted commas or finally when a highly gendered comment is referred to people for which gender identity recognition is one of the most important aspects of their lives. These articles put transsexual people in a negative light by depicting them as oversensitive and overreacting to something that, after all, was only done to have fun, diminishing the real impact these comments could have on transgender people. The newspaper explicitly takes the side of the two journalists by suggesting that they were attacked with no right cause, and that their freedom of speech was undermined.

If we turn to the popular press, the collocates retrieved for the PopCor are completely different. Firstly, they are more numerous at 14 per cent of the collocates under investigation. As we found for the analysis of the collocations of *transgender**, we have names of both fictional and non-fictional characters among the results. I will consider in more depth some of the collocates in order to identify linguistic patterns of representation in the use of *transsexual** in the PopCor in relation to the semantic category of *entertainment and celebrities*. We will first analyse the linguistic patterns that surround the collocate *Hayley*, a fictional character in the famous British soap opera *Coronation Street*, and then we will look at the linguistic patterns that accompany the collocate *Kellie*, referring to Kellie Maloney, found for the term *transgender** as well.

Hayley was found to occur eighteen times as a collocate of *transsexual**. Hayley Cropper is one of the characters of the traditional British soap opera *Coronation Street* and one of the first fictional characters to identify as a transsexual person in a British show, played by the cisgender actress Julie Hesmondhalgh. Newspapers talked about this character as the actress decided after fifteen years to leave the show. In order for this to happen, the directors of the show had to change the plot. Thus, Hayley was diagnosed with cancer and decided to take her own life before the cancer would take it. The media used this event to discuss the issue of euthanasia. All the articles reported positively on this character, using inclusive, non-discriminating language and coherent pronouns throughout the articles. The only instance of deadnaming is reported in the following example:

> (48) For 16 years ago, who would have expected **transsexual Hayley** – a woman formerly a man called Harold Patterson – to sustain a relationship with social misfit Roy Cropper for such a long time? (*The Daily Mirror*, 18 January 2014)

Perhaps it could be suggested that the gender identity of the actress playing Hayley could have influenced the discussion about her and therefore have facilitated the use of feminine pronouns on the part of the journalists, but there is no specific linguistic evidence to support this hypothesis.

The other collocate considered here is *Kellie*, occurring in a collocational pair with the term *transsexual** fourteen times, for a total of thirteen articles (two occurrences are in the same article). In this case, two different patterns were found. The first one, occurring in six articles, is shown in the following:

> (49) Tracey Maloney, 47, spoke of the traumatic' effect on the family after Frank – who now calls himself **Kellie** – revealed he was **transsexual**. The air stewardess admitted she would even have kept it a secret for the sake of their two daughters. (*Daily Mail*, 18 August 2014)

These articles use a mix of feminine and masculine pronouns and refer to Kellie both with her name assigned at birth and her chosen name. The other pattern, occurs in six articles, is shown in the following:

> (50) **Kellie** has lived as a **transsexual** for longer than the year transition period recommended by private clinics to ensure patients can cope with change […] As Frank, she managed world champ Lennox Lewis from 1989 until 2001. (*Daily Mirror*, 17 October 2014)

Here the article uses feminine pronouns and refers to Kellie as a woman throughout, but always uses the name assigned to her at birth. Example (50) shows how the deadname Frank is followed by female pronouns. Only one article shows no gender references. Both these patterns can be said to contribute to a negative discourse around transsexual people. The incoherent use of pronouns, titles and modifiers might generate misunderstanding in the reader. The use of pronouns that do not adhere to the identifying gender is strongly criticized by some transgender people and most guidelines for the use of non-discriminatory language advice to always use the pronouns that mirror the identifying gender of the person.

It is necessary to mention the fact that *Kellie* was retrieved both as a collocate of *transgender** and as a collocate of *transsexual**, meaning that both adjectives were used to refer to the same person in the PopCor. As mentioned in Chapter 4, this practice is not welcomed by many transgender people as it makes it a common practice to use the two terms interchangeably. In order to see to what extent this practice is used when it comes to celebrities, I went back to the corpus and turned to concordances to check the linguistic choices made for other names of celebrities that appeared in the collocation analysis in both sub-corpora. The mention of these characters is displayed in many different ways, by referring to the full fictional name, or the full name of the artist, to the first name, last name or nickname. Therefore, it would be impossible to give an exact number of the articles in which journalists chose to identify a person as *transgender* and the ones where they chose to identify them as *transsexual*. As a sample to identify this pattern, we will only consider those articles in which the full name is used. As far as *Kellie Maloney* we have ninety occurrences of the name in the PopCor, for a total of sixty-six different articles. Kellie Maloney is defined as a transgender person in fifteen articles, a transsexual person in eight articles, in one article she is referred to as both, and in two articles she is not defined in terms of her gender. The rest of the articles, forty-one in total, refer to her with phrases such as *gender-swap, gender reassignment, formerly known as* + deadname, *wants to be/lives like a woman* or *who was born male*. This pattern, which proved to be the most frequently used, seems to be an attempt to describe Kellie through the old binary vocabulary and categories which clearly do not apply in this case. Nonetheless, it reinforces the vision of transgender people as non-humans by simplifying gender identity to physical appearance. This type of representation recalls what Van Leeuwen (1996) defines as physical identification, a type of social actor representation strategy that categorizes social actors through physical details and characteristics. Although it is an inclusive strategy of representation, as we have argued previously in this study, transgender identity cannot and must not be reduced to what kind of genitals one person has.

A similar pattern was found to occur in the QualCor with the name *Kellie Maloney* occurring thirty-five times for a total of twenty-four articles. Here the most frequent pattern is again the one through which Kellie is defined by phrases such as the ones listed above. She is addressed as a transgender person in seven articles and as a transsexual in one article. Two articles chose to refer to her with the less compromising term *trans*. Among the findings, one particularly peculiar article was retrieved, here Kellie is addressed only as a woman; actually, the article insists on how wrong it is to even refer to her sex assigned at birth, as shown in the following example:

> (51) **Kellie Maloney** has always been a woman. She isn't becoming a woman. She isn't pretending to be a woman. She doesn't 'think' she is a woman. Nor is she magically transforming into a woman via some exotic and mysterious alchemical trickery. She says she's always felt different inside, but just couldn't explain it to anyone. Including herself. (*i*, 12 August 2014)

This article goes on to explain that transgender identity is not something that happens in one moment and that it is wrong to keep using undesired pronouns or references to the name assigned at birth, since the person does not recognize themselves in that description any longer. This article appeared on the *i* on 12 August 2014, and it would be beneficial to find an increasing number of articles like this one, except they should not be followed two days later by articles, in the same newspaper, which use phrases such as *formerly known as* + deadname.

When it comes to fictional transgender character Lili Elbe, discussed previously as well, we found the following pattern. *Lili Elbe* occurs eighteen times in the PopCor in eighteen different articles. She is never referred to as a transsexual person in the PopCor but as a transgender person in seven articles and through phrases such as *gender/sexual reassignment* and *first man to become a woman* in eleven articles. Once again, we can see the presence of a binary discourse, which tends to insinuate itself within the discourse about trans identity. In the QualCor the results are somehow different. *Lili Elbe* occurs thirty-eight times, for a total of thirty-four different articles. The QualCor presents only seven articles in which Lili is referred to with other phrases. She is mostly defined as a transgender person in twenty-five articles and as a transsexual person twice. Two examples of these patterns are as follows:

> (52) You can't picture either Toronto or Cannes according competition slots to both Tom Hooper's The Danish Girl, a biopic of the **transsexual** artist **Lili Elbe** with Eddie Redmayne in the title role, and Laurie Anderson's Heart of a Dog, the experimental musician and performance artist's first feature in almost 30 years, since her 1986 concert film Home of the Brave. (*Daily Telegraph*, 2 September 2015)

> (53) The Danish Girl, the biopic of **transgender pioneer Lili Elbe**, is to be screened at the White House as part of an event honouring 'champions of change' in the LGBT community, it has been announced. (*The Guardian*, 23 November 2015)

Example (52) is taken from *The Daily Telegraph* while example (53) is from *The Guardian*. They both contain a similar structure beginning with 'a biopic of …', although in *The Guardian* Lili Elbe is a transgender pioneer, and in *The Daily Telegraph* she is a transsexual artist. It is notable that some of the examples in which Lili is referred to as a transgender person are taken also from *The Daily Telegraph*, according to which the two terms can definitely and wrongly be used as synonyms, there are many examples in which they are used in this way in this newspaper.

Two more celebrities are worth mentioning here for the choices made by the newspapers: Rayon, the fictional transgender character who appears in the film *Dallas Buyers Club*, played by cisgender actor Jared Leto; and Labour candidate Emily Brothers, one of the first Labour party politician to identify as a transgender person.

In the PopCor, *Rayon* appears seven times in six different articles; she is defined as a transgender person in four articles and referred to as a woman in only two articles. In the QualCor *Rayon* occurs twenty-three times, in a total of ten articles. Rayon is described in *The Guardian* first as a *transgender Aids activist*, as shown in example (54) below, then as *transgender patient* (29 August 2013) and a few days later as a *transsexual drug addict*, as can be seen in the following:

> (54) Jared Leto, this year's odds-on favourite for the best supporting actor Oscar for his role as the drastically emaciated **transgender Aids activist Rayon** in Dallas Buyers Club is recalling the first time he 'road-tested' Rayon in public. (*The Guardian*, 1 February 2014)

> (55) He's matched by Jared Leto as **Rayon**, a **transsexual drug addict** who goes into business with Woodroof and carries the responsibility of broadening the shit-kicking cowboy's world view. (*The Guardian*, 9 September 2013)

Another aspect worth pointing out is the choices made by the journalists when deciding the nouns that would follow the adjective *transgender* and *transsexual* in these articles. In fact, while the transgender character is represented as a *patient* and an *activist*, the transsexual character is a *drug addict*, attributing to the two adjectives a different and opposing evaluation. The first being compassionate and positive and the second negative and unsympathetic. Here not only the newspaper builds on the idea that the two terms can be used interchangeably but also depicts a positive prosody around transgender people opposed to a negative one for transsexual individuals.

This pattern was found not only when speaking about characters in films but also when addressing actual human beings. As anticipated, the last celebrity considered here is the Labour party MP Emily Brothers, references to whom were retrieved among the collocates as well. *Emily Brothers* appears in the PopCor three times in two different articles; she is referred to as a transgender person in one, and as transgendered in the other one. As already mentioned, this last term is not welcomed by all transgender people as it is seen as a way to dehumanize the person using this nominalized version of the adjective. In the QualCor the name occurs fifteen times in a total of eleven different articles. Here, eight articles define her as a transgender person, one article as a transsexual person, and two articles do not specify her gender. Despite the fact that the two terms were used as synonyms only once, it is notable that it is the same newspaper doing it. In fact, the candidate, who became famous for being blind and identifying as transgender, is depicted in *The Guardian* first as the *first transgender candidate* and later as the *first transsexual candidate*.

Once again, this proves that newspapers are still using terminology inappropriately and are in need of more specific guidelines. Baker has examined the use of transsexual and transgender as well, concluding that while *transsexual** is used in his data mostly to address 'fictional characters and/or appear in contexts that are designed to entertain members of the public', *transgender** is more commonly 'used on "real" or non-entertaining people' (2014a: 255). This pattern does not apply to the TCUK as we have shown that there are no defined and repeated patterns when it comes to using the two terms.

To summarize, we could say that the representation of transgender people in the entertainment and celebrity world should not be underestimated because people from this world are frequently at the centre of attention, setting the standards for others and becoming role models in many cases. The way public figures are reported on is essential and, most of all, influential. Unfortunately, the TCUK shows that the discourse is still confused and in some cases counterproductive as it does not set a good example for people to follow, neither in the use of terminology nor in the way transgender identity is represented.

The following section discusses the representational patters related to *celebrities and entertainment* in the Canadian press.

Canada

The Canadian press presents a reduced number of collocates related to this category, and most importantly these are only available for the terms *transgender**

Table 5.4 *Entertainment and celebrities* in the TCC.

transgender*	transsexual*	trans
Rayon (15), Laverne (8), Rae (12), pioneer (10), singer-songwriter (10), dysphoria (12), Redmayne (10), Cox (12), Spoon (17), performer (9), clone (6), prostitute (16)	doomed (8), Buyers (8), Dallas (8), AIDS (6)	

and *transsexual**. Table 5.4 summarizes the collocates found in the TCC for this category.

Starting with the largest group of collocates in this category, those related to *transgender**, the first step is to group together those that discuss the same topic. *Pioneer* (10) and *Redmayne* (10) are two collocates, discussed for the TCUK as well, that refer to the film *The Danish Girl* (2015). All occurrences of the two collocates are included in articles which mainly praise the actor for his interpretation of the character. The use of pronouns is very limited and always coherent with the gender identity of the character discussed. There are no occurrences of Lili Elbe modified by the term transsexual, differently from what was highlighted in the TCUK. This was also confirmed through a concordance search of other articles which were not analysed in detail as they did not include the collocates but were searched to corroborate this finding via a direct concordance analysis of the terms Lili Elbe. When describing Lili, in these articles, we found phrases such as was *the first person to undergo sex reassignment surgery* or *trans pioneer* avoiding altogether the type of mixed representation that was found in the British data. The launch of this film was a very prominent event in the British press, which led to the publication of many articles and boosted discussion around the topic. The same does not seem to apply to the Canadian press, which does discuss it but does not give it the same level of prominence.

Three other collocates can be grouped together here as relating to the same person, *Rae* (12), *singer-songwriter* (10), *Spoon* (17). Rae Spoon is a Canadian musician and songwriter, as the collocates suggest, and identifies with the pronoun 'they'. In 2013 the Canadian filmmaker Chelsea McMullan produced the documentary *My Prairie Home* that narrates Rae's life history. All articles which contain the three collocates, except for one, are discussing the documentary which was presented at the Canadian Documentary Festival. In four examples, the articles actually specify the fact that the singer uses gender-neutral pronouns. The other articles either do not use pronouns at all or are respectful of the singer's choice. Similar to collocates analysed in the TCUK which are culturally specific (i.e. Kellie Malone, Julie Burchill), this one is peculiar of the Canadian scene and was found only here.

The collocates *Laverne* (8) and *Cox* (12) can also be analysed together as they refer to the same person. The articles in which the collocates are included speak about the roles played by the actress, mainly in *Orange is the New Black* (2015). The use of pronouns is consistent with the gender identity of the actress, and again we find a positive pattern which highlights the fact that finally a trans role is being played by a trans actress and how Laverne Cox is a model for many trans people.

The rest of the collocates cannot be grouped and refer to different topics. The collocate *performer* (9) refers to some of the celebrities that have been discussed in this section, namely Laverne Cox and Rae Spoon, in line with the same representational pattern.

The collocate *clone* (6) refers to a character in one episode of the Canadian TV series *Orphan Black* (2013), the articles in which the collocate appears are almost all the same published in different newspapers and discuss the innovation of having a trans character and the feelings the actor had in playing the role.

The collocate *dysphoria* (12) in ten out of the twelve occurrences refers to the sixth studio album by the American punk rock artist Laura Jane Grace and her band, Against Me!, released in 2014 with the title *Transgender Dysphoria Blues*. In the articles associated with this collocate, we find for the first time in the TCC an occurrence of the practice described many times for the TCUK of deadnaming. The article, appearing oi the *Calgary Herald* on 14 July 2015, talks about Laura Jane Grace and her past, and it is in this context that her name assigned at birth is mentioned. Apart from this mention, pronoun use always reflects the singer's gender identity. The collocate appears in eight different articles, in five of which we observe this pattern of referring to the name assigned at birth.

The collocate *prostitute* (16) refers in thirteen of the sixteen times to Kitana Kiki Rodriguez, an American transgender actress, famous for playing the role of Sin-Dee Rella, a transgender sex worker who discovers her boyfriend and pimp has been cheating on her, in the film *Tangerine* (2015). The articles mainly discuss the film and, in this case, given the character, it is a necessity to specify that the person is transgender and a sex worker to describe the plot of the film.

At first glance, the collocate could be seen as providing a negative representation of the character, but the concordance analysis reveals the content of the articles.

The last collocate in this group is *Rayon* (15), it relates to the character played by Jared Leto in the film *Dallas Buyers Club* (2013), similar collocates were analysed in the TCUK as well. This is the only collocate that relates to a topic which is also discussed in relation to the term *transsexual**, which will be analysed next. All the occurrences of this collocate are found within articles which mainly praise the actor who was nominated for a number of awards following the interpretation. In line with the representational patterns highlighted in the TCUK, the representation of Rayon was also considered. Differently from the British data, only one article defines Rayon as a drug addict, depicting the character negatively, while six articles use the phrase *patient with AIDS*, the rest of the articles do not define Rayon in terms of her illness.

The collocates of *transsexual** retrieved in this category of representation all relate to the film we discussed for the last collocate of *transgender**: *doomed* (8), *Buyers* (8), *Dallas* (8), *AIDS* (6). Before even looking at the concordances of these collocates, it is necessary to point out the fact that we find here the same character being defined both as transgender and transsexual. While earlier most of the articles had, nonetheless, a more positive representation which either depicted the character as a patient or simply as a person, here the first collocate which is also the strongest collocate of the *transsexual**, is *doomed*, an adjective which carries a negative connotation per se, meaning hopeless or ill-fated. In addition to the negative prosody which the term already carries, all the articles in which the collocate is found, the role of the character is briefly mentioned and the main discussion is again taken over by the praising of the actor, no explanation to why this character is 'doomed' is given. The collocates *Buyers* and *Dallas* are all contained in the same examples as doomed. The last collocate of this category is *AIDS*, this always refers to the same film (except in one concordance line in which the term is actually used as a verb), and it is used to describe Rayon's character as 'a transsexual with AIDS'. Again, here we see a problematic representation which puts together a transsexual person and this illness which still is a stigma for many people within the LGBTIQ+ community.

It is possible to argue within this category that the same type of representation, that of backgrounding (Van Leeuwen 1996: 39), associated to this category in the TCUK, applies for the TCC. Trans identities are mentioned in the background, with minor references to them. It is still noticeable that there is a difference between the two data sets, as in the Canadian press the articles tend to discuss the importance that trans identities representation in audiovisual production has, as it works toward the acknowledgement and normalization of trans people and helps taking it away from stigmatization. This is the same reason why I believe this category is extremely important in this discussion because film and in general fictional representations are one of the ways in which many people come across the discussion related to transgender identities. This category is much less prominent in the Canadian press in comparison to the British press, but all in all, it follows the same type of positive prosody we have highlighted so far in the TCC.

This first part of Chapter 5 addressed two of the categories that emerged from the collocation analysis, both these categories related to the collective representations of transgender identities. The next part described those linguistic patterns related to the category defined as *LGBTIQ+ group and labels*, here we saw that the main pattern used to represent trans identity is that of association, grouping together people from different backgrounds or from different groups which society sees as minorities and supposes to have the same necessities. Then we dealt with the representation of trans identities through their association with celebrities and fictional characters. Individuals who do not fall into the celebrity category, those that anybody could relate to in terms of experience and lifestyle, were never found to be dealt with in this group of collocates. One of the problems with these types of representation, which also emerges in the discussion of some articles in the TCC, is that there is rarely a mention of individuals to whom actual trans people can relate.

Representation of individuals will be at the centre of attention in the next section, which is completely dedicated to the British press as none of the collocates found in the TCC could be grouped in this category.

Crime stories: Victims vs perpetrators in the TCUK

Talking about crime in newspapers has been a priority since the beginning of the nineteenth century when the first dissemination of court reporting can be traced back to. Consistently, the use of crime stories to increase the circulation of newspapers for their sensationalizing effect is no hidden practice (Chermak 1994). Transgender people have not been exempted from this practice, as the collocation analysis demonstrates. What is most interesting to point out from the start is that this category of representation was only retrieved in the British section of the data. The collocation analysis carried out for the three search terms investigated did not produce any results in TCC that could be included within this semantic category of representation. In light of this, the results presented in this section only relate to the TCUK. As for the other sections, the British data was investigated here taking into account the two sub-corpora: QualCor and PopCor. Table 5.5 shows the collocates which were grouped together in the category *crime stories*.

As a first analytic description, it is notable how this category only interests the terms *transgender** and *trans*, showing no collocates for the term *transsexual**. Moreover, from the number of collocates, we can also conclude that crime stories in relation to transgender people are mostly discussed by the quality press, as the PopCor contains few results that fitted this category. Another aspect which differs from previous categories, and will become even more evident in the following sections, is the fact that the popular and the quality press use different language to talk about the issues discussed here, in fact, as shown in Table 5.5, there are no collocates in common between the two sub-corpora (QualCor and PopCor).

The category discussed in this subsection, *crime stories*, includes stories involving crime, injustice and death. Starting our analysis from the QualCor, and those collocates emerging from the analysis of the term *transgender**, we can see that one of the main stories narrated relates to the suicide of transgender teen girl from Ohio Leelah Alcorn. Among the collocates considered for this analysis, there are four terms relating to her story: *Ohio* (9), *teen* (5/16^2), *Leelah* (11) and *Alcorn* (11). These collocates refer to twelve different articles in the QualCor, mostly (8/12) released by *The Guardian*. Through a concordance search, it was

Table 5.5 *Crime stories* in the TCUK.

	QualCor	Terms Occurring in Both Sub-corpora	PopCor
transgender*	intimidate (6), homicide (6), Ohio (9), teen (16), dies (7), Leelah (11), Alcorn (11), limit (6), murders (6), Theroux (6)		academic (7), killer (6)
transsexual*			
trans	suicide (13), kids (8)		

possible to see that this event was discussed in a higher number of articles; however, since we are interested in the collocational patterns, we will refer here only to the articles that contain the collocates. The story is presented in different contexts, one of these is shown in the following example:

> (56) The White House's action came in response to a petition inspired by the death of a **transgender** teenager from **Ohio, Leelah Alcorn**, who stepped in front of a tractor-trailer one night last December. Her suicide note referred to visits to Christian therapists who told her she was 'selfish and wrong'. (*The Guardian*, 11 April 2015)

Leelah's last wish,[3] expressed in the note she left before committing suicide – to fix society and for her choice to be a wake-up call for everyone – seemed to have been taken into account in part. Example (56) shows one of the patterns related to Leelah in one of the ways she is mentioned. Following her suicide, Obama decided to take action toward the banning of the so-called conversion therapy, which is common in many states in the United States. Conversion therapy is a practice, adopted mainly in religious contexts, which tries to 'change' people from the LGBTIQ+ community and convert them back to heteronormativity, treating sexual and gender preference as a disease to cure. Another topic that was discussed, as a consequence of Leelah's suicide, is the question of parenting genderqueer children. We find mentions of the collocate in relation to the creator of TV series *Transparent*, Jill Soloway, who dedicates her award win for the show to her transgender parent and to the memory of Leelah.

As mentioned earlier, *The Guardian* is the newspaper in the QualCor mainly covering this news, and it does it in a strongly sympathetic way. Most of the articles in which the facts about Leelah's death were narrated were not primarily about telling her story. These articles, contrarily, discussed the fact that her death expedited talking about issues related to transgender identity and to the struggle that transgender people must face in order to have their identity recognized. The prosody retrieved in these articles shows an inclusive and compassionate discourse on the part of the newspapers. This prosody is supported by the context in which the collocates were retrieved, where phrases such as the following were found: *sparks outcry, they struggle to find a place, calling for legal changes, nationwide soul-searching, we need more tools [...] to survive and thrive, magnificence Leelah, never needed to be 'fixed', massive shame*. The newspapers chose to show their support to transgender people, in light of Leelah's death, highlighting a supportive and compassionate discourse and at the same time a willingness to fight and end inequality for the transgender community. *The*

Guardian reveals a supportive pattern in language choices also by pointing out issues such as the use of pronouns and misgendering. Some articles point to the fact that Leelah's mother perpetuates one of the behaviours that contributed to the girl's decision to take her own life, by misgendering her and using the pronouns which refer to her sex assigned at birth. As we underlined and discussed in much detail in Chapter 4, this practice is strongly disapproved of by many transgender people, including Leelah.

Since the patterns that have been described so far only pertained to those articles published by *The Guardian*, I decided to look more in detail at the other newspapers and at the linguistic choices adopted by these in relation to the event. The collocation analysis suggested that *The Times* and the *i* also covered this story. However, neither the *i* nor *The Times* did it when it happened in January 2015, but only in April of the same year in relation to the news about Obama, discussed for the previous examples. Both newspapers were limited to describing the event, choosing not to cover it at the time of its occurrence. It could be argued that the choice to discuss the event later was made for political reasons as it was mentioned in relation to the former President of the United States. Moreover, the choice of not giving an opinion or not discussing the event when it happened, and thus not showing support for this girl and her death, says a lot about the newspapers. This story not only responds to some of the most relevant news values, such as negativity (Bell 1991), where a story with an adverse ending is narrated as it attracts the interest of the readers, but also, as we pointed out at the beginning of this section, a crime story is always a good story.

The fact that none of the collocates retrieved were found in *The Daily Telegraph* becomes a reason to turn to concordances and look into this newspaper. The term *Leelah* occurs in the QualCor thirty-five times, of which three appeared in one article from *The Daily Telegraph*. The newspaper covered the news in January, differently from the *i* and *The Times*, but example (57) shows the type of linguistic choices adopted by this newspaper:

(57) A TEENAGER left an impassioned suicide note after his devoutly Christian parents rejected his request to become a woman.
  Josh Alcorn – who used the name **Leelah** – threw himself under a lorry near his home outside Cincinnati, Ohio, at 2am last Sunday, leaving behind a bitter 1,000-word note about his life […] When 14, he recalled, he 'cried with happiness' after discovering the existence of other transgender people, but his mother, Carla, said the desire to become a girl was 'a phase' and that 'God doesn't make mistakes'. After the suicide, Mrs Alcorn still appeared unable to accept that her child wanted to become female. (*The Daily Telegraph*, 2 January 2015)

The journalist refers to the teenager as 'Josh Alcorn – who used the name Leelah', ostensibly delegitimizing Leelah's choice of gender representation, and then goes on to refer to her with masculine pronouns, a sensitive topic when it comes to transgender identity, as pointed out in Chapter 4. In this example, and throughout the article, the journalist refers to Leelah as wanting to 'become a woman', which is essentially the main reason why the teenager killed herself, as she was not trying to become a woman, she was a woman in the wrong body, reiterating what is possibly the most recurrent narrative in transgender identity representation. The choices made around reporting Leelah's parents' words are also notable. In fact, whilst according to *The Daily Telegraph*, Mrs Alcorn 'appeared unable to accept that her child' was transgender, according to the *i*, 'her strict Christian parents had refused to accept her', and *The Guardian* limited its coverage of this aspect of the story to reported speech and to highlighting that the mother 'repeatedly referred to Leelah with male pronouns'. The three newspapers, through these different linguistic choices, depict the parents in different ways. In *The Daily Telegraph* they are represented as not having the ability to accept Leelah's gender identity, in the *i* the words *strict* and *refused* reinforce the description of the parents more negatively by stressing the way they treated their daughter, while *The Guardian* more explicitly criticizes their behaviour and judges the way they parented Leelah.

The rest of the collocates that are part of this category bring up another pattern related to crime. The collocates *intimidate* (6), *homicide* (6), *dies* (7), *murders* (6), all refer to death as a crime committed by someone. It is interesting to see how transgender people are represented as agents or patients (Van Leeuwen 1996) in the articles in which these collocates were found. In these examples, the way in which a role is allocated to a social actor can 'rearrange the social relations between participants' (Van Leeuwen 1996: 43). Representing transgender people as the victims, thus the patients of so much violence, builds around this identity a positive prosody and a supportive narrative, while representing transgender people as the actors of violence sorts the opposite effect.

The only collocate which is not part of this pattern is *limit* (6), which refers to an article published by *The Guardian* (4 February 2015) that strongly criticizes the choice of a Philippine eSports league to limit the number of gay and transgender competitors in all-female tournaments.

Furthermore, two collocates which reinforce this representation of transgender people as patients of violence are *homicide* and *murders*. Most of the articles in which these collocates appear are again from *The Guardian*, evidence which backs up the hypothesis of this newspaper using a more supportive discourse.

The terms *homicide* and *murders*, both refer to articles in which the newspaper discusses the homicide rate of transgender people in the United States denouncing the ever-growing percentage of transgender people murdered and the fact that nothing is being done to fix it. The context in which the collocate *intimidate* is found is a direct quote from Obama's speech following the ban for LGBTIQ+ athletes to participate in the Soci Winter Olympics. Transgender people are represented here as victims of the crimes or, recalling the terminology used previously, as patients. Baker (2014a) finds similar patterns but in relation to transsexual people. He argues that transsexual people are represented

> as involved with a range of different types of activities, some of which can be linked together. For example, the representation of this group of people as victims, either of prejudice or physical violence, perhaps helps to explain the presence of other categories receiving help, struggling for equality and gaining acceptance and approval. (Baker 2014a: 226–227)

The pattern found in the QualCor seems to suggest something different. As a matter of fact, it really mirrors the will of the newspapers, especially *The Guardian*, to discuss this issue and try to raise awareness about the violence that is happening to transgender people.

If we turn to the PopCor, we will see that the discourse is different and at times opposite. The PopCor only has two collocates for *transgender** in this category, that is, *academic* (7) and *killer* (6). The former is related to the case of a researcher who was stabbed almost to death in Scotland, while the latter gives a completely different representation of transgender people from the one retrieved in the QualCor. In that sub-corpus transgender people are the victims of this pattern of violence, in the PopCor they become the perpetrators, for instance:

(58) CRUEL & WICKED;
 Transgender killer guilty of neighbour's murder. (*The Sun*, 16 August 2014)

Transgender people shift from being the patients, those toward whom the violence is committed, to being the agents of violence in these articles. Once again, we can claim exclusivity for one newspaper. All occurrences were found in *The Sun*. The prosody surrounding this news is negative and judgemental as we can see in example (58). Although this is due in part to the topic discussed – it goes without saying that a killer is by no means eligible for praising – what we think should be pointed out here is the function of the adjective transgender. Stories such as this one have an extremely high degree of negativity and thus respond to many news values with no further additions made. Nonetheless, adding the gender identity of the killer, in this specific situation, enhances ordinary things to extraordinary, making the story even more sensational. In fact, knowing if the subject is transgender or not does not add any needed information to the plot of the story itself, but increases the level of sensationalism, appealing even more to the readership. Role allocation here has a crucial function, as we shift from the supportive and inclusive discourse presented in the QualCor, where transgender people are the patients of violence, to a negative and defamatory discourse presented in the PopCor, were transgender people are represented as actors of the violence.

The pattern of violence and crime is found also among collocates of the term *trans*. The discourse here goes back to the QualCor and to the inclusive and awareness raising discourse examined above. One of the collocates of the term *trans* is, in fact, *suicide* (13). This collocate occurs in articles that discuss the fact that one of the consequences of transphobia is ultimately suicide. It is inserted in a context in which it takes on an informative function: the article is explaining the problem of suicide in the transgender community.

The other collocate retrieved for this category in relation to *trans* in the QualCor is *kids* (8). Differently from the Canadian data, this is the first explicit mention of the topic of young transgender people. Once again, *The Guardian* covers the story with little, almost no, competition at all. The eight occurrences of the collocate were found in seven articles, six of which were published by *The Guardian*, and only one by the *i*. Here the newspaper tackles the sensitive question of transgender identity in children, for which society is split in half: on the one hand those who support and fully agree with the fact that children who identify as transgender should have all the help and support they need, and those who believe that children do not have the ability to fully understand their gender identity.

The Guardian works here as a sort of moderator by explaining both sides of the coin. It is interesting to note that it gives voice to transgender people or to experts in the field of medicine or psychology through whom they attempt to explain to their readers the insights of transgender identities thanks to personal testimony. This discourse is supported by one collocate retrieved for the term *transgender** in the QualCor, *Theroux* (6). Louis Theroux is a journalist who produced a documentary on the lives of some transgender children, and who is repeatedly brought up to support the hypothesis that children do have an understanding of their gender identity. The type of discourse constructed here is personal; the journalist draws on real life experiences in order to give the idea that transgender identity is not an abstract concept, by giving a name and a face to the person, it suddenly becomes real. According to Van Leeuwen (1996), there is a shift here in linguistic strategies that goes from a representation in terms of categorization to one in terms of nomination. Therefore, we are no longer reading about the community, or the suicide rate or any other category through which this identity was being described, but about real people and real children. This shift does not apply only to this last collocate but to all the collocates discussed in this section, as an inclusive and non-discriminatory discourse requires a different role allocation. Transgender people should not be categorized as murderers or prostitutes or by any other appellative but nominated through their names, stories and feelings. In fact, while the collective representation described in the previous sections draws more on impersonalization strategies, here personalization is more evident and effective for the type of discourse being conveyed.

This section has focused on the agent vs patient representation of transgender people in the TransCorUK in relation to *crime stories*, the following and last section focuses on two different semantic categories of representation: *laws and rights* and *awareness and support*. Both of these categories are discussed in the same section as they have the common theme of addressing rights, laws and awareness raising for trans identities.

Awareness and support for trans people in the TransCor

The introduction to this research argues that some significant events channelled and facilitated the discussion about transgender identity in the press, sometimes from a negative perspective, sometimes not. Some of these major shifts related to laws and regulations related to transgender identities are examined in the following section, which groups together collocates from the category defined as *laws and rights*. A different pattern that is somehow related to this one in terms of the final aim that the articles have is that of *awareness and support*, discussed in the following section.

Laws and rights

United Kingdom

The collocates that can be included within this category in the TCUK were found only for the term *transgender** and relate to three important topics: (1) the question of transgender people serving in the military; (2) the issue of the placing of transgender people in gender-appropriate prisons; and lastly, (3) the bathroom bill, which caused controversy all around the world in the last year. The collocates under investigation in this section are displayed in Table 5.6.

Table 5.6 *Laws and rights* in the TCUK.

	QualCor	Terms Occurring in Both Sub-corpora	PopCor
transgender*	inmate (6), bathrooms (7), serve (22), inmates (7), prisoner (9), personnel (7)		prisoners (10), soldier (11), officer (11), army (13), toilets (6), Hannah (5)
transsexual*			
trans			

The first striking difference is the use of dissimilar terms to describe the same phenomenon in the two sub-corpora. The QualCor talks about *bathrooms* and the PopCor about *toilets*; the QualCor tackles the issue of *inmates* and *prisoners*, while the QualCor only refers to *prisoners*; and while the QualCor uses a verb process, *serve*, to discuss the topic of the army, the PopCor uses nouns such as *soldier, army* and the reference to one specific officer, *Hannah Winterbourne*. These choices can be related to the different linguistic register each genre has, considering the dichotomy of quality vs popular. Furthermore, they also respond to the tendency of the popular press to make an attempt at highlighting the human side of stories in order to catch the attention of the readers who can more easily relate to the topic discussed. This section aims to uncover the context in which these terms are used.

Starting from the QualCor and the issue of gender-neutral toilets, which emerged in relation to the collocate *bathrooms* (7), *The Guardian* distinguishes itself again for being the newspaper which talked the most about it and which made less questionable linguistic choices. The articles that contain the term *bathroom* as a collocate of the term *transgender**, except for one article in the *i* and one in *The Times*, were retrieved from *The Guardian* in contexts such as the following:

(59) Proponents of the ordinance point out that sexual assault is, of course, already illegal in any situation, and the city has long had a law that specifically bans entering a restroom of the opposite sex with malicious intent. Nor is there any evidence of **transgender** people entering **bathrooms** to commit assault in other cities following the passage of similar laws. (*The Guardian*, 8 October 2015)

Example (59) is an extract from an article that deals with this issue. In the example, the newspaper's point of view regarding this topic emerges, as the following analysis proves. The article discusses the bill that the state of Florida was considering, which bans people from using bathrooms according to their gender identity and established that these should be used according to the gender assigned at birth. After reporting on the different points of view and some statements made by the politician who became the spokesperson for this bill, the journalist clearly asserts that 'there is no evidence' on how transgender people use bathrooms to commit assaults, and therefore the bill does not make any sense in relation to the motivation they are giving. In a different article, the newspaper also defines the bill as *anti-transgender*, again stating its position toward the issue, supported by the use of quotation marks around the term *wrong*, to underline the fact that this definition is totally arbitrary. *The Guardian* proves once again its inclusive policy, and in this case also its overt political stance by criticizing a law.

On the other hand, the PopCor discusses this issue with reference to a different collocate of *transgender**, namely *toilets* (6). The analysis of the QualCor showed the predominance of one newspaper among others that mostly covered the issue discussed. The situation in the PopCor is slightly different compared to the QualCor, as we do find examples from all the newspapers, but a more productive pen from *The Sun* is noticeable. We can detect different patterns of representation in the PopCor.

Firstly, we notice the use of the terms *transgenderists* and *transgendered* in two articles, which underline a choice from the newspaper that is not in line with the guidelines consulted for this research about terminology. These guidelines, in fact, suggest that referring to transgender identity with those terms is a disliked behaviour, as some transgender people might perceive them as demeaning and de-humanizing. The issue is dealt with in *The Sun* as a joke, as we can see in example (60).

> (60) I appreciate life can be tricky for **transgenderists** who arrive at the **toilets** and are unsure about which one to use. But I do have a suggestion. Have a quick look in your trousers. If there is a sausage-shaped tube in there, use the men's. If there isn't, use the ladies'. (*The Sun*, 23 February 2013)

> (61) T-shirts bearing the proud logo 'Je ne suis pas Charlie' will be available from the concession stall next to the **transgendered toilets**. (the *Daily Mail*, 8 December 2015)

In fact, the comment that follows the collocate can be found to be rather offensive. This type of representation suggests a negative prosody around the issue as it constructs the question as futile and unimportant, something that people are bragging about but not an actual problem that needs to be solved. Example (61) shows a different context in which the collocate is found, the article is about a totally different topic, and the toilet issue is mentioned without any relevant reason. One last thing, which is also one main difference between the lexical choices in the two sub-corpora, is the use of 'transgender' to pre-modify 'toilet' or 'bathroom'. The QualCor never uses this construction, which we believe is incorrect as toilets do not have gender but are used by people who are defined on the basis of their gender, whether identifying or assigned at birth. This issue takes us back to the question of the use of terminology. 'Transgender' is an adjective that refers to gender identity, and just like 'gay' and 'lesbian', or 'male' and 'female' should not be used in relation to objects, for instance toilets, which neither have a gender nor a sexual identity. This type of use sets an example that implies a negative application of this adjective, which should refer to human beings and not objects.

Another topic that emerged from this category of collocates refers to transgender people serving in the military and recent events which made headlines in reference to this.

The QualCor presents two collocates of *transgender** that refer to military service for trans people, *serve* (22) and *personnel* (7). The latter collocate is displayed in articles which discuss the 2015 policy on transgender people in the United States underlining the fact that the United Kingdom has been open to transgender soldiers long before the United States. The other collocate that deals with this topic in relation to *transgender** in the QualCor is *serve*. The twenty-two occurrences of the verb *serve* were found in eight different articles, one of which was not related to the issue of the army and transgender people. Of the seven articles that will be discussed here, one appeared in the *i*, one in *The Daily Telegraph* and five in *The Guardian*, which proves once again to be the most attentive newspaper with regards to the topic of transgender people. *The Guardian* discusses the topic in three different contexts. In one article, the main issue dealt with is the fact that the United States was at the time considering whether transgender people could be allowed to serve in the army. The newspaper chooses to describe the event through the direct words of the US Defense Secretary, underlining specific words of his statement such as the verb *deal with* and the terms *presumption, effectiveness* and *readiness*. It could be argued that by highlighting these specific words *The Guardian* was trying to present the United States in a negative way. The spokesperson uses the verb *deal with*, which carries a negative prosody in the sense that it implies that the United States is facing a problem that is being caused by transgender people.

Furthermore, he uses the terms 'effectiveness' and 'readiness' to point to two fundamental characteristics for soldiers that will not presumably be undermined by the fact that a person identifies as transgender. The way the sentence is structured implies a sort of uncertainty about the fact that transgender people are actually able to have these characteristics and therefore serve in the military. *The Daily Telegraph* reports the same quote but in a more extended way. The Defence Secretary maintains that this decision 'is a step in the right direction', an additional piece of information that *The Guardian* chooses to cut out. The article in *The Daily Telegraph* – which in this case, differently from other examples presented above, adopts a very positive and inclusive perspective toward the inclusion of transgender people in the army – goes on by quoting an additional extract from the speech of the Defence Secretary who declares that gender identity should no longer be a relevant parameter in the army. Opposing this, *The Guardian* leaves out this information and repeatedly insists on the fact that other countries, including the UK, have been open to transgender people in the army for a long time. In an attempt to be inclusive, *The Guardian* represents the United States in a more negative way. The articles analysed build on the discourse presented earlier according to which *The Guardian* is raising awareness about transgender identity, by informing people on an additional step forward by the British air force, which was considering allowing transgender women to serve in close combat as a way to bring equality and fairness among soldiers. Other articles choose to follow the strategy of telling personal narratives in order to, somehow, normalize the topic of transgender identity.

Once again, we see here *The Times* choosing not to discuss this topic. What sometimes is perceived as neutrality is actually a clear standpoint on an issue. The newspaper, by not talking about it is stating that they support the current situation and do not attempt at creating an inclusive ground of representation. The different approach taken by *The Daily Telegraph,* on the other hand, reveals its preference to support political stances more than people; the positive representation of US policies seems to be the central interest of the newspaper, while *The Guardian* once again stands out for its inclusivity and interest.

The PopCor refers to this topic through four different collocates: *soldier* (11), *officer* (11), *army* (13) and *Hannah* (6), focusing specifically on this last collocate, which refers to army officer Hannah Winterborne, whose story seems particularly relevant for the PopCor. The collocates occur in a total of fourteen articles. The PopCor takes on a different perspective to the discussion of this topic. As a matter of fact, all the articles in which the collocates were found talk about a specific person, differently from the QualCor which tackles the issue in more general terms. Examples (62) and (63) show the context in which the collocates were found.

(62) I've served in Afghanistan but becoming a woman was the hardest battle;
EXCLUSIVE: **ARMY'S** FIRST **TRANSGENDER OFFICER**
TRANSGENDER Army officer Hannah Winterbourne yesterday told how becoming a woman was tougher than being on the front line in Afghanistan.
Hannah, 27, who was born a boy, made the momentous decision while on a tour of duty at Camp Bastion. (*The Sun,* 19 January 2015)

(63) Sex-changing of the guard;
Meet Cpt Hannah Winterbourne. Brave, bold ... and Britain's 1st **transgender Army officer.** (*Daily Mirror,* 19 January 2015)

The case of Captain Winterbourne provided a great source of inspiration for the popular press, starting from the headlines. Examples (62) and (63) were taken from different popular newspapers. As mentioned previously, the categories of collocates discussed in this chapter were found in the PopCor throughout the newspapers with less exclusivity compared to the QualCor, although once again *The Sun* is the more productive newspaper. In a way, all four newspapers use an army related metaphor to describe the officer. *The Sun* (62) describes becoming a woman as the 'hardest battle'; *The Daily Mirror* (63) creates a pun making reference to the famous changing of the guards to point to a sex change; *The Express* also refers to sex change but with the derogatory phrase *sex-swap*; whereas the *Daily Mail* focuses on clothes, pointing to the change of shoes that followed Winterbourne's transition. One thing that all the examples provided here have in common is the reference to the body, hair, make-up, shoes, skin and the aspect that has changed after transition. The physical appearance seems to be the most important aspect in these articles and not the fact that some rights have been finally achieved for transgender people who are now free to join the army without fearing discrimination. *The Sun* seems to be less interested in the appearance of Winterbourne though it makes reference to her sex assigned at birth. Other articles included in the PopCor that related to this issue talk about other people. As pointed out above, the strategy adopted here is to narrate the experience of one person. The narration, in all cases, is similar to the one displayed in the examples, with great focus on body and use of terminology which transgender people may dislike, such as the phrase *sex-swap*.

The issue of prisons and transgender people was also tackled in the TCUK. The QualCor sub-corpus shows as collocates of *transgender** the terms *inmate* (6), *inmates* (7) and *prisoner* (9).

On this topic, we find more than one newspaper putting forward their point of view. A supportive discourse seems to be used in all the articles through phrases such as the following: *to ensure there is not a lot of isolation, change from the current segregation, silence on abuse, cruelty and violence facing*. The QualCor seems to have a very positive prosody when it comes to gender-appropriate prisons, sustaining the idea that the prison should be chosen according to gender preference and not the sex assigned at birth.

While the QualCor displays this narrative of support toward transgender people detained in prisons, the PopCor shows an opposite type of discourse. Firstly, it is notable that the PopCor only uses the term *prisoner* to refer to this issue. This term carries a negative prosody that implies the guilt of the person defined as such. Secondly, the collocate, found in eight different articles, is always used in contexts that offer a negative representation of transgender individuals. The claim, retrieved in these articles, against transgender people mainly plays on the fact that they are using taxpayers' money to get special treatment while they are in prison. Transgender people are defined as murderers and the phrase 'sex swap' is repeatedly used, together with continuous references to the sex assigned at birth. The PopCor does not show a supportive discourse in this case.

This section has addressed the way in which laws and rights regarding transgender people were discussed by the British press. Generally speaking, I was able to retrieve a more inclusive discourse from the QualCor but a less positive narrative from the PopCor, which not only tends to pinpoint the discussion on individuals rather than the collectivity but also makes arguable representational choices. Next, I will discuss the same semantic category of representation in the Canadian press.

Canada

Table 5.7 presents the TCC collocates for the category *laws and rights*.

Table 5.7 *Laws and rights* in the TCC.

transgender*	*transsexual**	*trans*
C-279 (6), inmates (42), inmate (7), revision (8), pledge (7), re (9)	Russia (6), gender (6)	advocate (6), advocacy (9), filed (6), activists (6), rights (33)

Differences and similarities in the representation of trans identities 155

We can immediately observe that collocates in this category are found for all three terms in the Canadian press, differently from the British press which only shows collocates for the term *transgender** in this category.

In the first groups, collocates of *transgender**, we find six items. One of these collocates, *C-279* (6), refers directly to a law, a historical bill first presented in 2013 and passed in 2015, to amend the Canadian Human Rights Act and the Criminal Code with reference to gender identity. This bill was set to include, within the Human Rights Act, gender identity as a prohibited ground of discrimination and as a protected category in the Criminal Code. The six articles that present this collocate do not really go into detail in explaining what it is but simply mention it by its name, this implies that the bill is popular among the readers of the newspapers, people know what this bill refers to and the maximum information added to the article is a descriptor such as 'transgender bill' or 'transgendered rights bill'. The articles tend to discuss the implication of this bill or the opinions of different politicians. The following example is representative of some of the discussion that happens around this collocate:

> (64) One tweeter said she is 'married to a huge bully of LGBQT folk,' and thus, shouldn't be offering her support, and many pointed to the government's stalled progress on Bill **C-279** – a transgendered rights bill – as the reason why the prime minister's wife has no business showing support for gay and trans youth. (*National Post*, 10 April 2015)

The articles are more interested in discussing the different political parties supporting or not supporting the bill rather than the bill itself and the implications it might have for trans people. In this example, we also see the use of the term *transgendered*; this term is found throughout the TCC 187 times. I have argued a number of times in this book that this term can be seen as problematic and is unwelcomed by some people that identify as transgender. Despite the use of this term, positive patterns associated to trans identities have been found throughout the corpus, this certainly does not justify the use of given words, but at the same time, we also have to acknowledge that the number of occurrences of this variation of the term transgender is less than 6 per cent of the total occurrences retrieved by searching for *transgender** in the TCC, a minimal percentage. It could be argued that in reference to the discussion related to this law, we can, again, identify the phenomenon described earlier of backgrounding (Van Leeuwen 1996), where the social actors involved in this representation are not really at the centre of the discussion, and the attention is switched toward politics.

Two other collocates that can be analysed together are *inmates* (42) and *inmate* (7), articles in which these collocates are found discuss the delicate issue of trans people in prisons. Different from the examples retraced in the TCUK, here the collocates are related to articles that introduce a new policy that has been put in place in British Columbia, which imposes that prison should group inmates based on their gender identity rather than their sex assigned at birth. We also learn from the concordances that this law establishes that if an inmate cannot be moved from where they are staying for health or safety reasons, then they must be put in a single cell and not be forced to share common areas if this means making the person feel unsafe. If we compare this law to those enforced in other countries in this situation, we will see that Canada is far ahead in terms of making life safer for inmates identifying as transgender. The articles in which these collocates are found also make reference to the old policy saying that it would put inmates at risk of sexual harassment and assault. This pattern is found for all fifteen collocates retrieved from *The Globe and Mail* and for the four collocates found in the *Toronto Star*. In the collocates found in the *National Post*, all nine examples point to a different topic related to prison. These articles refer to the complaint raised by an inmate that reported being harassed by the guards in the prison where she was held. This led the Department of Public Safety and Correctional Services to launch a campaign aimed at educating prison guards on how to deal with transgender inmates. There is a potentially problematic representation retrieved in the examples related to this collocate, which is displayed in the following extract:

(65) He said the state also has since developed policies for handling transgender **inmates**. (*National Post*, 25 September 2015)

The verb *handling* used to refer to people objectifies them and depicts them in a way that dehumanizes transgender inmates. I refer to this as potentially problematic as it is not possible to establish whether this verb is used because they are speaking of a transgender person or, more generally, an inmate. In both cases, it is negative and undermining, but it is impossible to establish whether the pattern is strictly related to the representation of transgender identity or not. As could be expected, the other collocate, which is in the singular form, refers to more personal stories, mentioning the Manning case and two stories of trans women detained in a male prison. The articles report on the negative impact that this had on the lives of these people. We can include these articles among those which carry a positive representation of this issue; in fact, they support trans people and become a platform to condemn the choices that go against transgender people's rights.

Related to the term *transsexual** two collocates were found for this category, *Russia* (6) and *gender* (6). The first collocate takes us outside the boundaries of

Canada, to discuss a law in Russia that bans trans people, among many others, from getting a driving licence, the articles all express their outrage for the absurdity of the law. For the first time in the TCC, we find pieces that are directly related to countries that are not Canada or the United States. The articles criticize the law and discuss the negative impact that this has on the lives of trans people. The second collocate refers to another law, the one that allows people to use their identifying gender on documents without going through gender confirmation surgery, this law was discussed in more detail in Chapter 4.

For the term *trans* five collocates that fit into this category were retrieved. Four of these collocates, *advocate* (6), *advocacy* (9), *filed* (6) and *activists* (6), follow a similar pattern in their use. In fact, while at first glance, they might appear to be more fitted for the semantic category discussed in the next and final section, the concordance lines show a different pattern. The examples relating to these collocates actually refer to someone advocating, supporting or attempting to modify or challenge an old law and suggest new, more inclusive measures to enhance transgender people's lives. The following examples show the collocates in context:

(66) Trans **advocacy** groups and health care professionals who are experts in trans issues proposed amendments to the bill in order to remove the obstacles to legal gender recognition. (*The Gazette*, 10 August 2013)

(67) The B.C. Human Rights Tribunal has agreed to review complaints **filed** by the Trans Alliance Society and a handful of transgender and intersex individuals, who argue that doctors should stop assigning the sex of a baby based on a quick inspection of the baby's genitals at birth when there's a possibility they may identify under a different gender, or no gender, years later. (*Vancouver Sun*, 26 May 2015)

Both these examples point to the type of discourse associated with these collocates, where someone related in some way to transgender identities (an ally or a trans person) advocates for transgender rights. The actors depicted in these examples are mainly groups, such as 'advocacy groups' in example (66) or the Trans Alliance Society in example (67).

The last collocate in this group for this category sits, somehow, in between the semantic category of representation discussed here and the one being discussed in the following section, *rights* (33). This collocate is associated with two major topics, the C-279 bill discussed previously, and activism to achieve rights for trans people. Generally speaking, the prosody associated with this collocate is also positive; the articles that mention the topic are supportive of the new bill and advocate toward it. In three examples, the articles discuss a member of the Conservative Party who publicly announces she would vote against, but the articles respond by interviewing advocates of trans rights and including quotes from them. The discourse is supported by phrases such as 'the bill would be a significant step forward for protecting trans rights in the country' (*Calgary Herald*, 20 August 2015), 'advancing the rights of trans people' (*The Gazette*, 10 August 2013), 'the policy helps protect the rights of trans people' (*National Post*, 27 January 2015). Reported speech from advocates is a pattern found in all the articles which contain this collocate. This is a frequently used strategy in News Discourse, which helps depict the fact reported as more legitimate because an expert is endorsing it. In fact, while advocates for trans rights might not necessarily be lawyers or scholars, they are recognized as specialists or at least are part of those accessed voices (Bell 1991) which are heard and given space in newspapers.

The semantic category of representation discussed in this section, once again, highlights the considerable difference between the two datasets considered in this book, while the UK continues to address the negative and discriminatory laws that have been put in place, or the fact that lawmakers are beginning to consider adapting laws to make them more inclusive, the Canadian scenario is already at the point where they recognize that, for example, the problem with inmates is not due to the inmates themselves but to the fact that guards are not adequately prepared to face this different situation, or referring to laws by their name and assuming that the readers are aware of the laws without further need to explain what the law is about.

This chapter concludes with a section that discusses issues about transgender identity awareness and support toward trans people.

Awareness and support

United Kingdom

The last category emerging from the collocation analysis dealt with in this chapter is defined as *awareness and support*. This category is present throughout the TCUK with collocates both in the QualCor and in the PopCor. It is notable that these collocates are used mainly with reference to the terms *transgender** and *trans*, as we can see from Table 5.8.

The main semantic pattern to which this category of collocates hints at is retraceable in articles that deal with the development of awareness toward issues

Table 5.8 *Awareness and support* in the TCUK.

	QualCor	Terms Occurring in Both Sub-corpora	PopCor
*transgender**	recognizing (7), center (12), tipping (6)		Beaumontsociety (7), Beaumont (19), org (10), supports (6), campaigners (7), issues (28), society (24), support (38), rights (18), www (8), families (7), counseling (6), equality (9), uk (20), feelings (8)
*transsexual**	rights (10)		against (7)
trans	visible (6), advocacy (6), activist (8), watch (13), experiences (8), Stonewall (11), issues (18), movement (9), media (20), transition (8), respect (6), pride (7), experience (9)		

related to transgender identities and explain ways in which cisgender people can be supportive of transgender people. The collocates, in particular, relate to major events that include transgender people and the whole LGBTIQ+ community, for example gay pride, but more extensively, this category encompasses terms that refer to different organizations which fight every day in order to achieve rights for transgender people. The collocates included in this category relate to a very positive and inclusive discourse surrounding transgender people; therefore, we believe it is surprising to find such a strong presence of these collocates in the PopCor in reference to *transgender** considering the results highlighted in the previous sections.

In line with the structure of all the analyses that the sections on the TCUK have presented so far, we will start by addressing the QualCor. This sub-corpus was found to have, in relation to the term *transgender**, only three collocates: *Tipping* (6), *center* (12) and *recognising* (7). These terms refer, to a certain extent, to a prosody and a stance on the part of the newspapers that can express support for the transgender community.

The collocate *tipping* refers to the phrase *transgender tipping point*. The articles in which this phrase was mentioned all refer to the fact that transgender issues are becoming more and more popular in newspapers nowadays. The articles tend to explain the origins of this phrase, which appeared for the first time in May 2014 on the front cover of the magazine *TIME*, dedicated to Laverne Cox. One article continues by referring to *Orange is the New Black*, suggesting that it is thanks to this series that Cox was launched into the public eye, becoming a symbol for transgender people. The *i* seems to be very positive about this visibility that the transgender community is having thanks to the media. The newspaper affirms that society is getting closer to adopting a more inclusive and accepting behaviour.

The Guardian, on the other hand, seems to be distancing itself from the assertion of trans people experiencing violent and discriminatory behaviour through the use of the term *apparent*, the greater context of the article actually insists on the fact that violence against transgender people is still a very relevant problem and that although *TIME* might be suggesting that the tipping point for transgender rights has been reached this is not truly the case, if we consider the percentage of deaths of transgender people by suicide or murder. The main difference between the *i* and *The Guardian* lies exactly here, while the former agrees on the fact that the tipping point for transgender people has arrived, the latter strongly disagrees with this and denies any visibility and awareness regarding transgender issues by declaring that transgender individuals do not feel like this changing point has actually arrived as violence against them continues to grow.

A different discourse is retraceable in the other two newspapers under investigation in the QualCor. *The Times* does not discuss the *transgender tipping point* at all, whereas *The Daily Telegraph* considers this phrase in an article with the headline: 'Boys will be girls, and girls will be boys: Transgender times' (17 April 2015). The article makes reference to the cover of *TIME*, as the other two examples presented do, but it goes on to define transgender identity as a *must-have accessory* and in a way diminishes the issue by describing it as something temporary, and almost like a game, if we consider the headline that discursively positions gender as a joke. This article makes use of sophisticated language, with terms such as *balk at, watershed* and *echoed*, which are not very commonly used in everyday language. Moreover, the construction of the sentence appears very long in relation to the basic English syntax structure, and it contrasts the oversimplification and the initial wordplay in the headline. As a result, the headline downgrades the issue to a less significant matter, while the body of the article seems to try to masquerade a stance, from the newspaper, that could be criticized by activists for the rights of transgender people.

The other two collocates included in this category in relation to *transgender** were found in a different context. The use of the verb *recognise* implies on the part of the journalists that they are, in a way, acknowledging and validating transgender identity. In all four newspapers, we found examples of this kind of inclusive discourse in which transgender identity or transgender people's rights are presented as something that is being, or needs to be, recognized. This is done by acknowledging specific issues such as the fact that gender identity is something very complex and should not be put in a box or by describing the situation in other parts of the world where transgender people are still experiencing a status of profound disadvantage. The prosody used in these sentences is positive, and it seems like the journalists are trying to create a bond or make a connection between the reader and the struggle that transgender people face in their everyday lives. To achieve this goal, phrases such as *welcomed, human rights, experience life-changing discrimination, needs*, and *difficult to share*, referring to an inclusive discourse, were found in the examples. Most of the examples quote someone, which can be seen as a way to give a voice to a person who is actually facing the problems discussed, or to people struggling to be recognized, and not just an interpretation of what each newspaper believes a transgender person feels. Following these findings, and the observation of a supportive narrative, it is possible to come to the conclusion that in the newspapers included in the QualCor, despite the cases of language misuse pointed out in previous examples, the articles are mostly meant to do no harm, and are not interested in giving a negative representation of the transgender community. Nonetheless, the linguistic patterns highlighted demonstrate the lack of consistency or awareness that different journalists and editors working for the same newspaper have in discussing transgender identities, possibly due to a lack of information and dissemination of inclusive and non-binary language practices among the newspapers' staff. This claim is not meant to be general, but it is valid for the examples under investigation only.

The last collocate, *center*, is in a way similar in use to *recognising*, as both, although found in different contexts, have a positive function in terms of discourse construction. The term appears in all occurrences as a collocate of *transgender** in the phrases 'National Center for Transgender Equality' or 'Transgender Law Center'. These places are not specifically mentioned as a way of advertising them or explaining to a wider audience their function or the reasons why they exist, but are used as a reference to acknowledge the role of specific people in some situations. The context in which the collocates occur seems to suggest that people from these institutions are being asked to give their opinions regarding the news story, as a source of authority and also providing attribution to the news story. Nonetheless, the repeated occurrence of these two phrases serves the function of introducing the two centres to the audience. Generally speaking, although the articles do not specifically advertise the centres, they are always mentioned in sentences that deal with transgender awareness or rights, contributing to the building of the inclusive discourse retraceable throughout the examples presented so far in this section.

The PopCor, on the other hand, has a very high number of collocates in this category. Most of the terms name support groups or websites that transgender people can refer to for assistance, namely the Beaumont Society and Stonewall. org, together with other terms that all recall acceptance and efforts to promote equality. The two collocates that refer to the Beaumont Society are actually the second and third strongest collocates of *transgender** in the PopCor. The collocates of *transgender** in the PopCor belonging to the category of *awareness and support* are: *Beaumontsociety* (7), *Beaumont* (19), *org* (10), *supports* (6), *campaigners* (7), *cruel* (5), *issues* (28), *society* (24), *support* (38), *rights* (18), *www* (8), *families* (7), *counseling* (6), *equality* (9), *uk* (20) and *feelings* (8). Some of these collocates refer to the Beaumont Society,[4] a non-profit transgender support group established in the UK in 1966. The collocates which refer to this are *Beaumontsociety, Beaumont, org, society, www* and *uk*. One of the most recurrent contexts is the reference to its email contact: *www* or *uk*. It is notable that these collocates only occurred in *The Sun* and in the first two years (2013, 2014) of the collection. The collocates were found in a very specific context, a special correspondence column called 'Dear Deidre'. A common way in which the collocates occur is through Deidre, the writer of the column, who suggests that her readers refer to this support group in order to deal with issues that transgender people or their family may face. Some of the concordances also show the use of the terms *transgendered* instead of *transgender*. Previously in this study I pointed out some guidelines that suggest that *transgendered* is an adjective that is not always considered acceptable by transgender people as some feel that this form tends to dehumanize people. However, in this case, if we consider the Beaumont Society website, we will notice that this term is very often used there and obviously not in a derogatory way. This point sustains our initial statement regarding the use of terminology as a very subjective matter, upon which people have different and sometimes distant understandings. Nonetheless, these collocates, in contrast to other results found in *The Sun*, show a very positive discourse toward support and awareness on the part of this newspaper.

One of the collocates discussed so far was also found in a different context worth mentioning, that is, *UK*. The following example shows the other context in which this collocate occurred:

(68) For every 10 **transgender** cases in the **UK** there is only one where a woman wants to live as a man. (*Daily Mirror*, 4 January 2015)

When it was not part of the email address of the Beaumont Society, the collocate was retrieved in articles such as the one shown in example (68). This example highlights a collective representation of transgender people, with a reference to the United Kingdom. The structure of the articles which contain this collocate used with this function generally see the use of numbers that count how many transgender people are involved in specific events or are in the UK. The use of numerals is very common in the journalistic genre as it responds to the need to sensationalize events by associating them to a large number of people, what Johan Galtung and Mari H. Ruge (1965) define as 'news making standards'. This type of representation also recalls a strategy employed in the representation of social actors pointed out by Van Leeuwen (1996), defined as aggregation. This strategy is 'often used to regulate practice and to manufacture consensus opinion, even though it presents itself as merely recording facts' (Van Leeuwen 1996: 49).

Of the remaining collocates which form this category, we will look in more detail at the two most frequently occurring ones, that is, *issues* (28) and *support* (38). The prosody surrounding the collocate *issues* in the PopCor is very positive as it is accompanied by terms and phrases such as *sensitive, learn about, teaching about, information about, serious,* and *advice on*, which all contribute to sending a message that signals the necessity to support more and more the awareness on transgender identities, to help people understand what it means to be transgender and what everybody should do to support transgender people. This discourse is reinforced by the use of the collocate *support* found in phrases such as *transgender support group* (8/38), *support the transgender community* (11/38) and *support transgender people* (7/38).

With just two collocates, this discourse was found, in a small percentage, with reference to the term *transsexual** as well. The collocate retrieved for the

QualCor, *rights* (10), and the one retrieved for the PopCor, *against* (7), both have a very positive prosody. The articles discussing these collocates describe events organized in support of transsexual people and argue about their importance.

The term *trans*, differently from the other two terms analysed, presents many collocates for this category, but only in the QualCor. These collocates are: *visible* (6), *advocacy* (6), *activist* (8), *watch* (13), *experiences* (8), *Stonewall* (11), *issues* (18), *movement* (9), *media* (20), *transition* (8), *respect* (6), *pride* (7) and *experience* (9).

As it was the case for the term *transgender** some of the collocates here (*watch, Stonewall, media*) refer to organizations and groups that fight for transgender people's rights such as Stonewall,[5] a support group for LGBTIQ+ people, and Trans Media Watch,[6] a charity dedicated to improving transgender and intersex issues' coverage in the media. Other collocates such as *experiences* and *experience*, found in the phrase *experience/s of trans people* and supported by terms such as *explain, understand, share* and *disclose*; or *issues*, found in the phrase *trans issues* surrounded by verb processes such as *campaigning for, have been neglected, integrate, written about, talked about* and *care passionately about*; or also *respect*, found neighbouring terms such as *deserve, treated with*, and *shows*, function, as mentioned above, as bricks to the building of an inclusive and supportive, above all, positive, discourse surrounding the representation of transgender people.

The next and final section of this chapter presents similar results emerging from the analysis of the TCC.

Canada

The semantic category of representation *awareness and support* is strongly present in the Canadian press. This does not come as a surprise given the very positive representational patterns and linguistic choices highlighted so far in the sections discussing results from the TCC. What is unexpected is to find no collocates for this category referred to in the search term *transsexual**. This absence in relation to this term was observed as well in the British press. This category also appears to be the one with the most results, especially for the term *trans*. Collocates that fall within this category in the TCC are summarized in Table 5.9.

Starting with the collocates of *transgender**, some of the collocates are explored in more detail here. *Tipping* (7) relates to the same topic discussed earlier for the TCUK. The type of discussion within the articles that include

Differences and similarities in the representation of trans identities 165

Table 5.9 *Awareness and support in the TCC.*

transgender*	transsexual*	trans
remembrance (7), tipping (7), accommodating (6), accommodate (13), discriminate (6), awareness (21), protect (20), advocates (13), competed (6), discussing (8), argues (6)		Pulse (10), alliance (11), awareness (10), equality (15), issues (24), voice (7), society (21), Ontario (10), culture (6), discrimination (7), activist (6), member (6), experiences (9), experience (8), identity (11), especially (6), feel (11), program (7), coming (7), rent (6)

this collocate is different from what we observed in the British press. In four out of six articles related to this collocate the topic is discussed in reference to the reality drama *Becoming Us* (2015), aired on ABC Family, which follows the lives of a family in the United States where one of the parents comes out as a trans woman. These articles all put forward the idea that the increasing representation of trans identities in the media is positive and favours the popularization and destigmatization of this topic. In one article, though, published by *The Globe and Mail* on 23 April 2015, the discussion around the use of this phrase 'transgender tipping point' is stretched much further than the reference to this show or to the front page of *TIME* magazine. Judith Butler's theories on gender performance are discussed in the article, and the journalist questions whether the issue has gone too far. While they acknowledge that all the achievements reached so far for trans people are positive they question the right to allow children to decide about their gender identity. There is a constant back and forth in this article between positive and supportive representation and negative ones, as we go from constructions such as 'but performance is not all that gender is, although that's what some thinkers in the trans/queer community proclaim' where the quantifier *some* and the verb *proclaim* implicitly suggests the author is critical of this idea, to constructions such as 'but the emergence of transgender life in mainstream culture invites an appreciation of issues and struggles that are as complex as those in a Dostoyevsky novel' where the journalist acknowledges the struggle that trans people face on a daily basis.

In the analysis of the concordances related to the collocates in this group, this example is the only problematic one. The collocates *accommodating* (6) and *accommodate* (13) both refer in all examples except one to students or children, and all discuss the will of schools to adopt strategies that can help transgender children feel safer and less discriminated in this environment. The collocate *awareness* (21), which in some examples occurs in the phrase Transgender Awareness Week, is always modified by the verbs *rising, growing* and *increasing*. The collocate *protect* (20) is used in phrases such as 'a policy to protect transgender people' in all but three examples. The seventeen examples which include this phrase are modified by verbs such as *support, adopt, agree to, bring in* or phrases such as 'put policies in place to protect'. In one example, the action of adopting such policies is evaluated as laudable. The collocate *remembrance* (7) occurs in all seven examples in the phrase 'Transgender Day of Remembrance' described as a day which 'marks lives lost' or 'commemorates individuals who have lost' or highlight that a 'candlelight vigil' has been organized for the occasion. All in all, apart from the one example discussed in relation to the collocate tipping, the prosody retrieved around these collocates is very positive and supportive of transgender people's lives and pushing toward a growing awareness on the topic.

Moving on to the twenty collocates of *trans* in this category, it is possible to observe a variety of topics related to it, differently from the British data where the collocates in this category were mainly related to specific organizations for trans rights, here we observe that the discussion shifts to address trans rights from a legal perspective. Given the high number of collocates, I will try to group those which carry a similar representation or present interesting patterns.

Starting from the collocate *Pulse* (10), which is the strongest collocate for this term, it refers to an Ontario-based research project (Trans Pulse Project) that released a study on the trans population in Ontario looking at the number of trans people who have children. The study proves that 27 per cent of trans people in the province are within this group. Related to this is the collocate *Ontario* (10). The articles in which this collocate is present discuss different studies and data related to the transgender population in the province. The articles appear in *The Globe and Mail* (5), the *National Post* (2), *Calgary Herald* (2), and the *Times & Transcript* (1) and provide information that goes from the suicide rate for trans people in the province to health-related issues. The articles are informative and provide a thorough discussion of the data presented, with experts giving opinions. Interestingly, the information presented is very specific to the Ontario province, but the articles are published in two national newspapers and in two newspapers published respectively in the province of Alberta and New Brunswick. There is no clear explanation behind these choices apart from the fact that presumably this information is not available for the other provinces. We can argue that its laudable to choose to discuss these issues even if not directly related to the territory covered by the newspapers as a way to give space to the dissemination of this type of information. Against this backdrop, it is interesting to observe the presence of the collocate *awareness* (10). Despite the very positive patterns highlighted throughout the corpus, the articles related to this collocate actually argue in favour of raising awareness more, the collocate is found in the sentence 'if more had an awareness of trans issues' four out of ten times and actually points out that we still do not know enough about transgender identities.

Many are the attempts at raising awareness found in the corpus, some are related to the collocates in this semantic category of representation, such as *experiences* (9) and *experience* (8). The articles that included these collocates reported on the lives of trans people, the difficulties that they face on a daily basis, and the fact that they are becoming more and more visible. The collocate *program* (7), also relates to this informative function retrieved in the corpus, in fact, the articles in which this collocate is included relate the problem of homeless transgender children presented above in relation to the collocate *youth* in the category *personal details*. *Program* is related to a plan to organize events in which people can exchange clothes to donate to organizations which support young homeless transgender people.

The discussion on trans awareness is supported on different levels, three of the collocates in this category are related to one collocate – *clone* – which we discussed earlier in this chapter in relation to *entertainment and celebrities*. The three collocates are *voice* (7), *culture* (6) and *feel* (11), most of the occurrences of these collocates appear in articles which include an interview to the main actress of the Canadian TV series *Orphan Black*. At one point in the plot the character discovers she has a brother who is a transgender man. The actress who plays this role, in these articles explains her experience in playing a transgender character and says she 'feel[s] like trans culture's voice is louder now', in line with the growing awareness toward this topic.

The last collocates in this category I will discuss here are *alliance* (11), *equality* (15), and *society* (21), which mostly co-occur in either the phrase Trans Equality Society or Trans Alliance Society. These are two organizations based respectively in Edmonton, Alberta, and in Vancouver, British Columbia. The collocates resemble those found in this category in the TCUK in the way they refer directly to organizations that fight for trans rights, but the patterns identified in relation to the content of the articles that include the collocates are very different. While in the British press, these articles aim to inform people of the presence of these organizations and how they can be contacted, in the Canadian press, the articles inform people about the fights these organizations are carrying out. Articles related to the Trans Equality Society of Alberta discuss issues related to the Human Rights Act and the bill that changes the act to eliminate the presence of gender identity on ID documents, arguing in favour of passing this bill (the same bill was discussed a number of times in relation to the Canadian data earlier in this chapter). Similarly, articles that include the collocate related to the Trans Alliance Society discuss the request from advocates of this organization to remove the gender indication from birth certificates, the main difference is that these articles also report on news about members of the public and of politicians who do not agree with the bill and how this organization is working to compete with those voices.

All in all, we can argue that again we find a very positive prosody associated to the topic of trans identities in this category of representation, the discussion presented by the articles analysed is also balanced as they talk about both positive and negative views on the topic and argue in favour of trans rights and raising awareness.

This section has presented two semantic categories of representation that might seem very similar, therefore grouped in the same section, but are in some traits very different. The results presented in this section denote an ever-growing effort, regardless of the reasons behind these choices, of an inclusive and non-discriminating type of discourse presented by both the British and the Canadian press. In the TCUK, we see that each newspaper has a different way of introducing the discourse on transgender identities and this, despite the at times questionable choices, is a giant leap forward toward the erasure of transphobia and discrimination. The TCC has a more general positive and endorsing representation of trans people, with articles that take the discussion even further than simply mentioning issues related to trans identities.

Unfortunately, the current political and economic situation worldwide restrains our positive expectations toward a more inclusive and non-discriminatory society due to the major political and ideological shifts our society is witnessing, with the rise of strongly conservative parties in many European and non-European countries. However, the press still works as one of the main references for people, and we should keep advocating for its educational and informative function.

Among the over 400 collocates analysed through their concordances in this study some were excluded, either for not presenting any relevant results, or because the discourse surrounding them was similar to other results presented. Nonetheless, I believe that the major discursive and representational patterns in the narrative around transgender identities, in the time span considered for this study, were highlighted and discussed in Chapters 4 and 5.

The following, and final chapter will try to sum up all the results discussed in addressing the research questions that guided the study, with a particular focus on an attempt to provide a more straightforward answer to these questions and more specifically to address the impact that the press, through the discussion about transgender identities, has had on society. The next chapter seeks to also look at future steps for this research and discuss some of the theoretical and methodological issues related to the study.

6

Conclusion

The contribution of the press

This research began with many doubts, countless questions, and a few hypotheses. Nearly all of the doubts were clarified, most of the questions answered and many of the hypotheses proved to be either false or biased. The long process that resulted in the writing of this book started in 2015 with the formulation of the research questions presented in Chapter 1, as follows:

1. How is language used in the British and the Canadian press to represent transgender people between 2013 and 2015?
   a. In the British press, to what extent does language change with reference to the main class distinction between popular and quality press?
2. In what ways do newspapers differ in terms of language when covering news stories about transgender people with reference to:
   a. frequency and context of use of naming strategies (nouns and pronouns); and
   b. semantic prosodies (e.g. use of descriptors, such as adjectives or descriptions of grammatical agency via verbs).
3. How do the findings relate to the social context and social practices in the UK and Canada?

The next step in the process that led to this book was the creation and compilation of the TransCorUK (TCUK) and later the linguistic analysis of the extensive amount of data collected. In light of the results that the analysis of the British newspapers produced, I then decided to create another set of data as a means of comparison for my results and, thus, expanded the investigation of the press by compiling a new dataset, the TransCorCanada (TCC), collected from the Canadian press. The analysis of these two sub-corpora led to two different sets of conclusions with regard to how trans identities are discussed in the press. On the one hand, I was able to highlight some understandings that can be generalized in relation to the representation of transgender identities, while on the other hand, other results were found to be exclusively relevant in relation to the types of newspapers, country or time span considered in this study. Additionally, some considerations could also be drawn about the theoretical and methodological framework in which this study is set.

In this section I will explore in more detail issues related to the former set of results, which also address the first and second research questions. The section that follows discusses issues related to the methodological and theoretical framework, while the last section of this chapter will attempt to answer the third research question and draw some final conclusions also with regard to further development of this work in the future.

One of the most important aspects that this research further confirms is that transgender identities cannot be defined and categorized according to one specific set of labels comprehensive of all individuals who identify as transgender. As I pointed out in Chapter 1, the manner in which transgender identity is expressed is very subjective, and people who identify using this label articulate their identity in many different ways. I believe that it is necessary for researchers who dedicate their investigations to the study of transgender identities, and more in general to the representation of all identities, to bear in mind that it is problematic to generalize on labels and categorizations when it comes to the definition of identities, whether these are related to gender, sexuality or any other aspect of one's self. The examples and the analysis presented in this study contribute to proving this hypothesis. The different types of representations retrieved are a tangible linguistic proof of the variety of ways in which each transgender individual can be represented and prefers to represent their own self. I argue throughout this book that there are specific terms that are connected to trans identities, such as *transsexual* or *transgendered*, which are not well received by all members of the trans community, nonetheless we find instances of people self-identifying with those very terms.

The analysis of the use of terminology related to transgender identities, presented in the first section of Chapter 4, revealed an evolution in the use of the terms under investigation. Despite the more prominent use of *trans* in recent years, and the frequent use of *transsexual*, *transgender* remains the most common term used to refer to trans identities. I also observed a less frequent use of those terms that can be perceived as discriminatory and defamatory, although at the same time the TransCorUK shows a reappropriation of these terms (see the case of *tranny*) in the representation of these identities, as mentioned above.

As pointed out in Chapter 3, already in 1988 Ronald Carter underlined the importance of lexical choices, which can be seen as the 'items which attract most attention' (Carter 1988: 9) and are, nonetheless, ideologically connoted. The way in which people are referred to, or named, 'can have significant impact on the way in which they are viewed', posits John Richardson (2007: 49). Lexical choices position the social actors not only within a specific social group but also characterize the individual indexically, that is to say, in relation to the social occasion or event in which they are being represented.

The characterization of transgender individuals in the TransCor is also reinforced by the different semantic patterns of representation retrieved across the corpus through a combination of collocation and concordance analysis. Seven different patterns emerged in this study and are discussed in this book. Similar to what was pointed out by Costas Gabrielatos and Paul Baker with reference to the representation of RASIM in the UK press, where the authors note that the interest in these social actors in the media is delineated by an occasional/seasonal attraction due to the sociopolitical situation in the country (Gabrielatos and Baker 2008: 17), the analysis of the TransCor revealed that there were major events or issues channelling the discussion on transgender identities, from the release of films and TV series that included transgender characters, to more formal events such as the issuing of laws or the release of studies on the trans population presenting data related to transphobia or suicide rates.

Linguistic strategies through which the representations of trans individuals in the press are carried out were previously identified by Baker (2014a), whose study represents the starting point for the one described in this book, but also by Thomas J. Billard (2016). The latter describes four main categories through which trans people are described in the press in the United States, as pointed out in Chapter 2. These categories include misgendering and misnaming; misrepresentation (through pathologization) of trans identities; use of puns and mockery; and the sexualization of the transgender body (Billard 2016: 4196). The linguistic strategies related to these categories were found in the TransCor as well, as the analysis chapters underline.

This study goes beyond the level of lexical choices and looks at the type of discourses within which the representation of trans identities is embedded by analysing the semantic categories of representation identified within the TransCor, which reveal the different linguistic patterns used by the press to mention transgender people in the United Kingdom and in Canada. These range from the use of *personal details* and *implying verbs* to describing transgender individuals (Chapter 4) to different forms of collective representation. One of these, *LGBTIQ+ group and labels* is used to describe trans people by creating an association between transgender identity and LGBTIQ+ groups or labels related to identities through the use of intersectionality in reference to other groups that society considers minorities (Chapter 5).

The *entertainment and celebrity* world is another major context through which transgender identities are discussed in the press in a way that collectivizes trans identities. The increasing number of transgender film stars, and that of shows, films and TV series, featuring a transgender character, made this environment extremely productive in creating news stories dealing with this identity; this promptly became a fertile ground for news production.

The last part of the analysis (Chapter 5) brought forward three additional semantic patterns of representation, which in a way take us back to a more 'traditional' news reporting. In fact, these are all related to covering crime stories or political/official events that relate, in one way or another, to transgender people. From the analysis of *crime stories*, a category peculiar to the TCUK, it emerged that transgender people tended to be represented differently: as victims in the quality press and as agents of violence in the popular press.

Laws and rights for transgender people are also a topic that generated copious amounts of news articles, topics in these stories expanded from issues related to gender-neutral toilets, to military service for transgender people and gender-appropriate prisons. In such cases, a strongly inclusive narrative emerged. One major difference was identified between the two sub-corpora, while the British data addresses the topics showing a more politically oriented type of stance rather than having a merely informative function, the Canadian press has a tendency to highlight the legal achievement for trans people and the advancement made in society from this perspective.

The last semantic pattern retrieved in the analysis of the TransCor is related to *awareness and support*. This result, while expected for the Canadian data, came as a surprise for the British press. In fact, although I initially hypothesized that the popular press would produce the most negative results in terms of the representation of transgender people, this category proved me wrong. Many of the collocates related to raising awareness and creating a support network for transgender people and their families were unexpectedly retrieved in the section of the corpus including articles from newspapers that fall within the popular press category.

More broadly, we can conclude that the press, in the time span considered, presented both positive and negative linguistic behaviours. The two datasets considered for the analysis proved to be very different in the way in which they represent trans identities. The Canadian press presents a very inclusive and non-discriminatory representation throughout the three years considered with very few exceptions made, while the British press includes a number of different linguistic choices, positive and negative. Among the negative linguistic and semantic choices identified within the TransCorUK, I can definitely list the habit, shown by all newspapers, to refer to transgender people by their name assigned at birth. Additionally, the use of pronouns which refer to the sex assigned at birth was frequent and often mixed within the same article. From my analysis, neither of these practices are found in the TCC. Furthermore, another practice retrieved throughout the TransCorUK was the use of *transgender* and *transsexual* as synonyms, a practice condemned by many guidelines offered for the use of non-discriminatory language, for its implications linking identity to physical appearance. Along the same line, I also found the presence – and this practice is also retrieved in the Canadian press especially with reference to the use of the term *transgendered* – of terminology considered to be offensive or non-inclusive. Two more aspects are peculiar of the British data in the TransCorUK, the first is the reference, not only through the use of the term *transsexual* but also through the many occurrences of terms such as *sex change*, of a discourse that goes back to the medical and/or physical aspect related to transgender identity. It could be argued that these aspects are, nonetheless, related to the discourse of trans identity, but become problematic when they are addressed as the sole aspect related to this identity. The second pattern retrieved, which can be included among the negative ones, is the use of trans identity as a mean to sensationalize news. In fact, a number of stories present this pattern whereby the articles provide information about the gender identity of the social actor represented which is in no way relevant to the story being told.

On a more positive note, the press also works as a platform to discuss, acknowledge and include transgender identities, a topic which in many cases is still perceived as a taboo. A peculiarity of the Canadian data is the prominence of the discussion on trans children, with the aim of finding more and more ways to make life easier and more inclusive for young people.

Newspapers, in the three years under investigation, were able to initiate discussion about support groups and events to raise awareness, but most of all, spark the conversation on transgender people in society. For this reason, despite the patterns of non-inclusive representation, I believe that the interest taken by the press in the representation of trans identities can be regarded as a positive step toward inclusiveness and the acknowledgement of trans identities.

Corpus-based approaches to the analysis of gender identities

In this book I make use of corpus-based methodologies to analyse the representation of gender identities. Against the backdrop of a number of diverse theoretical frameworks, different methodologies were combined together to carry out the analysis and interpret the results presented in this book, including the use of two different pieces of software for corpus analysis.

In light of this, some reflections are required. The analyses presented in this book consider a variety of elements. First, the critical literature review regarding the field of language and gender identity demonstrates how this is a fast-growing and continuously evolving field. It also proves that, although issues related to transgender identities have been interrogated for a very long time, it is only in the last two decades that linguistic analysis has been carried out to investigate these types of identities. Numerous compelling studies on language in relation to transgender identities in the last five years have been valuable instruments in the growth and further understanding of these identities, but the fast-changing reality in which we live urges scholars to continue in this direction.

If we turn to the field of News Discourse, also thoroughly addressed in this work, the discussion shows that many of the theoretical issues proposed over half a century ago are today still relevant for the analysis of the language of the news, while some others have inevitably evolved into new and updated perspectives on the use of language in journalism. For instance, despite the constant evolution of language, many of the features defining the quality and popular press in the British context still apply to the two genres of news writing, as well as the news making standards, more generally speaking, which still look for newsworthiness and refer to those same news values first proposed by Johan Galtung and Mari H. Ruge (1965) and later by Allan Bell (1991), Monika Bednarek and Helen Caple (2012) and other scholars (see Chapter 2).

At the same time, other theoretical standpoints, such as some of the categorizations of the British press presented in Chapter 2, no longer apply. Among these, the dichotomy according to which newspapers are grouped in relation to their size (broadsheets vs tabloids) can be criticized, as the newspaper formats have changed through the years. Similarly, the up-, mid- and down-market distinction – which takes into account the readership's socio-economic status – seems to be somehow deceptive, especially following the rise of the circulation of newspapers online, which has enabled people from all social classes and geographical provenance to access news. As far as the Canadian press is concerned, the close relationship with the news from the United States is strongly present in the data, proving that this bond is still a fundamental one in Canadian news production. The articles retrieved for the TCC were generally discussing national news or US-based news, and very rarely were news about the rest of the world found. This peculiarity cannot be generalized for the Canadian press as a whole but could be traced back to the fact that the corpus only includes articles on a specific topic, in order to generalize this result further analysis of the Canadian news production is required. Another peculiarity of the Canadian sub-corpus is the high number of duplicates found, that were not excluded as they were published in different newspapers, that is to say, while duplicates in the British press were normally different editions of the same article published on the same day in the same newspaper (and for this reason excluded from the corpus, as specified in Chapter 3), in the Canadian corpus the same edition of an article was published in different newspapers and thus counted as a different reproduction of the topic.

Lastly, CBDA proved to be a very useful methodology in uncovering ideological stances and linguistic patterns in the large amount of data considered in this book. As pointed out in Chapter 2, the critical approach adopted for the analysis presented in this research proved to be functional, since the representation of gender identities has many political and ideological implications that need to be questioned in order to fully attempt to grasp the related issues. For this purpose, the corpus collected for the analysis, the TransCor, was searched to pinpoint different discursive and linguistic choices. As observed by Heiko Motschenbacher, corpus-based '(critical) discourse analysis […] has been playing an increasingly prominent role' in the study of language used to represent gender and sexual identities, as it allows for the exploration of larger datasets, for methodological triangulation and it reduces the researchers bias (Motschenbacher 2018: 148). This study is an example of this, as all three criteria have been met, the corpus as a whole includes nearly five million words, different methodological approaches which combine qualitative and quantitative analytical tools were employed and my bias toward expected results were proven wrong. The most relevant aspect in the use of this technique in this book is that it allowed me, to put it in Baker's words, to 'show how certain innocuous-sounding words or phrases may be relatively frequent but contain particular negative (or positive, A/N) associations due to their repetition' in specific contexts (Baker 2018: 265).

The use of two different pieces of software served the purpose of exploring different methodological approaches as well; for example, while AntConc is a computer-based software, CQPweb is a web browser-based one. Testing the efficacy and applicability of the two pieces of software on the one hand proved useful in relation to the results obtained and the exploration of different analysis techniques (see, for example, the use of restricted queries, or the fact that CQPweb allows to exploit the metadata in the corpus in different ways from AntConc), while on the other hand it also positions the book as a possible didactic tool for those who wish to engage with basic corpus analysis.

As a way to sum up the major results that emerged from the analysis of the TransCor, the following section introduces one last reflection on the impact on society of the representation of transgender identities in the press. In fact, while the results presented in Chapters 4 and 5, and summarized in this and the previous section try to give an answer to the first two research questions the following and last section tries to address the third and final research question that focuses primarily on the social aspect of this research.

Trans fashion or trans awareness? Concluding remarks

Can the sudden rise of popularity in the discussion of issues related to transgender identities in the press be regarded as a new fashionable topic or is it related to the increasing rise in awareness toward this expression of gender identity? This is the overarching question that engendered this work and guided it throughout. However, as the compilation of the TransCor progressed, and with it the close reading of the articles in it, this question grew stronger in my mind.

Starting with observations on the UK, this section will attempt to retrace the response of society to the growing acknowledgement of transgender identity.

In Great Britain, legislation appertained to transgender people dates back to 2010 (Polese and Zottola 2019). The Equality Act (2010) was passed as a follow-up to a previous act issued in 2004, the Gender Recognition Act, as specified in Chapter 1. The latter is the first legal document concerning gender reassignment and transgender identity produced in the UK, while the 2010 Act provides recommendations in cases of discrimination and inequality for transgender people. Despite the issues discussed in the two laws, Vanda Polese and I (2019) have concluded that in the years under scrutiny the issue was still strongly dealt with in terms of gender reassignment processes and the bureaucratic aspects that concern them rather than in terms of a relevant argument on identity and non-discriminatory behaviours toward transgender people. In line with these findings, the House of Commons, in the person of Nicky Morgan, Minister for Women and Equalities, on 14 January 2016 published a document that summarizes the then-current legal situation of transgender people in the UK. The document states that while we recognise the importance of the Gender Recognition Act as pioneering legislation when it was passed, it is clear that the Act is now dated. The medicalised approach regarding mental-health diagnosis pathologises trans identities; as such, it runs contrary to the dignity and personal autonomy of applicants. (Women and Equalities Committee 2016: 7).

This document highlights the necessity for the UK to upgrade its laws concerning transgender identity, although the existence of this material proves an effort in this direction. As a further step forward, countless non-profit organizations and inquiries that monitor the situation regarding transphobia and transgender rights and support have been sponsored in the last few years. A document announcing the top inclusive employers in 2017 has been produced by the organization Stonewall.[1] As of today, the organization All About Trans[2] is the most active in monitoring the representation of transgender people in the media.

Despite all this, violence against transgender people does not seem to be decreasing. According to an article found on the *Independent* online published on 28 July 2016,[3] transphobic hate crimes reported to the police in the UK increased from 215 in 2011 to 582 in 2015. To the best of my knowledge, official figures on violence, hate crimes, and suicide rates for transgender individuals, or on the actual number of people who identify as transgender in the UK, are not available, but some data emerged from those organizations that work in favour of transgender people.

Stonewall (2017a) conducted a survey proving that eight out of ten transgender children have been bullied in schools across the UK. The Office for National Statistics determined that 15 per cent of the overall number of police reports on hate crime in 2014 were to the detriment of transgender people (Home Office 2015[4]). In a report published by Stonewall in 2018,[5] it is stated that 41 per cent of trans people in the UK have experienced a hate crime in the last 12 months, and that crime against trans people is significantly underreported. If we turn to Canada the situation does not seem to be much different. In an article published for *The Conversation* (a network of non-profit media outlets that publish articles written by academics and researchers) on 19 August 2019,[6] Abigail Curlew, a researcher in security and surveillance at Carleton University, describes the situation of hate crimes for trans people in Canada as being on the rise. The researcher affirms that official data on trans people are not available in Canada as these are mostly included within the more general label of gender and sexual crimes (as happens for the UK), but reports on surveys conducted by organizations that work with transgender people do present some figures. One of these surveys, for example, shows that 98 per cent of the 433 participants that took part in a survey conducted in 2013 by the Trans Pulse Project in Ontario (discussed in Chapter 5) have reported at least one experience of transphobia. Against this backdrop, it is clear that the press has an ever-growing role in the dissemination and acknowledgement of issues related to transgender identities and must continue in this role. The discussion on these issues will, hopefully, come to an end only when we will no longer feel the need to refer to them as problematic.

Point eight of the National Union of Journalists (NUJ) code of conduct states that a journalist should produce 'no material likely to lead to hatred or discrimination on the grounds of a person's age, gender, race, colour, creed, legal status, disability, marital status, or sexual orientation' (NUJ 2011). Some of the linguistic patterns retrieved in the TransCor suggest that, at times, this assertion is undermined, as negative representations of transgender identities are offered to the readers, which contribute to the reinforcement of hate and transphobia. In a recent follow-up study on the representation of trans people in the British press published by Baker (2019) as a blog entry and commissioned by Mermaids UK,[7] the scholar states that, at a surface level, there seems to have been improvements in 2018 and 2019, in the sense that he retrieved less occurrences of sexualization or mockery of trans people and more stories on transphobia and inclusivity, but at the same time he also observed many articles that were unreasonably critical and aggressive toward trans people, leading him to conclude that the British press has shifted from 'an openly hostile and ridiculing stance on trans people towards a carefully worded but still negative stance' (Baker 2019).

The analysis presented in this book shows that this behaviour is mainly retrieved in the British data, while the Canadian press always worked, in the three years investigated, as an inclusive and non-discriminatory platform.

It can be argued that transgender identities entered the wider media discussion as a form of fashion, mainly a curiosity toward a topic that society could still not grasp, adding to a need to sensationalize news and use diversity to attract the readers' attention – as we have seen has been done historically by the press with any subject, object or concept which differed from the stereotyped, binary and heteronormative representation in vogue. As fashion faded out, as it always does, the stakes were up for the topic of transgender identities. What used to be fashion became awareness and, as the analysis of the TransCor revealed, by displaying the evolution of the articles in the three years under investigation, the press took on an important function of raising knowledge on this issue.

As a way to continue this work many paths could be followed. In the first place, enlarging data collection to cover articles up until a more recent time would allow one to explore how the representation changed or evolved in the present. Another aspect which could further enlighten the representation of trans identities in the press could be a multimodal one, as images in the news are generally employed to complement the meaning and ideas that are being put forward. As Giuseppe Balirano posits, 'multimodal analyses are also needed to critically examine both the verbal and visual representation of the roles, identities, activities and relations of social actors' (2017: 157). Finally, it could be useful to compare the representation of trans people in the press in the countries considered in this book and in other countries which publish both in English and in other languages as well.

On a more social level, the hope is that works such as this one, or the many others that were discussed in this book that tackle similar issues, could be useful to those who are at the top of the news production chain, who could benefit from scholarly analyses like this one and begin to build a more inclusive and non-discriminatory news society.

Notes

Chapter 1

1. The term is deliberately in italics, as the question about what 'normality' is remains unsolved.
2. Throughout this work the phrase 'news story' is used according to the definition given by Galtung and Ruge (1973). They suggest a list of elements of newsworthiness (further discussed in Chapter 2) which can theoretically be defined as criteria that an event should meet in order to be considered as newsworthy and included in the news cycle. This process, therefore, turns an event into a news story. This definition also recalls the narrative function of the news story which follows a narrative schema that differs from that of face-to-face narration (Polese 2004: 76–77).

Chapter 2

1. See for example the '3Ds' referring to three paradigms developed starting from 1922: *Deficit* (Jespersen 1922), *Dominance* (Lakoff 1975) and *Difference* (Tannen 1990).
2. For further reading about verbal processes see Eggins (2004), Halliday and Matthiessen (2013) and Thompson (2013).
3. A tagged corpus is a corpus that has been annotated during compilation, the most common form of tagging is by part-of-speech (POS). POS tagging a corpus means labelling each word with its grammatical category (Reppen 2010: 35).
4. WikiLeaks is a multinational media organization, founded in 2006 by Julian Assange. The aim of the organization is to collect, analyse and divulge censored and restricted official documents (see WikiLeaks 2015).
5. In Corpus Linguistics a token is the smallest single linguistic unit, i.e. a word, punctuation, or anything between spaces (Hunston 2002: 17).
6. AntConc and other corpus tools developed by Lawrence Anthony and in collaboration with other scholars can be retrieved at Laurence Anthony's Website 2019.
7. See News Media Canada 2018.
8. Bold had been added to the table to indicate the chosen newspapers.
9. The TransCorCan is available through the server found at http://cqpweb2.makeba.org/transcorca/.

Chapter 3

1. The Observer's Paradox is a concept introduced by William Labov in 1972. As a sociolinguist working in the United States, Labov maintained that sociolinguistics has the aim of studying the way people talk when they are not observed, to catch the true nature of interaction. The only way to do this was to record them, but he noticed that the moment people became aware of being recorded they would change their linguistic behaviour, making the recording useless or the results of the analysis altered.
2. Among others see Baker (2006, 2010), Baker and McEnery (2005), Baker, Gabrielatos and McEnery (2013b), Baker and Levon (2015), Partington (2012, 2015), Venuti and Nisco (2015), and Facchinetti et al. (2015).
3. This is true not only for British newspapers but also it is a growing trend worldwide.
4. *The Guardian* launched a Berliner size, in between a broadsheet and a tabloid, whilst *The Daily Telegraph* kept the broadsheet format.
5. Despite playing a pivotal role in Canada nowadays, indigenous Canadian press will not be taken into consideration in this study. For further information on the topic see among others Mongibello (2018), Clark (2014), Anderson and Robertson (2011), Alia (2011) and Harding (2006). For studies on the French-Canadian press see among others Vessay (2016), Young and Dugas (2012) and Gagnon (2006).
6. Which includes the provinces of Newfoundland and Labrador, Nova Scotia, New Brunswick and Prince Edward Island.
7. Which includes the provinces of Manitoba, Saskatchewan and Alberta.
8. Some material in this section were originally published in Zottola (2018b).
9. The * next to a search term is defined in Corpus Linguistics as the 'wild card', it allows the term itself to be searched for, as well as all its morphological declinations. Here some exceptions were made and not all different declinations of each were kept for the purpose of the analysis. The search for *transgender** includes the terms: transgender, transgenders, transgendered, transgenderism.
10. The search for *transsexual** includes the terms: transsexual, transsexuals, transexual, transexuals, transsexuality, transsexualism.
11. The search for *sex change** includes the terms: sex change, sex changes, sex-change, sex-changes.
12. The search for *transvestite** includes the terms: transvestite, transvestites.
13. The search for *gender reassignment** includes the terms: gender reassignment and gender reassignments.
14. The search for *cross-dresser** includes the terms: cross-dresser, cross-dressers, cross dresser, cross dressers.
15. The search for *trann** includes the terms: tranny, trannie, trannies.

16 The search for *shemale** includes the terms: shemale, shemales.
17 For definitions of the terms it is possible to see GLAAD n.d.-b.
18 The first number indicates the raw frequencies of the term *transgender**, the second those of *transsexual**.
19 Different sources specify that many transgender people do not prefer the use of the term *transsexual*, see GLAAD n.d.-b; gires 2019; National Center for Transgender Equality 2020b.
20 As some of the terms have very high frequency figures, I have used 10 per cent as a sample to identify the general pattern. The sample used was randomized. To obtain the random sample with AntConc I used a function that sorts the concordance lines to show only every (N)th row in the KWIC list (specifically every 10th for *transgender**, every 9th for *trans* and every 9th for *transsexual**), while for CQPweb I used the built-in randomizer function.
21 Bold is added in all examples throughout Chapters 5, 6 and 7 to highlight the collocates.

Chapter 4

1 As the analysis was conducted by dividing the TCUK into two sub-corpora, the second column (QualCor) contains the collocates retrieved from the quality press while the last column (PopCor) contains those collocates retrieved from the popular press. The third column (terms occurring in both sub-corpora) contains those terms that occurred as collocates of *transgender**, *transsexual** and *trans* in both sub-corpora.
2 It is notable to point out that the two acronyms are not found in the TCUK.

Chapter 5

1 Examples taken from articles published from the same newspaper on the same day are marked by a letter following the date in order to distinguish them.
2 Of the sixteen occurrences of the term as collocates of *transgender**, only five refer to the Alcorn case.
3 She ended her suicide note with a plea for action: 'My death needs to be counted in the number of transgender people who commit suicide this year. I want someone to look at that number and say "that's fucked up" and fix it. Fix society. Please' (*The Guardian*, 5 January 2015).
4 For more about the Beaumont Society, see Beaumont 2018.
5 For more information, see Stonewall n.d.
6 For more information, see Trans Media Watch n.d.

Chapter 6

1. For further information, see Stonewall 2017b.
2. For further information, see All About Trans 2020.
3. For further information, see Yeung 2016.
4. For further information, see Corcoran, Lader and Smith 2015.
5. For further information, see Bachmann and Gooch 2018.
6. For the full article, see Curlew 2019.
7. A non-profit organization that works mainly with trans youth. For more on the study, see Baker 2019.

References

Aarts, Jan and Theo van den Heuvel. (1982), 'Corpus-based Syntax Studies', *Gramma: tijdschrift voor taalkunde in Nijmegen*, 7 (2–3): 153–174.

Aarts, Jan and Willem Meijs. (1984), *Corpus Linguistics: Recent Developments in the Use of Computer Corpora in English Language Research*, Amsterdam: Rodopi.

Adampa, Vasiliki. (1999), 'Reporting of a Violent Crime in Three Newspaper Articles: The Representation of the Female Victim and the Male Perpetrator and their Actions; A Critical News Analysis'. *Centre for Language in Social Life Working Paper No. 108*, Department of Linguistics and Modern English Language, Lancaster University.

Alia, Valerie. (2011), *Uncovering the North: News, Media and Aboriginal People*, Vancouver: University of British Columbia Press.

All About Trans. (2020). Available online: http://www.allabouttrans.org.uk (accessed 9 September 2020).

Allan, Stuart. (1999), *News Culture*, Buckingham, UK, and Philadelphia, PA: Open University Press.

Anderson, Benedict. (1983), *Imagined Communities: Reflections on the Origin and Spread of Nationalism*, London: Verso.

Anderson, Mark Cronlund and Carmen L. Robertson. (2011), *Seeing Red: A History of Natives in Canadian Newspapers*, Winnipeg: University of Manitoba Press.

Anthony, Lawrence. (2014), *AntConc* (Version 3.4.4m) [Computer Software], Tokyo: Waseda University. Available online: http://www.laurenceanthony.net/ (accessed 30 December 2016).

Audit Bureau of Circulations (ABC). (2015), *Regional Publications: Combined Total Circulation Certificate*. January. Available online: http://www.abc.org.uk/Certificates-Reports/Our-Reports/ (accessed 16 September 2015).

Audit Bureau of Circulation (ABC). (n.d.). Available online: http://www.abc.org.uk/ (accessed 9 September 2020).

Aultman, B. Lee. (2014), 'Cisgender', *Transgender Studies Quarterly*, 1 (1–2): 61–62.

Bachmann, Chaka L. and Becca Gooch. (2018), *LGBT in Britain: Trans Report*. Stonewall and YouGov. Available online: https://www.stonewall.org.uk/system/files/lgbt_in_britain_-_trans_report_final.pdf (accessed 9 September 2020).

Baer, Brian J. (2016), 'Translation, Transition, Transgender. Framing the Life of Charlotte von Mahlsdorf', *Transgender Studies Quarterly*, 3 (4): 506–523.

Bagemihl, Bruce. (1997), 'Surrogate Phonology and Transsexual Faggotry: A Linguistic Analogy for Uncoupling Sexual Orientation from Gender Identity', in Anna Livia and Kira Hall (eds), *Queerly Phrased: Language, Gender, and Sexuality*, 380–401, Oxford: Oxford University Press.

Baker, Sarah Jane. (2017), *Transgender behind Prison Walls*, Hook: Waterside Press.

Baker, Paul. (2002), 'Construction of Gay Identity via Polari in the Julian and Sandy Radio Sketches', *Lesbian and Gay Review*, 3 (3): 75–84.

Baker, Paul. (2003), 'No Effeminates Please: A Corpus-based Analysis of Masculinity via Personal Adverts in *Gay News/ Times* 1973–2000', in Bethan Benwell (ed.), *Masculinity and Men's Lifestyle Magazines*, 243–260, Oxford: Blackwell.

Baker, Paul. (2005), *Public Discourses of Gay Men*, London: Routledge.

Baker, Paul. (2006), *Using Corpora in Discourse Analysis*, London: Continuum.

Baker, Paul. (2008), *Sexed Texts: Language, Gender and Sexuality*, London: Equinox.

Baker, Paul. (2010), 'Representations of Islam in British Broadsheet and Tabloid Newspapers 1999–2005', *Language and Politics*, 9 (2): 310–338.

Baker, Paul. (2012), 'Acceptable Bias? Using Corpus Linguistics Methods with Critical Discourse Analysis', *Critical Discourse Studies*, 9 (3): 247–256.

Baker, Paul. (2014a), 'Bad Wigs and Screaming Mimis: Using Corpus-assisted Techniques to Carry out Critical Discourse Analysis of the Representation of Trans People in the British Press', in Christopher Hart and Piotr Cap (eds), *Contemporary Critical Discourse Studies*, 211–235, London: Bloomsbury.

Baker, Paul. (2014b), *Using Corpora to Analyze Gender*, London: Bloomsbury.

Baker, Paul. (2018), 'Language, Sexuality and Corpus Linguistics', *Journal of Language and Sexuality*, 7 (2), 263–279.

Baker, Paul. (2019), 'Representing Trans People in the UK Press – A Follow-up Study', Corpus Approaches to Social Science (CASS), 26 November. Available online: http://cass.lancs.ac.uk/representing-trans-people-in-the-uk-press-a-follow-up-study-professor-paul-baker/ (accessed 9 September 2020).

Baker, Paul and Erez Levon. (2015), 'Picking the Right Cherries?: A Comparison of Corpus-based and Qualitative Analyses of News Articles about Masculinity', *Discourse and Communication*, 9 (2): 221–336.

Baker, Paul and Tony McEnery. (2005), 'A Corpus-based Approach to Discourses of Refugees and Asylum Seekers in UN and Newspaper Texts', *Language and Politics*, 4 (2): 197–226.

Baker, Paul and Tony McEnery. (2015), *Corpora and Discourse: Integrating Discourse and Corpora*, London: Palgrave.

Baker, Paul, Costas Gabrielatos and Tony McEnery. (2013a), 'Sketching Muslims: A Corpus Driven Analysis of the Representation Around the Word "Muslim" in the British Press 1998–2009', *Applied Linguistics*, 34 (3): 255–278.

Baker, Paul, Costas Gabrielatos and Tony McEnery. (2013b), *Discourse Analysis and Media Attitudes: The Representation of Islam in the British Press*, New York: Cambridge University Press.

Baker, Paul, Costas Gabrielatos, Majid KhosraviNik, Michal Krzyzanowski, Tony McEnery and Ruth Wodak. (2008), 'A Useful Methodological Synergy? Combining Critical Discourse Analysis and Corpus Linguistics to Examine Discourses of Refugees and Asylum Seekers in the UK Press', *Discourse and Society*, 19 (3): 273–306.

Balirano, Giuseppe. (2017), 'Who's Afraid of Conchita Wurst? Drag Performers and the Construction of Multimodal Prosody', in Maria Grazia Sindoni, Janina Wildfeuer and Kay O'Halloran (eds), *Mapping Multimodal Performance Studies*, 154–179, London: Routledge.

Balirano, Giuseppe and Maria Cristina Nisco. (2016), 'A Corpus-based Discourse Analysis of *Refugee** in EU Legal Texts', in Girolamo Tessuto (ed.), *Constructing Legal Discourses and Social Practices: Issues and Perspectives*, 106–128, Newcastle upon Tyne: Cambridge Scholars Publishing.

Barker-Plummer, Bernadette. (2013), 'Fixing Gwen', *Feminist Media Studies*, 13 (4): 710–724.

Barthes, Roland. (1964), *Elements of Semiology*, London: Cape Editions.

Bartley, Leanne and Encarnacion Hidalgo-Tenorio. (2015), 'Constructing Perceptions of Sexual Orientation: A Corpus-based Critical Discourse Analysis of Transitivity in the Irish Press', *Estudios Irlandeses*, (10): 14–34.

Bartley, Leanne and Encarnacion Hidalgo-Tenorio. (2016), 'To Be Irish, Gay, and on the Outside: A Critical Discourse Analysis of the Other after the Celtic Tiger Period', *Journal of Language and Sexuality*, 5 (1): 1–36.

Beaumont. (2018), 'About Us'. Available online: https://www.beaumontsociety.org.uk/about-us.html (accessed 16 September 2020).

Bednarek, Monika. (2006), *Evaluation in Media Discourse: Analysis of a Newspaper Corpus*, London: Continuum.

Bednarek, Monika. (2008), 'An Increasingly Familiar Tragedy: Evaluative Collocation and Conflation', *Functions of Language*, 15 (1): 7–34.

Bednarek, Monika and Helen Caple. (2010), 'Double-take: Unpacking the Play in the Image-Nuclear News Story', *Visual Communication*, 9 (2): 211–229.

Bednarek, Monika and Helen Caple. (2012), *News Discourse*, London: Continuum.

Bell, Allan. (1991), *The Language of News Media*, Oxford: Blackwell.

Bem-vindo. (2008–2018), 'TransCor Canada'. Available online: http://cqpweb.makeba.org/ (accessed 9 September 2020).

Besnier, Niko. (2003), 'Crossing Genders, Mixing Languages: The Linguistic Construction of Transgenderism in Tonga', in Janet Holmes and Miriam Meyerhoff (eds), *The Handbook of Language and Gender*, 279–301, Malden, MA: Blackwell.

Biber, Douglas. (1993), 'Representativeness in Corpus Design', *Literary and Linguistic Computing*, 8 (4): 243–257.

Billard, Thomas J. (2016), 'Writing in the Margins: Mainstream News Media Representations of Transgenderism', *International Journal of Communication*, 10: 4193–4218.

Borba, Rodrigo. (2019), 'The Interactional Making of a "True Transsexual": Language and (Dis)identification in Trans-specific Healthcare', *International Journal of the Sociology of Language*, 256: 21–55.

Brownlees, Nicholas. (2016), '"News also Came by Letters": Functions and Features of Epistolary News in English News Publications of the Seventeenth Century', in

Joad Raymond and Noah Moxham (eds), *News Networks in Early Modern Europe*, 394–419, Leiden: Brill.

Brownlees, Nicholas. (2017), 'The Concept of Periodicity in English Pamphlet News', in Giovanni Ciappelli and Valentina Nider (eds), *La Invencion de las Noticias las Relaciones de Sucesos entre la Literatura y la informacion (Siglos XVI–XVIII)*, 77–88, Trento: Università degli Studi di Trento.

Bucholtz, Mary and Kira Hall. (2005), 'Identity and Interaction: A Sociocultural Linguistic Approach', *Discourse Studies*, 7 (4–5): 585–614.

Burns, Christine. (2018), *Trans Britain: Our Journey from the Shadows*, London: Unbound.

Burnes, Theodore R. and Mindy M. Chen. (2012), 'The Multiple Identities of Transgender Individuals: Incorporating a Framework of Intersectionality to Gender Crossing', in Ruthellen Josselson and Michele Harway (eds), *Navigating Multiple Identities: Race, Gender, Culture, Nationality, and Roles*, 113–128, Oxford: Oxford University Press.

Butler, Judith. (1988), 'Performative Acts and Gender Constitution: An Essay in Phenomenology and Feminist Theory', *Theatre Journal*, 40 (4): 519–531.

Butler, Judith. (1990), *Gender Trouble: Feminism and the Subversion of Identity*, 2nd edition, New York: Routledge.

Butler, Judith. (1993), *Bodies that Matter*, New York: Routledge.

Butler, Judith. (1997), *Excitable Speech: A Politics of the Performative*, New York: Routledge.

Butler, Judith. (2004), *Undoing Gender*, New York: Routledge.

Byerly, Carolyn and Karen Ross. (2006), *Women & Media: A Critical Introduction*, Malden, MA: Blackwell.

Caldas-Coulthard, Carmen Rosa and Rosamund Moon. (2010), '"Curby, Hunky, Kinky": Using Corpora as Tools for Critical Analysis', *Discourse & Society*, 21 (2): 99–133.

Caldas-Coulthard, Carmen Rosa and Theo van Leeuwen. (2002), 'Stunning, Shimmering, Iridescent: Toys as the Representation of Gendered Social Actors', in Lia Litosseliti and Jane Sunderland (eds), *Gender Identity and Discourse Analysis*, 91–110, Amsterdam: John Benjamins.

Capuzza, Jamie C. (2015), 'What's in a Name? Transgender Identity, Metareporting, and the Misgendering of Chelsea Manning', in Leland G. Spencer and Jamie C. Capuzza (eds), *Transgender Communication Studies: Histories, Trends, and Trajectories*, 93–110, Lanham, MD: Lexington Books.

Capuzza, Jamie C. and Leland G. Spencer. (2017), 'Regressing, Progressing, or Transgressing on the Small Screen? Transgender Characters on U.S. Scripted Television Series', *Communication Quarterly*, 65 (2): 214–230.

Carter, Cynthia, Gill Branston and Allan Stuart. (1998), *News, Gender and Power*, London: Routledge.

Carter, Ronald. (1988), 'Front Pages: Lexis, Style and Newspaper Reports', in Mohsen Ghadessy (ed.), *Registers of Written English: Situational Factors and Linguistic Features*, London: Pinter Publishers.

Chermak, Steven M. (1994), 'Body Count News: How Crime Is Presented in the News Media', *Justice Quarterly*, 11 (4): 561–582.

Chomsky, Noam. (1965), *Aspects of the Theory of Syntax*, Cambridge, MA: MIT Press.

Cixous, Helen. (1975), *Le Rire de la Méduse*, Paris: Hónore Champion.

Clark, Brad. (2014), 'Framing Canada's Aboriginal Peoples: A Comparative Analysis of Indigenous and Mainstream Television News', *Canadian Journal of Native Studies*, 34 (2): 41–64.

Clarke, Kate. (1992), 'The Linguistics of Blame: Representations of Women in *The Sun* Reporting of Crimes of Sexual Violence', in Michael Toolan (ed), *Language, Text and Context: Essays in Stylistics*, 208–224, London: Routledge.

Crenshaw, Kimberlé. (1991). 'Mapping the Margins: Intersectionality, Identity Politics, and Violence against Women of Colour', *Stanford Law Review*, 43(6): 1241–1279.

Crystal, David and Derek Davy. (1969), *Investigating English Style*, London: Longman.

Conboy, Martin. (2002), *The Press and Popular Culture*, London: Sage.

Conboy, Martin. (2006), *Tabloid Britain: Constructing a Community through Language*, Abingdon: Routledge.

Conboy, Martin. (2007), *The Language of the News*, Abingdon: Routledge

Conboy, Martin. (2010), *The Language of Newspapers: Socio-Historical Perspectives*, London: Continuum.

Concilio, Arielle A. (2016), 'Pedro Lemebel and the Translatxrsation: On a Genderqueer Translation Praxis', *Transgender Studies Quarterly*, 3 (4): 462–484.

Corcoran, Hannah, Deborah Lader and Kevin Smith. (2015), *Hate Crime, England and Wales: 2014/15*. Home Office, 13 October. Statistical Bulletin 05/15. Available online: https://www.gov.uk/government/uploads/system/uploads/attachment_data/file/467366/hosb0515.pdf (accessed 9 September 2020).

Cory, D. Walter. (1965), 'The Language of the Homosexual', *Sexology*, 32 (3): 163–165.

Cotter, Colleen. (2010), *News Talk: Investigating the Language of Journalism*, Cambridge: Cambridge University Press.

Curlew, Abigail. (2019), 'Transgender Hate Crimes Are on the Rise even in Canada'. *The Conversation*, 20 August. Available online: https://theconversation.com/transgender-hate-crimes-are-on-the-rise-even-in-canada-121541 (accessed 9 September 2020).

Dashti, Laleh and Mehrpour Saeed. (2017), 'Representation of Social Actors in J. Krishnamurti and Alan Watts's Philosophical Speeches: A Critical Discourse Analysis', *Journal of Applied Linguistics and Language Research*, 4 (4): 5–59.

Davari, Safoura and Mohammad Raouf Moini. (2016), 'The Representation of Social Actors in Top Notch Textbook Series: A Critical Discourse Analysis Perspective', *International Journal of Foreign Language Teaching and Research*, 4 (13): 69–82.

Davies, Mark. (2008–), *Corpus of Contemporary American English (COCA)*. Available online: https://corpus.byu.edu/coca/ (accessed 9 September 2020).

Delemarre-van de Waal, Henriette and Peggy Cohen-Kettenis. (2006), 'Clinical Management of Gender Identity Disorder in Adolescents: A Protocol on Psychological and Paediatric Endocrinology Aspects', *European Journal of Endocrinology*, 155: S131–S137.

Derrida, Jacques. (1967), *De la grammatologie*, Paris: Éditions de Minuit.
Derrida, Jacques. (1976), *Of Grammatology*, Baltimore, MD: Johns Hopkins University Press.
Di Martino, Emilia. (2017), 'Painting Social Change on a Body Canvas: Trans Bodies and their Social Impact', in Paul Baker and Giuseppe Balirano (eds), *Queering Masculinities in Language and Culture*, 149–173, London: Palgrave.
Doan, Petra L. (2010), 'The Tyranny of Gendered Spaces: Reflections from beyond the Gender Dichotomy', *Gender, Place and Culture*, 17 (5): 635–654.
Duguid, Alison and Alan Partington. (2018), 'Absence: You Don't Know What You're Missing. Or Do You?', in Charlotte Taylor and Anna Marchi (eds), *Corpus Approaches to Discourse: A Critical Review*, 38–59, London: Routledge.
Durrant, Philip and Doherty Alice. (2010), 'Are High Frequency Collocations Psychologically Real? Investigating the Thesis of Collocational Priming', *Corpus Linguistics and Linguistics Theory*, 6 (2): 125–155.
Eckert, Penelope and Sally McConnell-Ginet. (1992), 'Communities of Practice: Where Language, Gender, and Power All Live', in Kira Hall, Mary Bucholtz and Birch Moonwomon (eds), *Locating Power: Proceedings of the 1992 Berkeley Women and Language Conference*, 89–99, Berkeley, CA: Berkeley Women and Language Group.
Efe, Ibrahim and Omer Ozer. (2015), 'A Corpus-based Discourse Analysis of the Vision and Mission Statements of Universities in Turkey', *Higher Education Research & Development*, 34 (6): 1110–1122.
Eggins, Suzanne. (2004), *An Introduction to Systemic Functional Linguistics*, 2nd edition, London: Pinter.
Facchinetti, Roberta, Nicholas Brownlees, Birte Bös and Udo Fries. (2015), *News as Changing Texts: Corpora, Methodologies and Analysis*, Newcastle upon Tyne: Cambridge Scholars Publishing.
Fairclough, Norman. (1989), *Language and Power*, London: Longman.
Fairclough, Norman. (1992), *Discourse and Social Change*, Cambridge: Blackwell.
Fairclough, Norman. (1995), *Media Discourse*, London: Hodder.
Fairclough, Norman. (2005), *Analysing Discourse*, London: Routledge.
Fairclough, Norman and Ruth Wodak. (1997), 'Critical Discourse Analysis', in Teun van Dijk (ed.), *Discourse as Social Interaction*, 258–284, London: Sage.
Fairclough, Norman, Jane Mulderrig and Ruth Wodak. (2011), 'Critical Discourse Analysis', in Teun van Dijk (ed.), *Discourse Studies: A Multidisciplinary Introduction*, 357–378, London: Sage.
Ferraresi, Adriano. (2018), 'Who Writes the Story Matters: Transgender Identity through the Lens of Citizen Journalism', in Giuseppe Balirano and Oriana Palusci (eds), *Miss Man? Languaging Gendered Bodies*, 190–214, Cambridge: Cambridge Scholars Publishing.
Ferraresi, Adriano and Silvia Bernardini. (2019), 'Building EPTIC: A Many-Sided, Multi-purpose Corpus of EU Parliament Proceedings', in Irene Doval (ed.), *Parallel Corpora for Contrastive and Translation Studies*, 123–139, Amsterdam: John Benjamins.

Firth, John R. (1957), *Papers in Linguistics 1934–1951*, London: Oxford University Press.
Fowler, Roger. (1991), *Language in the News: Discourse and Ideology in the Press*, London: Routledge.
Foucault, Michel. (1972), *Archeology of Knowledge and the Discourse on Language*, New York: Pantheon Books.
Foucault, Michel. (1980), *The History of Sexuality: An Introduction*, Paris: Édition Gallimard.
Freud, Sigmund. (1953), *A General Introduction to Psychoanalysis*, New York: Pocket Books.
Gabriel, Kay. (2016), 'Untranslating Gender in Trish Salah's *Lyric Sexology Vol. 1*', *Transgender Studies Quarterly*, 3 (4): 524–544.
Gabrielatos, Costas and Paul Baker. (2008), 'Fleeing, Sneaking, Flooding: A Corpus Analysis of Discursive Constructions of Refugees and Asylum Seekers in the UK Press, 1996 – 2005', *Journal of English Linguistics*, 36 (1): 5–38.
Gagnon, Chantal. (2006), 'Language Plurality as Power Struggle, or: Translating Politics in Canada', *Target*, 18 (1), 69–90.
Galtung, Johan and Mari H. Ruge. (1965), 'The Structure of Foreign News: The Representation of the Congo, Cuba and Cyprus Crises in Four Norwegian Newspapers', *Journal of Peace Research*, 2 (1): 64–90.
Galtung, Johan and Mari H. Ruge. (1973), 'Structuring and Selecting News', in Stanley Cohen and Jock Young (eds), *The Manufacture of News: Social Problems, Deviance and the Mass Media*, 62–72, London: Constable.
Garside, Roger, Geoffrey Leech and Geoffrey Sampson, eds. (1987), *The Computational Analysis of English*, London: Longman.
Ghadessy, Mohsen. (1988), *Registers of Written English: Situational Factors and Linguistic Features*, London: Pinter Publishers.
gires. (2019), 'Terminology'. May. Available online: https://www.gires.org.uk/terminology#Transsexual (accessed 9 September 2020).
GLAAD. (n.d.-a). Available online: https://www.glaad.org (accessed 9 September 2020).
GLAAD. (n.d.-b), 'GLAAD Media Reference Guide – Transgender'. Available online: https://www.glaad.org/reference/transgender (accessed 9 September 2020).
Gouveia, Carlos Alberto M. (2005), 'Assumptions about Gender, Power and Opportunity: Gays and Lesbians as Discursive Subjects in a Portuguese Newspaper', in Michelle M. Lazar (ed.), *Feminist Critical Discourse Analysis: Gender, Power and Ideology in Discourse*, 229–250, London: Palgrave Macmillan.
Granger, Sylviane, Estelle Dagneaux and Fanny Meunier. (2002), *International Corpus of Learner English*, Louvain: Presses universitaires de Louvain.
Green, Eli R. (2006), 'Debating Trans Inclusion in the Feminist Movement', *Journal of Lesbian Studies*, 10 (1–2): 231–248.
Gries, Stefan T. (2008), 'Dispersion and Adjusted Frequencies in Corpora', *International Journal of Corpus Linguistics*, 13 (4): 403–437.
Gupta, Kat. (2019), 'Response and Responsibility: Mainstream Media and Lucy Meadows in a Post-Leveson Context', *Sexualities*, 22 (1–2): 31–47.

Hall, Kira. (1997), '"Go Suck your Husband's Sugarcane!": Hijras and the Use of Sexual Insult', in Kira Hall and Anna Livia (eds), *Queerly Phrased: Language, Gender, and Sexuality*, 430–460, Oxford: Oxford University Press.

Hall, Kira. (2002), 'Unnatural Gender in Hindi', in Marlis Hellinger and Hadumod Bussman (eds), *Gender across Languages: The Linguistic Representation of Women and Men*, 133–162, Amsterdam: John Benjamins.

Hall, Kira. (2013), '"It's a Hijra!": Queer Linguistics Revisited', *Discourse & Society*, 24 (5): 634–642.

Hall, Kira, and Anna Livia. (1997), *Queerly Phrased: Language, Gender and Sexuality*, New York: Oxford University Press.

Hall, Kira, and Veronica O'Donovan. (1996), 'Shifting Gender Positions among Hindi-Speaking Hijras', in Victoria L. Bergvall, Janet M. Bing and Alice F. Freed (eds), *Rethinking Language and Gender Research: Theory and Practice*, 228–266, London: Longman.

Hall, Kira and Lal Zimman. (2010), 'Language, Embodiment and the "Third Sex"', in Carmen Llamas and Dominic Watt (eds), *Language and Identities*, 166–178, Edinburgh: Edinburgh University Press.

Hall, Stuart. (1996), 'Introduction: Who Needs "Identity"?', in Stuart Hall and Paul du Gay (eds), *Questions of Cultural Identity*, 1–7, London: Sage.

Halliday, Michael A.K. and Christian M.I.M. Matthiessen. (2013), *Hallidays' Introduction to Functional Grammar*, 4th edition, Abingdon: Routledge.

Hardie, Andrew. (2012), 'CQPweb: Combining Power, Flexibility and Usability in a Corpus Analysis Tool', *International Journal of Corpus Linguistics*, 17 (3): 380–409.

Harding, Robert. (2006), 'Historical Representations of Aboriginal People in the Canadian News Media', *Discourse & Society*, 17 (2): 205–235.

Hartner, Marcus. (2015), 'Imagining Transgender: Reinscriptions of Normativity in Duncan Tucker's *Transamerica* and Jackie Kay's *Trumpet*', *FIAR*, 8 (1): 109–122.

Henry, Harry. (1983), 'Are the National Newspapers Polarizing?', *Admap*, 19 (10): 484–491.

Hess, Linda M. (2017), '"My Whole Life I've Been Dressing Up Like a Man": Negotiations of Queer Aging and Queer Temporality in the TV Series Transparent', *European Journal of American Studies*, 11 (3). https://doi.org/10.4000/ejas.11702.

Hidalgo-Tenorio, Encarnation. (2011), 'Critical Discourse Analysis: An Overview', *Nordic Journal of English Studies*, 10(1): 183–210.

Home Office. (2015), *Hate Crime, England and Wales 2014/15*, Statistical Bulletin 05/15, October. Available online: https://www.report-it.org.uk/files/ho_hate_crime_statistics_201415.pdf (accessed 16 September 2020).

Horak, Laura. (2014), 'Trans on YouTube. Intimacy, Visibility, Temporality', *Transgender Studies Quarterly*, 1 (4): 572–585.

Hoskan, Özlem. (2006), 'The Media Portrayal of Homosexuality in the Turkish Press between 1998 and 2006', PhD Thesis, Institute of Social Sciences, Ankara, Turkey. Available online: http://etd.lib.metu.edu.tr/upload/12608008/index.pdf (accessed 1 July 2017).

Hunston, Susan. (2002), *Corpora in Applied Linguistics*, Cambridge: Cambridge University Press.

Hunston, Susan. (2007), 'Semantic Prosody Revisited', *International Journal of Corpus Linguistics*, 12 (2): 249–268.

Irigaray, Luce. (1985), *This Sex Which Is Not One*, Ithaca, NY: Cornell University Press.

Irvine, Judith and Susan Gal. (2000), 'Language Ideology and Linguistic Differentiation', in Paul Kroskrity (ed.) *Regimes of Language: Ideologies, Polities, and Identities*, 35–83. Santa Fe, NM: SAR Press.

Isani, Shaeda. (2011), 'Of Headlines and Headlinese: Towards Distinctive Linguistic and Pragmatic Genericity'. *Asp*, 60. Available online: https://asp.revues.org/2523 (accessed 24 November 2016).

Jacques, Juliet. (2015), *Trans: A Memoir*, London: Verso.

Jarrin, Alvaro. (2016), 'Untranslatable Subjects: Travesti Acces to Public Health Care in Brazil', *Transgender Studies Quarterly*, 3 (4): 357–375.

Järvinen, Timo. (1994), 'Annotating 200 Million Words: The Bank of English Project', in *Proceedings of the 15th International Conference on Computational Linguistics*, Vol. 1, 565–568, COLING 94 Organizing Committee. Kyoto: International Committee on Computational Linguistics. Available online: http://aclweb.org/anthology/C94-109 (accessed 20 September 2017).

Jaworska, Sylvia. (2017), 'Corpus Approaches: Investigating Linguistics Patterns and Meanings', in Colleen Cotter and Daniel Perrin (eds), *The Routledge Handbook of Language and Media*, 93–108, New York: Routledge.

Jaworska, Sylvia and Ramesh Krishnamurthy. (2012), 'On the F Word: A Corpus-based Analysis of the Media Representation of Feminism in British and German Press Discourse, 1990-2009', *Discourse & Society*, 23 (4): 401–431.

Jespersen, Otto. (1922), *Language: Its Nature, Development and Origin*, London: Allen & Unwin.

Jones, Lucy. (2016), 'Language and Gender Identities', in Siân Preece (ed.), *The Routledge Handbook of Language and Identity*, 210–224, Abingdon: Routledge.

Jones, Lucy. (2019), 'Discourses of Transnormativity in Vloggers' Identity Construction', *International Journal of the Sociology of Language*, 256: 85–101.

Joseph, John. (2016), 'Historical Perspectives on Language and Identity', in Siân Preece (ed.), *The Routledge Handbook of Language and Identity*, 19–33, Abingdon: Routledge.

Josephson, Jyl and Einarsdottir Porgerdur. (2016), 'Language Purism and Gender: Icelandic Trans* Activists and the Icelandic Linguistic Gender Binary', *Transgender Studies Quarterly*, 3 (4): 376–387.

Jucker, Andreas H. (1992), *Social Stylistics: Syntactic Variation in British Newspapers*, Berlin: Mouton de Gruyter.

Kim, Kyung Hye. (2014), 'Examining US News Media Discourses about North Korea: A Corpus-based Critical Discourse Analysis', *Discourse & Society*, 25 (2): 221–224.

Kirk, John M. (2009), 'Word Frequency Use or Misuse?', in Dawn Archer (ed.), *What's in a Word-List? Investigating Word Frequency and Keyword Extraction*, 17–34, Farnham: Ashgate.

Kiss, Charlie. (2017), *A New Man*, Leicester: Troubador Publishing.

Koller, Veronika. (2009), 'Analysing Collective Identity in Discourse: Social Actors and Contexts', *Semen Revue de semio-linguistique des textes et discours*, 27. https://doi.org/10.4000/semen.8877.

Kuhar, Roman. (2003), *Media Representation of Homosexuality: An Analysis of the Print Media in Slovenia, 1970–2000*, Ljubljana: Peace Institute. Available online: https://www.mirovni-institut.si/wp-content/uploads/2014/08/media_representations_of_homosexuality.pdf (accessed 9 September 2020).

Kulick, Don. (1998), *Travesti: Sex, Gender, and Culture among Brazilian Transgendered Prostitutes*, Chicago: University of Chicago Press.

Kulick, Don. (1999), 'Transgender and Language: A Review of the Literature and Suggestions for the Future', *Journal of Lesbian and Gay Studies*, 5 (4): 605–622.

Labov, William. (1972), *Sociolinguistic Patterns*, Philadelphia: University of Pennsylvania Press.

Lacan, Jacques. (1977), *Écrits: A Selection*, New York: W. W. Norton & Co.

Lakoff, Robin. (1975), *Language and Woman's Place*, New York: Harper & Row.

Laurence Anthony's Website. (2019), 'AntConc'. Available online: http://www.laurenceanthony.net/software.html (accessed 9 September 2020).

Leech, Geoffrey. (1992), 'Corpora and Theories of Linguistic Performance', in Jan Svartvik (ed.), *Directions in Corpus Linguistics: Proceedings of the Nobel Symposium 82, Stockholm, 4–8 August 1991*, 105–122, Berlin: Mouton De Gruyter.

Leech, Geoffrey. (2007), 'New Resources, or Just Better Old Ones?', in Marianne Hundt, Nadja Nesselhauf and Carolin Biewer (eds), *Corpus Linguistics and the Web*, 134–149, Amsterdam: Rodopi.

Lehmann, Hans-Martin, Peter Schneider and Sebastian Hoffmann. (2000), 'BNCweb', in John M. Kirk (ed.), *Corpora Galore: Analysis and Techniques in Describing English*, 259–266, Amsterdam: Rodopi.

Leigh, Irene (2009), 'Identity and the Power of Labels', in *A Lens on Deaf Identities*, Oxford: Oxford Scholarship Online. https://doi.org/10.1093/acprof:oso/9780195320664.003.0001.

Leino, Unni. (2016), 'Conceptualizing Sex, Gender, and Trans: An Anglo-Finnish Perspective', *Transgender Studies Quarterly*, 3 (4): 448–461.

Leung, Helen Hok-Sze. (2016), 'Always in Translation: Trans Cinema across Languages', *Transgender Studies Quarterly*, 3 (4): 433–447.

LexisNexis. (n.d.), 'LexisNexis Academic'. Available online: https://www.lexisnexis.com/communities/academic/default.aspx (accessed 9 September 2020).

Litosseliti, Lia. (2002), '"Head to Head": Gendered Repertoires in Newspaper Arguments', in Lia Litosseliti and Jane Sunderland (eds), *Gender Identity and Discourse Analysis*, 129–148, Amsterdam: John Benjamins.

Livia, Anna. (2000), *Pronoun Envy: Literary Uses of Linguistic Gender*, Oxford: Oxford University Press.

Llamas, Carmen and Dominic Watt. (2010), 'Introduction', in Carmen Llamas and Dominic Watt (eds), *Language and Identities*, 166–178, Edinburgh: Edinburgh University Press.

Louw, Bill. (1993), 'Irony in the Text or Insincerity in the Writer? The Diagnostic Potential of Semantic Prosodies', in Mona Baker, Gill Francis and Elena Tognini-Bonelli (eds), *Text and Technology: In Honour of John Sinclair*, 48–95, Philadelphia, PA: John Benjamins.

Louw, Bill and Carmela Chateau. (2010), 'Semantic Prosody for the 21st Century: Are Prosodies Smoothed in Academic Contexts? A Contextual Prosodic Theoretical Perspective', in *JADT 2010: 10th International Conference on Statistical Analysis of Textual Data*. Available online: https://pdfs.semanticscholar.org/494c/bdda7c5c85b96dd1e676794b1976bfc96f00.pdf (accessed 9 September 2020).

McCarthy, Michael and Anne O'Keeffe. (2010), 'Historical Perspective: What are Corpora and How Have They Evolved?', in Anne O'Keefe and Michael McCarthy (eds), *The Routledge Handbook of Corpus Linguistics*, 3–13, London: Routledge.

McEnery, Tony and Andrew Hardie. (2012), *Corpus Linguistics: Method, Theory and Practice*, Cambridge: Cambridge University Press.

McEnery, Tony and Andrew Wilson. ([1996] 2001), *Corpus Linguistics: An Introduction*, 2nd edition, Edinburgh: Edinburgh University Press.

McEnery Tony, Richard Xiao and Yukio Tono. (2006), *Corpus-based Language Studies: An Advanced Resource Book*, London: Routledge.

Milani, Tommaso. (2010), 'What's in a Name? Language Ideology and Social Differentiation in a Swedish Print-mediated Debate', *Journal of Sociolinguistics*, 14 (1): 116–142.

Milani, Tommaso. (2013), 'Are "Queers" Really "Queer"? Language, Identity and Same-Sex Desire in a South African Online Community', *Discourse & Society*, 24 (5): 615–633.

Milani, Tommaso. (2017), *Queering Language, Gender and Sexuality*, Sheffield: Equinox eBooks.

Mongibello, Anna. (2018), *Indigenous People in Canadian TV News: A Corpus-based Analysis of Mainstream and Indigenous News Discourses*. Naples: Paolo Loffredo Iniziative Editoriali.

Morley, James and Alan Partington. (2009), 'A Few Frequently Asked Questions about Semantic – or Evaluative – Prosody', *International Journal of Corpus Linguistics*, 14 (2): 139–158.

Morrish, Elisabeth and Helen Sauntson. (2007), 'Camp Codes and Subtle Outing: How the British Broadsheets Press Learned Slang', in Elizabeth Morrish and Helen Sauntson (eds), *New Perspectives on Language and Sexual Identity*, 166–197, Basingstoke: Palgrave.

Motschenbacher, Heiko. (2010), *Language, Gender and Sexual Identity: Poststructuralist Perspectives*, Amsterdam: John Benjamins.

Motschenbacher, Heiko. (2018), 'Corpus Linguistics in Language and Sexuality Studies', *Journal of Language and Sexuality*, 7 (2): 145–174.

Mulderrig, Jane. (2011), 'Manufacturing Consent: A Corpus-based Critical Discourse Analysis of New Labour's Educational Governance', *Educational Philosophy and Theory*, 43 (6): 562–577.

Namaste, Viviane K. (2000), *Invisible Lives: The Erasure of Transsexual and Transgendered People*, Chicago: University of Chicago Press.

National Center for Transgender Equality. (2020a). Available online: http://www.transequality.org (accessed 9 September 2020).

National Center for Transgender Equality. (2020b), 'Issues'. Available online: http://www.transequality.org/issues/resources/transgender-terminology (accessed 9 September 2020).

National Union of Journalists (NUJ). (2011), 'NUJ Code of Conduct'. Available online: https://www.nuj.org.uk/about/nuj-code/ (accessed 9 September 2020).

News Media Canada (NMC). (2020), 'Daily Newspaper Circulation Data'. Available online: https://nmc-mic.ca/about-us/ (accessed 25 November 2018).

Nisco, Maria Cristina. (2016), *Agency in the British Press: A Corpus-based Discourse Analysis of the 2011 UK Riots*, Newcastle upon Tyne: Cambridge Scholars Publishing.

O'Donnell, W.R. and Loreto Todd. (1980), *Variety in Contemporary English*, London: Allen & Unwin.

OED Online. (2018), s.v.v. 'Cis-', 'Trans-' 'Identity', 'Transgender'. Oxford University Press. Available online: https://oed.com/ (accessed 11 August 2018).

O'Halloran, Kieran. (2009), 'Inferencing and Cultural Reproduction: A Corpus-based Critical Discourse Analysis', *Text & Talk*, 29 (1): 21–51.

Partington, Alan S. (1998), *Pattern and Meaning: Using Corpora for English Language Research and Teaching*, Studies in Corpus Linguistics 2, Amsterdam: John Benjamins.

Partington, Alan S. (2004), '"Utterly Content in Each Other's Company": Semantic Prosody and Semantic Preference', *International Journal of Corpus Linguistics*, 9 (1): 131–156.

Partington, Alan S. (2012), 'The Changing Discourses on Antisemitism in the UK Press from 1993 to 2009: A Modern-Diachronic Corpus-assisted Discourse Study', *Journal of Language and Politics*, 11 (1): 51–76.

Partington, Alan S. (2015), 'Corpus-assisted Comparative Case Studies of Representations of the Arab World', in Paul Baker and Tony McEnery (eds), *Corpora and Discourse Studies: Integrating Discourse and Corpora*, 220–243, London: Palgrave Macmillan.

Partington, Alan S. (2017), 'Evaluative Clash, Evaluative Cohesion and How We Actually Read Evaluation in Texts', *Journal of Pragmatics*, 117: 190–203.

Partington, Alan S., Alison Duguid and Charlotte Taylor. (2013), *Patterns and Meaning in Discourse: Theory and Practice in Corpus-Assisted Discourse Studies (CADS)*, Amsterdam: John Benjamins.

Pearce, Ruth. (2018), *Understanding Trans Health: Discourse, Power and Possibility*, Bristol: Policy Press.

Pearce, Ruth, Igi Moon, Kat Gupta and Deborah Lynn Steinberg. (2019), *The Emergence of Trans: Cultures, Politics and Everyday Lives*, London: Routledge.

Polese, Vanda. (2004), *Language in the Spotlight News Manufacturing and Discourse*, Naples: Arte Tipografica Editrice.

Polese, Vanda and Stefania D'Avanzo. (2012), 'Hybridisation in EU Academic Discourse: The Representation of EU Social Actor(s)', in Stefania M. Maci and Michele Sala (eds), *Genre Variation in Academic Communication: Emerging Disciplinary Trends*, 231–259, Bergamo: CELSB.

Polese, Vanda and Angela Zottola. (2019), 'Language and Law at Stake: An Investigation into Transgender People's Rights and Identity Representation in the UK', *International Journal of Psycholinguistics*, 19 (1): 79–96.

Potts, Amanda and Anne Lise Kjaer. (2015), 'Constructing Achievement in the International Criminal Tribunal for the Former Yugoslavia (ICTY): A Corpus-based Critical Discourse Analysis', *International Journal of Semiot Law*, 29: 525–555.

Preece, Siân. (2016), *The Routledge Handbook of Language and Identity*, Abingdon: Routledge.

Raymond, Janice. (1979), *The Transsexual Empire: The Making of the She-Male*, London: Women's.

Rayson, Paul, Dawn Archer, Scott L. Piao and Tony McEnery. (2004), 'The UCREL Semantic Analysis System', in *Proceedings of the Workshop on Beyond Named Entity Recognition Semantic Labelling for NLP Tasks, in Association with 4th International Conference on Language Resources and Evaluation* (LREC 2004), 25 May 2004, Lisbon, Portugal, 7–12.

Reppen, Randi. (2010), 'Building a Corpus: What Are the Main Considerations?', in Anne O'Keefe and Michael McCarthy (eds), *The Routledge Handbook of Corpus Linguistics*, 31–37, London: Routledge.

Richardson, John. (2007), *Analysing Newspapers: An Approach from Critical Discourse Analysis*, London: Red Globe Press.

Rose, Emily. (2016), 'Keeping the Trans in Translation: Queering Early Modern Transgender Memoirs', *Transgender Studies Quarterly*, 3 (4): 485–505.

Sardinha, Tony. (2000), 'Semantic Prosodies in English and Portuguese: A Contrastive Study', *Cuadernos de Filologia Inglesa*, 9 (1): 93–110.

Saussure, Ferdinand de. (1916), *Cours de Linguistique general*, Lausanne: Payot.

Scott, Mike. (2010), 'What Can Corpus Software Do?', in Anne O'Keefe and Michael McCarthy (eds), *The Routledge Handbooks in Applied Linguistics*, 136–151, London: Routledge.

Seymour-Ure, Colin. (1996), *The British Press and Broadcasting, since 1945*, Oxford: Blackwell.

Sherpe, Jens. (2015), *The Legal Status of Transsexual and Transgender Persons*, Cambridge: Intersentia.
Shoemaker, Sydney. (2006), 'Identity & Identities', *Daedalus*, 135 (4) (Fall): 40–48.
Sinclair, John. (1987), *Looking Up*, London: Collins COBUILD.
Sinclair, John. (1991), *Corpus, Concordance, Collocation*, Oxford: Oxford University Press.
Sinclair, John. (1996), 'The Search for Units of Meaning', *Textus*, 9 (1): 75–106.
Sparks, Colin. (1999), 'The Press', in Jane Stokes and Anna Reading (eds), *The Media in Britain: Current Debates and Developments*, 41–60, London: Macmillan.
Spencer, Leland G. (2015), 'Introduction: Centering Transgender Studies in Communication Scholarship', in Leland G. Spencer and Jamie C. Capuzza (eds), *Transgender Communication Studies: Histories, Trends, and Trajectories*, ix–xxii, Lanham, MD: Lexington Books.
Stig, Johansson, Geoffrey Leech and Helen Goodluck. (1978), *Manual of Information to Accompany the Lancaster-Oslo/Bergen Corpus of British English, for Use with Digital Computers*, Oslo: Department of English, University of Oslo.
Stokes, Jane and Anna Reading. (1999), *The Media in Britain: Current Debates and Developments*, London: Macmillan.
Stone, Sandy. (1991), 'The Empire Strikes Back: A Posttranssexual Manifesto', in Julia Epstein and Kristina Straub (eds), *Body Guards: The Cultural Politics of Gender Ambiguity*, 280–304, New York: Routledge.
Stonewall. (2017a), *School Report (2017)*. Available online: http://www.stonewall.org.uk/school-report-2017 (accessed 9 September 2020).
Stonewall. (2017b), 'UK Workplace Equality Index'. Available online: http://www.stonewall.org.uk/workplace-equality-index (accessed 9 September 2020).
Stonewall. (2018), *LGBT in Britain: Trans Report*. Available online: https://www.stonewall.org.uk/system/files/lgbt_in_britain_-_trans_report_final.pdf (accessed 16 September 2020).
Stonewall. (n.d.), 'About Us'. Available online: http://www.stonewall.org.uk/about-us (accessed 16 September 2020).
Stryker, Susan. (1994), 'My Words to Victor Frankenstein above the Village of Chamounix: Performing Transgender Rage', *Journal of Lesbian and Gay Studies*, 1 (3): 227–254.
Stryker, Susan. (1998), 'Transgender Issues: An Introduction', *Journal of Lesbian and Gay Studies*, 4 (2): 145–158.
Stryker, Susan. (2008), 'Transgender History, Homonormativity, and Disciplinarity', *Radical History Review*, 100: 145–157.
Stryker, Susan and Aren Aizura. (2013), *The Transgender Studies Reader 2*, New York: Routledge.
Stryker, Susan and Stephen Whittle. (2006), *The Transgender Studies Reader*, London: Routledge.

Stubbs, Michael. (1983), *Discourse Analysis: The Sociolingusitics Analysis of Natural Language*, Chicago: University of Chicago Press.

Stubbs, Michael. (1995), 'Collocations and Semantic Profiles: On the Cause of the Trouble with Quantitative Methods', *Function of Language*, 2 (1): 1–33.

Stubbs, Michael. (1997), 'Whorf's Children: Critical Comments on Critical Discourse Analysis', in Ann Ryan, and Alison Wray (eds), *Evolving Models of Language*, 100–116, Clevedon: Multilingual Matters.

Stubbs, Michael. (2002), 'Two Quantitative Methods of Studying Phraseology in English', *International Journal of Corpus Linguistics*, 7 (2): 215–244.

Sullivan, Lou. (1990), *Information for the Female to Male Cross Dresser and Transsexual*, Lansing, MI: Ingersoll Gender Center.

Talbot, Mary. (1995), *Fictions at Work – Language and Social Practice in Fiction*, London: Longman.

Tannen, Deborah. (1990), *You Just Don't Understand: Women and Men in Conversation*, New York: Morrow.

Taylor, Charlotte. (2008), 'What is Corpus Linguistics? What the Data Says', *ICAME Journal*, 32: 179–200.

Taylor, Charlotte. (2013), 'Searching for Similarity Using Corpus-assisted Discourse Studies', *Corpora*, 8 (1): 81–113.

Thompson, Geoff. (2013), *Introducing Functional Grammar*, 3rd edition, Abingdon: Routledge.

Tognini-Bonelli, Elena. (2001), *Corpus Linguistics at Work*, Amsterdam: John Benjamins.

Trans Media Watch. (n.d.), 'Trans Media Watch Home'. Available online: http://www.transmediawatch.org/ (accessed 16 September 2020).

Tribble, Christopher. (2010), 'What Are Concordances and How Are They Used?', in Anne O'Keefe and M. McCarthy (eds), *The Routledge Handbook of Corpus Linguistics*, 167–183, London: Routledge.

Trump, Donald [@realDonaldTrump]. (2017), 'After consultation with my Generals and military experts, please be advised that the United States Government will not accept or allow transgender individuals to serve in any capacity in the U.S. Military …', Twitter, July 26. Available online: https://twitter.com/realDonaldTrump/status/890193981585444864 (accessed 3 August 2017).

Van Dijk, Teun. (1988a), *News Analysis: Case Studies of International and National News in the Press*, Hillsdale, NJ: Lawrence Erlbaum Associates.

Van Dijk, Teun. (1988b), *News as Discourse*, Hillsdale, NJ: Lawrence Erlbaum Associates.

Van Dijk, Teun. (1991), *Racism and the Press*, London: Routledge.

van Leeuwen, Theo. (1996), 'The Representation of Social Actors', in Carmen Rosa Caldas-Coulthard and Malcolm Coulthard (eds), *Texts and Practice*, 32–70, London: Routledge.

van Leeuwen, Theo. (2005), *Introducing Social Semiotics*, London: Routledge.

van Leeuwen, Theo. (2007), 'Legitimation in Discourse and Communication', *Discourse & Communication*, 1 (1): 91–112.

Venuti, Marco and Maria Cristina Nisco. (2015), 'Languaging the Riots: A Corpus-based Investigation of the Rioters' Identity as Reported by the British Press', in Giuseppe Balirano and Maria Cristina Nisco (eds), *Languaging Diversity: Identities, Genres, Discourses*, 16–31, Newcastle upon Tyne: Cambridge Scholars Publishing.

Verschueren, Jef. (2001), 'Predicaments of Criticism', *Critique of Anthropology*, 21 (1): 59–81.

Vessay, Rachelle. (2016), *Language and Canadian Media: Representations, Ideologies, Policies*, London: Palgrave Macmillan.

Vipond, Mary. (2012), *The Mass Media in Canada*, 4th edition, Toronto: James Lorimer.

Webster, Lexi. (2018), 'I Wanna Be a Toy', *Journal of Language and Sexuality*, 7 (2): 205–236.

Webster, Lexi. (2019), '"I am I": Self-constructed Transgender Identities in Internet-mediated Forum Communication', *International Journal of the Sociology of Language*, 256: 129–146.

Whittle, Stephen. (1995), 'Outing – Shattering the Conspiracy of Silence', *Journal of Gender Studies*, 4 (2): 206–207.

Whittle, Stephen. (1996), 'Transsexualism in Society: A Sociology of Male-to-Female Transsexuals – Lewins', *Journal of Gender Studies*, 5 (2): 236–237.

Whittle, Stephen. (1998a), 'The Trans-cyberian Mail Way', *Social & Legal Studies*, 7 (3): 389–408.

Whittle, Stephen. (1998b), 'Gender Outlaw: On Men, Women and the Rest of Us', *Archives of Sexual Behavior*, 27 (5): 526–530.

Widdowson, Henry. (1998), 'The Theory and Practice of Critical Discourse Analysis', *Applied Linguistics*, 19 (1): 136–151.

Widdowson, Henry. (2005), *Text, Context, Pretext: Critical Issues in Discourse Analysis*, Oxford: Blackwell.

WikiLeaks. (2015), 'What is WikiLeaks'. 3 November. Available online: https://wikileaks.org/What-is-Wikileaks.html (accessed 9 September 2020).

Williams, Cristan. (2014), 'Transgender', *Transgender Studies Quarterly* 1 (1–2): 232–234.

Williams, Raymond. (1976), *Keywords: A Vocabulary of Culture and Society*, London: Croom Helm.

Willox, Annabelle. (2003), 'Branding Teena: (Mis)representations in the Media', *Sexualities*, 6 (3), 407–425.

Witten, Tarynnm and Stephen Whittle. (2004), 'TransPanthers: The Greying of Transgender and the Law', *Deakin Law Review*, 9 (2): 504–522.

Wodak, Ruth. (1997), *Gender and Discourse*, London: Sage.

Women and Equalities Committee. (2016), *Transgender Equality: First Report of Session 2015–16*, House of Commons. Available online: https://publications.parliament.uk/pa/cm201516/cmselect/cmwomeq/390/390.pdf (accessed 25 August 2018).

Xiao, Richard and Tony McEnery. (2006), 'Collocation, Semantic Prosody, and Near Synonymy: A Cross-Linguistic Perspective', *Applied Linguistics*, 271 (1): 103–129.

Yeung, Peter. (2016), 'Transphobic Hate Crimes in "Sickening" 170% Rise as Low Prosecution Rates Create "Lack of Trust" in Police'. *Independent*, 29 July. Available online: http://www.independent.co.uk/news/uk/home-news/transphobic-hate-crime-statistics-violence-transgender-uk-police-a7159026.html (accessed 9 September 2020).

Young, Nathan and Eric Dugas. (2012), 'Comparing Climate Change Coverage in Canadian English- and French-Language Print Media: Environmental Values, Media Cultures, and the Narration of Global Warming', *Canadian Journal of Sociology/Cahiers canadiens de sociologue*, 37 (1): 25–54.

Zimman, Lal. (2009), '"The Other Kind of Coming Out": Transgender People and the Coming Out Narrative Genre', *Gender & Language*, 3 (1): 53–80.

Zimman, Lal. (2012), 'Voices in Transition: Testosterone, Transmasculinity, and the Gendered Voice among Female-to-Male Transgender People', PhD Dissertation, University of Colorado, Boulder.

Zimman, Lal. (2013), 'Hegemonic Masculinity and the Variability of Gay-Sounding Speech: The Perceived Sexuality of Transgender Men', *Journal of Language & Sexuality*, 2 (1): 5–43.

Zimman, Lal. (2014), 'The Discursive Construction of Sex: Remaking and Reclaiming the Gendered Body in Talk about Genitals among Trans Men', in Lal Zimman, Jennifer L. Davis, and Joshua Raclaw (eds), *Queer Excursions: Retheorizing Binaries in Language, Gender, and Sexuality*, 13–34, New York: Oxford University Press.

Zottola, Angela. (2018a), 'Living as a Woman: The British Press on Trans Identity', in Giuseppe Balirano and Oriana Palusci (eds), *Miss Man? Languaging Gendered Bodies*, 168–189, Cambridge: Cambridge Scholars Publishing.

Zottola, Angela. (2018b), 'Transgender Identity Labels in the British Press (2013–2015): A Corpus-based Discourse Analysis', *Journal of Language and Sexuality*, 7 (2), 237–262.

Index

Aarts, Jan 47
abstraction strategies 103
activation strategies 101
activism 157
advocacy groups 157
affiliation strategies 102
aggregation strategies 103
AIDS 140
Aizura, Aren 19
Alcorn, Leelah 122, 142–5
All About Trans 7, 179
Allan, Stuart 25
anachronism strategies 103
Anderson, Benedict 114
'anonymous' individuals or groups 101
AntConc 39, 177, 178
appraisement strategies 102
Araujo, Gwen 24
assimilation strategies 103
association 101
asylum seekers 65
    see also RASIM
Audit Bureau of Circulation (ABC) 58
autobiographies 19
awareness and support 174, 178–81
    Canada 164–9
    United Kingdom 158–64

backgrounding strategies 104, 126, 140
bathrooms 148, 149, 150, 151
Baer, Brian J. 20
Baker, Paul 14, 17, 22–3, 24, 25, 26, 29, 32, 34, 46, 48, 52, 54, 65, 70, 80, 109, 115, 130, 137, 146, 173, 177, 180
balanced corpora 28
Balirano, Giuseppe 50, 181
Bank of English (BoE) 28
Barker-Plummer, Bernadette 24
Barthes, Roland 15
Bartley, Leanne 26, 66
Beaumont Society 7, 162, 163
beauty contests 113–14
Bednarek, Monika 54, 62, 63, 79, 176

Bell, Allan 54, 62, 63, 176
beneficialization 101
Besnier, Niko 19
Biber, Douglas 28
Billard, Thomas J. 24, 173
binary structures 16
'bisexual' 118
Borba, Rodrigo 22
Branson, Gill 25
Brazil 18, 20, 22, 113, 114
'Brazilian' 86, 88–9
British press 11, 12, 25, 35–8, 52, 54–8, 61–2, 64, 65, 176
    crime stories 141–8, 174
    defining transgender people 82–93
    entertainment and celebrities 123–37
    implying verbs 91–3
    LGBTIQ+ groups and labels 108–16
    NUJ code of conduct 180
    personal details 82–91
    TransCorUK (TCUK) 33–9, 67, 68, 70–4, 82, 86, 96, 97, 98, 99, 107, 108, 109, 117, 120, 122, 137, 138, 139, 140, 141–8, 149, 153, 156, 158, 159, 160, 164, 168, 171, 172, 174, 175
    UK vs Canada 67–75
'broadsheets' 56
Brothers, Emily 136, 137
Bucholtz, Mary 3, 4
bullying 179
Burchill, Julie 89, 130, 131
Burnes, Theodore R. 21
Butler, Judith 15, 165
Byerly, Carolyn 25

Caldas-Coulthard, Carmen Rosa 52, 105
Cameron, David 113
Canada 5, 6
    Americanization 59
    awareness and support 164–9
    defining trans identities in the Canadian press 93–100

entertainment and celebrities 137–41
identity labels 67–75
implying verbs 99–100
indigenous press 59, 60
laws and rights 154–8
LGBTIQ+ groups and labels 116–23
personal details 93–9
press 11, 12, 39–42, 58–60, 67–75, 175, 176–7, 180
TransCorCan (TCC) 39–43, 67, 69–74, 96, 98, 99, 107, 116, 118, 119, 122, 138, 139, 140, 141, 154, 155, 157, 165, 168, 171, 175, 177
transphobia and hate crimes 179–80
UK vs Canada comparisons 67–75
Caple, Helen 62, 63, 176
Capuzza, Jamie C. 21
Carter, Cynthia 25
Carter, Ronald 54, 62, 173
categories of representation 12, 158
categorization strategies 87, 102, 147–8
Catholics 82, 85
celebrities *see* entertainment and celebrities
Chateau, Carmela 80
Chen, Mindy M. 21
children 147, 165, 166, 175, 179
Chomsky, Noam 27
cinematic productions *see* films
circumstantialization strategies 101
cisgender: definition 3
citizen journalism 23
Cixous, Helen 16
classification strategies 102
CLAWS POS tagger 43
Clinton, Hillary 111
collective representation 107
collectivization strategies 103
collocation analysis 12, 32–3, 82, 85, 89, 90, 93, 94, 96, 97, 98
awareness and support 158, 159, 160, 161, 162, 163, 164, 166, 167, 169
crime stories 141, 143, 144, 145, 148
entertainment and celebrities 123, 125, 128, 129, 130, 131, 137
laws and rights 149, 154, 155, 156, 157
LGBTIQ+ groups and labels 109, 111, 117–22
see also semantic prosodies
collective representation

entertainment and celebrities
Canada 137–41
United Kingdom 123–37
LGBTIQ+ groups and labels
Canada 116–23
United Kingdom 108–16
color/colour 82, 83, 85, 90
coming out stories 21
communication and journalism studies 24
communicative behaviour 18
'community' 114
community of practice 14
Conboy, Martin 54, 56, 57
concordance analysis 12, 31–2, 33
connotation strategies 103
conversion therapy 121–2, 143
Corpus-based Discourse Analysis (CBDA) 46, 48–52, 64, 66, 177
Corpus Linguistics 12, 22, 27–9, 46, 47, 54, 66, 75
corpus-based and corpus-driven approaches 48
Critical Discourse Analysis and 46–8
see also Corpus-based Discourse Analysis; TransCor
Corpus of Contemporary American English (COCA) 28
Cory, D. Walter 14
Cotter, Colleen 54, 63
Cox, Laverne 21, 123, 139, 160
CQPweb 43, 177, 178
Crenshaw, Kimberlé 84
crime stories 141–8, 174, 179
Critical Discourse Analysis (CDA) 12, 46–7, 54
see also Corpus-based Discourse Analysis
'cross-dresser' 68, 69, 72, 74
Crystal, David 54
Curlew, Abigail 179
Currah, Paisley 18

Dashti, Laleh 105
D'Avanzo, Stefania 104
Davari, Safouri 104
Davy, Derek 54
deadnaming 129, 130, 133, 134, 135, 139
defamatory language 172
Derrida, Jacques 15, 16
determination strategies 101, 102, 103

deviation strategies 103
Di Martino, Emilia 21
diachronic corpora 29
dialectical-relational approach 46
DiNovo, Cheri 96
discourse 12, 45–6
discriminatory language 7, 172
distillation strategies 103
Doan, Petra L. 19
documentaries 138–9
'dysphoria' 6, 139

Eastern European migration 65–6
    see also RASIM
Eckert, Penelope 14
educational programmes 104
Elbe, Lili 125, 135–6, 138
Elliot, Hamilton 94, 95
entertainment and celebrities 123, 174
    Canada 137–41
    United Kingdom 123–37
Erasmus programme 104
ethnicity 65
EU legal texts 50
euthanasia 97, 133
evidentiality 63
exclusion strategies 104

Fairclough, Norman 45, 46, 53, 54
fashionable topics 178, 180
female-to-male (FTM) 3, 88
feminism 66
femininity 15, 52
Ferraresi, Adriano 23
films 8, 20–1, 124, 136, 137, 139, 140, 141
    The Danish Girl 124, 125, 135–6, 138
Finnish 20
Firth, John R. 32, 77
formalization strategies 102
Foucault, Michel 16, 45
Fowler, Roger 54, 57, 62, 63
France 5
freedom of speech 130–2
frequency lists 30–1
Freud, Sigmund 16
functionalization strategies 102

Gabriel, Kay 20
Gabrielatos, Costas 32, 54, 65, 80, 173
Galtung, Johan 63, 163, 176

gay community 14
'gay-sounding' speech 22
gender
    deconstruction 15, 16
    definition 7, 13
    sex and 2–3
gender confirmation surgery 72, 94, 97
gender 'dysphoria' 6, 139
gender identity labels *see* identity labels
gender performances 15, 16, 165
gender reassignment 87
    search term 68, 69, 70, 73
gender stereotypes 16
'gender-variant' 119
genericization strategies 103
German press 66
Ghadessy, Mohsen 54, 62
GLAAD 7, 86, 87
glamorization 128–9
Gouveia, Carlos Alberto M. 26
Grace, Laura Jane 139
Gries, Stefan T. 30
Gupta, Kat 23

Hague Programme 50
Hall, Kira 3, 4, 18, 19
Hardie, Andrew 32, 48
Hartner, Marcus 21
hate crimes 179
headlines 61
health-related issues 166
hegemonic power 16
    gender 'normality' 52
Henry, Harry 56–7
Hess, Linda M. 21
heteronormativity 16, 19
heterosexuality 46
Hidalgo-Tenorio, Encarnacion 26, 66
hijras 18, 19
Hok-Sze Leung, Helen 20
homicide 145–6
homophobia 25
homosexuality 66
honorification strategies 102
Horak, Laura 23
Hunston, Susan 33, 79

Icelandic 20
ID documents 168
identification strategies 102

identity
    definition 1–2, 3–5
    post-structuralism 16
    subjectivity 9
identity labels 67–75
    choices in English 45–53
ideology 104
'imagined community' 114
immigrants 49, 65, 110–11
    see also RASIM
impersonalization strategies 101, 103, 148
implying verbs 12
    British press 91–3
    Canadian press 99–100
inclusion strategies 101
inclusive language 6, 9
indetermination strategies 101
indexicality 14
Indian hijras 19
individualization strategies 103, 104
information strategies 102
International Corpus of Learner English (ICLE) 28
International Criminal Tribunal for the Former Yugoslavia 51
intersectionality 84, 85, 90, 111, 174
intertextuality 49, 63
inversion strategies 103
Ireland 5, 26
    press 66
Irigaray, Luce 16

Jarrin, Alvaro 20
Jaworska, Sylvia 66
Jenner, Caitlyn 128, 129, 130
Jennings, Jazz 94
Jones, Lucy 23
Joseph, John 13
journals 18
Jucker, Andreas H. 54, 57

Kelner, Simon 131
keyword analysis 32, 51
Kjaer, Anne Lise 51
Koller, Veronika 105
Krishnamurti, Jiddu 105
Krishnamurthy, Ramesh 66
Kulick, Don 19
KWIC (key words in context) 31
Kyung Hie Kim 50

labels see identity labels
Lacan, Jacques 16
Lakoff, Robin 17
Lancaster/Oslo/Bergen (LOB) corpus 28
language teaching 104
Lavender linguistics 14, 16
laws and rights 174
    Canada 154–8
    UK 148–54, 178–9
lead development 61
Leap, William 14
Leech, Geoffrey 28, 48
legal texts 50, 51
lesbian communities 105
Leto, Jared 124, 136, 140
LexisNexis 34, 36, 37, 38
LGBTIQ+ groups and labels 107, 174
    Canada 116–23
    UK 108–16
linguistic practices 8–9, 10, 12, 13–14
    corpus linguistics 12, 22, 27–9
    see also TransCor
    gay community 14
    Lavender linguistics 14, 16
    paralinguistic features 28
    Queer Linguistics 16–17
    translation 20
Litosseliti, Lia 24
Livia, Anna 16, 19
Louw, Bill 78, 80
Lyons, Beth 121

male-to-female (MTF) 3, 88, 97
Maloney, Kellie 128, 129, 130, 132, 134–5
Malta 5
managerialism 50–1
Mandelson, Peter 25
Manning, Chelsea 34, 129, 156
masculinity 15, 52
McConnell-Ginet, Sally 14
McEnery, Tony 29, 32, 48, 54, 80
McMullan, Chelsea 138
Meadows, Lucy 23
media discourses 8
    see also films; news media; social media; TV
medical perspectives 18, 175
meetmarket 52
Mehrpour, Saeed 105
Meijs, Willem 47

memoirs 20
Mermaids UK 180
migrants 65, 85
   see also RASIM
Milani, Tommaso 15, 52
military service 85, 148, 149, 151–2
minorities 84, 85
misgendering 24, 173
misrepresentation 24, 173
modifiers 82
Moini, Mohammad Raouf 104
monitor corpora 28
Moon, Rosamund 52
Moore, Suzanne 89, 130, 131
Morgan, Nicky 178
Morrish, Elisabeth 25
Motschenbacher, Heiko 17, 177
Mulderrig, Jane 50
murder 145–6

Namaste, Vivienne 18
National Center for Transgender Equality 7
National Union of Journalists (NUJ) 180
negative stereotypes 23, 24
News Discourse 12, 53–4, 176
   British press 54–8
   Canadian press 58–60, 158
   language of newspapers 61–6
'news making standards' 163
news media
   Canada 39–42
   contribution of the press 171–5
   German press 66
   identity labels 67–75
   Irish press 66
   representation of gender identities 24–7
   semantic prosody *see* semantic prosodies
   UK *see* British press
   UK vs Canada 67–75
   US media 24, 50
Newspaper Canada 60
Nexis UK 66
Nisco, Maria Cristina 50, 64
nomination strategies 102, 148
non-discriminatory language 6, 9, 133–4, 175
non-inclusive practices 7

Nordic languages 20
normalization 141
North Korea 50

Obama, Barack 122, 143, 146
objectivation strategies 103
observer's paradox 53, 183
O'Donnell, W. R. 61–2
O'Halloren, Kieran 65–6
'openly' 82, 84, 85, 90
overdetermination strategies 103

paralinguistic features 28
participation strategies 101
Partington, Alan S. 54, 78–9, 80, 81
passivation strategies 101
pathologization 173
Pearce, Ruth 19
Pearson, Allison 89, 131
performativitiy 15, 16
personal details 12
   British press 82–91
   Canadian press 93–9
personalization strategies 101, 103, 148
physical identification strategies 102, 134
'pioneer' 128
Platell, Amanda 113
Polari 14
Polese, Vanda 104, 178
PopCor 36, 82, 83, 86, 88, 90, 108, 112, 114, 115, 128, 132, 134–7, 142, 146, 147, 149, 150, 152, 153, 154, 158, 159, 162, 163, 164
'popular' press 35, 37, 55, 56, 57, 132
   see also PopCor
Portugal 26
possessivation strategies 101
post-structuralism 15, 16
Potts, Amanda 51
'pre-op' 86–7
press *see* News Discourse; news media
prison inmates 148, 149, 153–4, 156, 158
pronouns 23, 133, 135, 139
prosody *see* semantic prosodies
Pullen, Olie 94

QualCor 36, 82–4, 86, 88, 90, 108, 109, 112, 123, 125, 128, 130, 134–7, 142, 144, 146, 147, 149–54, 158–61, 164
qualitative analysis 47, 48, 177

'quality' press 35, 37, 55, 56, 58, 127
    see also QualCor
quantitative analysis 47, 48, 177
'queer' 118–19
Queer Linguistics 16–17
Queer-Straight Alliance 94

race and ethnicity 65
RASIM 80, 173
    see also asylum seekers; immigrants;
        migrants; refugees
Reading, Anne 54
Redmayne, Eddie 125, 126
refugees 50, 65
relational identification strategies 102
research aims 8–10
research questions 10–11
Richardson, John 173
rights see laws and rights
Rodriguez, Kitana Kiki 139
Rose, Emily 20
Ross, Karen 25
Ruge, Mari H. 63, 163, 176

same-sex marriage 26
sample corpora 28, 29
sampling 31–2
Sardinha, Tony Berber 80
Saunston, Helen 25
Saussure, Ferdinand de 15
self-identification 23
semantic categories of representation 12
semantic prosodies 12, 77–81
    awareness and support 158, 161, 164
    crime stories 143, 145
    defining transgender people in the
        British press 82–93
    defining transgender people in the
        Canadian press 93–100
    implying verbs 91–3, 99–100
    laws and rights 154, 157
    personal details 82–91, 93–9
    'trans' 81, 82, 83, 90, 91, 93, 98, 99
    'transgender' 81–6, 90, 93, 95, 98, 101,
        126–8, 136, 141
    'transsexual' 81–3, 86, 87, 89–93, 97,
        99, 136
    transgender people as social actors 87,
        100–5
semi-formalization strategies 102

sensationalization 128–9
sex and gender 2–3
'sex change' 175
    search term 68, 69, 70, 71, 100
sex workers 88
sexual identities 13, 15
sexual orientation 66
Seymour-Ure, Colin 55
shared representation 15
'shemale' 34, 68, 69, 72, 73–4
signifiers 15
Sinclair, John 28, 48, 77–8, 79
single determination strategies 103
SketchEngines 51
Slovenia 26
social actor representations 12, 87,
    100–5
social media 23, 131
sociological perspectives 19
Sparks, Colin 55
specification strategies 103
Spencer, Leland G. 21
Spoon, Rae 138
stereotypes 23, 24, 65, 88
Stokes, Jane 54
Stone, Sandy 18
Stonewall 162, 164, 179
'straight' 121
Stryker, Susan 17, 18, 19
Stubbs, Michael 47, 48, 78
subjection strategies 101
suicides 90, 96, 98, 143–5, 147, 166
Sullivan, Lou 17–18
support see awareness and support
suppression strategies 104
symbolization strategies 103, 127
synchronic corpora 29

'tabloids' 56, 65
Talbot, Mary 45
Tampere Programme 50
Tannen, Deborah 17
'teens' 94–5
television see TV
terminology 1–3, 11, 67–75
Theroux, Louis 147
titulation strategies 102
Todd, Loreto 61–2
toilets 149, 150, 151
Tonga 19

Toronto International Film Festival (TIFF) Kids 94
toy advertisements 105
Tran, Mark 37
'trann': search term 68, 69, 72–3
'tranny' 172
  search term 73
'trans'
  collocation analysis of crime stories 141–8
  forms of collective representation 107
    entertainment and celebrities 124, 134
    LGBTIQ+ groups and labels 107, 116, 117, 121–2
  search term 68, 69, 70, 71, 172
  semantic prosodies 81, 82, 83, 90, 91, 93, 98, 99
Trans Alliance Society 157, 167, 168
trans awareness *see* awareness and support
Trans Equality Society 167, 168
trans fashion 178, 180
Trans Media Watch 164
Trans Pulse Project 166, 180
TransCor 9, 27–9, 102, 104, 173, 177, 178, 180
  association 101
  collocation 32–3
  concordance analysis 31–2, 33
  frequency lists 30–1
  keyword analysis 32
  sampling 31–2
  TransCorCan (TCC) 39–43, 67, 69–74, 96, 98, 99, 107, 116, 118, 119, 122, 138–41, 154, 155, 157, 165, 168, 171, 177
  TransCorUK (TCUK) 33–9, 67, 68, 70–4, 82, 86, 96–9, 107–9, 117, 120, 122, 137–49, 153, 156, 158–60, 164, 168, 171, 172, 174, 175
'transgender'
  collocation analysis of crime stories 141–8
  definition 1, 2–3
  forms of collective representation 107
    entertainment and celebrities 123–30, 137–40
    LGBTIQ+ groups and labels 108–15, 117–20

search term 67–71, 74
semantic prosodies 81–6, 90, 93, 95, 98, 101
Transgender Awareness Week 166
'transgender community' 103
Transgender Day of Remembrance 166
transgender individuals
  categorizations and labels 172
  recognition in countries around the world 5
    Canada 6
    UK: Gender Recognition Act 5, 178
    WHO definition 6
transgender men 21–2
transgender studies
  journals 18
  marginalization 18
'transgender tipping point' 160
transgender women 17–18
'transgendered' 86
translation 20
transphobia 180
'transsexual' 3
  forms of collective representation 107
    entertainment and celebrities 124, 130–7, 138, 140–1
    LGBTIQ+ groups and labels 108, 115–16, 117, 120–1
  search term 68–71
  semantic prosodies 81–3, 86, 87, 89–93, 97, 99
'transvestite' 3, 113, 114
  search term 68, 69, 74
travesti 18
'true transsexual' 22, 23
Trump, Donald 85
Turkey 26, 51
TV 8, 21, 123, 127, 137, 139, 167
  Orange is the New Black 8, 123, 139, 160
  soap operas 132
Twitter 8, 23
'two-spirited' 117, 119

Ukraine 5
United Kingdom
  awareness and support 158–64
  education policy 50
  Equality Act 5, 178

Gender Recognition Act 5, 178
identity labels 67–75
laws and rights 148–54, 178–9
press *see* British press
TransCorUK 33–9, 67, 68, 70–4, 82, 86, 96–9, 107–9, 117, 120, 122, 137–49, 153, 156, 158–60, 164, 168, 171, 172, 174, 175
United States
military service 151–2
US media 24, 50
USAS semantic tagger 43

van Dijk, Teun 54
van Heuvel, Theo 47
van Leeuwen, Theo 12, 100, 101, 102, 103, 104, 105, 109, 114, 116, 123, 126, 134, 147, 163
Verschueren, Jef 47
Vikander, Alicia 125
violent crime 145–7, 179
Vipond, Mary 59

vloggers 23
von Mahlsdorf, Charlotte 20

Wallner, Thomas 97
Watts, Alan 105
Webster, Lexi 23
Whittle, Stephen 17, 18
Widdowson, Henry 47
WikiLeaks 34, 182
Williams, Raymond 57
Winterbourne, Hannah 149, 152–3
Wmatrix 51
Wodak, Ruth 45
World Health Organization (WHO) 6

Xiao, Richard 80

YouTube 23

Zimman, Lal 21–2

www.ingramcontent.com/pod-product-compliance
Lightning Source LLC
Chambersburg PA
CBHW072235290426
44111CB00012B/2106